ATARI BASIC

More than a million people have learned to program, use, and enjoy microcomputers with Wiley paperback guides. Look for them all at your favorite bookshop or computer store:

BASIC, 2nd ed., Albrecht, Finkel, & Brown
BASIC for Home Computers, Albrecht, Finkel, & Brown
TRS–80 BASIC, Albrecht, Inman, & Zamora
More TRS-80 BASIC, Inman, Zamora, & Albrecht
ATARI BASIC, Albrecht, Finkel, & Brown
Data File Programming in BASIC, Finkel & Brown
APPLE BASIC: Data File Programming, Finkel & Brown
ATARI Sound & Graphics, Moore, Lower, & Albrecht
Using CP/M, Fernandez & Ashley
Introducton to 8080/8085 Assembly Language Programming, Fernandez & Ashley
8080/Z80 Assembly Language, Miller
Personal Computing, McGlynn
Why Do You Need a Personal Computer?, Leventhal & Stafford
Problem-Solving on the TRS–80 Pocket Computer, Inman & Conlan
Using Programmable Calculators for Business, Hohenstein
How to Buy the Right Small Business Computer System, Smolin
The TRS–80 Means Business, Lewis
ANS COBOL, 2nd ed., Ashley
Structured COBOL, Ashley
FORTRAN IV, 2nd ed., Friedmann, Greenberg, & Hoffberg
Job Control Language, Ashley & Fernandez
Background Math for a Computer World, 2nd ed., Ashley
Flowcharting, Stern
Introduction to Data Processing, 2nd ed., Harris

ATARI BASIC

BOB ALBRECHT
LE ROY FINKEL
and
JERALD R. BROWN

Dymax Corporation
Menlo Park, California

JOHN WILEY & SONS
New York • Chichester • Brisbane • Toronto • Singapore

Library of Congress Cataloging in Publication Data:

Albrecht, Robert L
Atari BASIC.

(Wiley self-teaching guides)
Includes index.

1. Atari 400 (Computer) — Programming.

2. Atari 800 (Computer) — Programming. (Computer program language) I. Finkel, LeRoy, joint author. II. Brown, Jerald, 1940- joint author. III. Title.

10 9 8 7 6

QA76.8.A8A4 001.6'424 79-12513

Printed in the United States of America

ISBN 0-471-06496-3

To the Reader

With the advent of integrated circuits and miniaturization in electronics, suddenly a complete computer, with all the peripherals or attachments needed to use it, can be purchased for as little as $600. Now a computer for your home, club, school or business is in the same price range as the less expensive stereo component systems! These inexpensive computers, among them the ATARI computers, use the computer language BASIC. This book will teach you how to write programs using the BASIC language, specifically for ATARI computers.

BASIC was originally developed at Dartmouth College by John Kemeny and Thomas Kurtz who recognized the need for an all-purpose computer language that would be suitable for beginning programmers whose educational backgrounds would be varied and diverse. Beginners All-purpose Symbolic Instruction Code (BASIC) was originally designed as a simple language which could be learned in a few short hours. With improvements over the years, the language now may take a few days to learn, but you will find that you can do nearly anything you want in BASIC.

If you *do* have an ATARI computer to use, be certain that the BASIC cartridge is installed in the computer, so it will understand instructions given in BASIC. It is the nature of progress to find ways of improving on things, and BASIC is no exception, so you may find that your BASIC has some extra statements and refinements that were not in the 8K ATARI BASIC we used in writing this book. So we encourage you to experiment and, if you get stuck, consult your reference manual. If that doesn't do it, call ATARI or write the authors, and you'll find people to point you in the right directions.

Also, notice that there is an appendix of functions. By Chapter 3 or 4, you should begin browsing the function appendix and your reference manual to enhance your understanding of the capabilities of your computer. Learn how to save (CSAVE) your programs on the cassette recorder, if you opted to include one on your computer system. As you progress to writing longer programs that are developed and modified, having an early version on tape saves tedious typing time.

And notice the ERROR message appendix. Believe us, you'll refer to it as often as we have for clues as to what we typed wrong, or where our logic temporarily foiled us. There is a saying among programming afficionados: "Keep on hackin'." So give it another try.

Now take a look at How to Use This Book, and then go on to learn BASIC!

How to Use this Book

With this book's self-instructional format, you'll be actively involved in learning BASIC for the ATARI computer. The material is presented in short numbered sections called frames, each of which teaches you something new about ATARI BASIC and gives you a question or asks you to write a program. Correct answers are given following the dashed line. For the most effective learning we urge you to use a thick paper to keep the answers out of sight until you have written your answer.

You will learn best if you actually write out the answers and try the programs out on the ATARI computer. The questions are carefully designed to call your attention to important points in the examples and explanations, and to help you learn to apply what is being explained or demonstrated.

Each chapter begins with a list of objectives—what you will be able to do after completing that chapter. If you have had some previous experience using BASIC and the objectives for that chapter look familiar, take the Self-Test at the end of that chapter first to see where you should start your close reading of the book. If you do well, study only the frames indicated for the questions you missed. If you miss many questions, start work at the beginning of the chapter.

The Self-Test can also be used as a review of the material covered in the chapter. You may test yourself immediately after reading the chapter. Or you may wish to read a chapter, take a break, and save the Self-Test as a review before you begin the next chapter. At the end of the book is a Final Self-Test which will allow you to test your overall understanding of ATARI BASIC.

This is a self-contained book for learning ATARI BASIC, but what you learn will be theoretical until you actually sit down at a computer terminal and apply your knowledge of the computer language and programming techniques. So we strongly recommend that you and this book get together with an ATARI computer. BASIC will be easier and clearer if you have even occasional access to a computer so that you can try the examples and exercises, make your own modifications, and invent your own programs for your own purposes. You are now ready to teach yourself how to use ATARI BASIC.

Contents

ATARI BASIC

CHAPTER ONE

Your ATARI Personal Computer

This chapter will introduce you to the ATARI 400 and the ATARI 800 Personal Computers for home, school, club, or business use. When you complete this chapter, you will have a thorough introduction to these two computers and the expansion components which are currently available for them. You will also be able to use the following words and phrases from the language of the computer world.

Computer language
BASIC and, specifically ATARI BASIC
CPU or Central Processing Unit
Disk drive
Keyboard
Screen or television screen
Printer
Program
Program recorder
ROM cartridge containing ATARI BASIC
Operating System program
ROM module
RAM memory
RAM memory module
BASIC statements
Line numbers

You may be using this book with either the ATARI 400 or the ATARI 800 personal computer system. The 400 computer console has a flat-panel keyboard and is used with your television set and, possibly, the optional ATARI 410 program recorder. The 800 computer console has a typewriter-like keyboard. Both consoles attach to your television set. There are other differences between the two systems which we will note as we go along.

Before you go any farther, it would be a good idea to set up your computer so that you can use it as you read this book. Packed in the carton with your ATARI 400 or 800 you will find the Operators Manual. This manual will tell you how to attach the television, turn on the power to your computer, and use the program cartridges which come with it. The Operators Manual contains a lot of information so don't feel you must read every word of it right away. But do get your computer "up and running in BASIC" if you haven't done so before, and then come back to this book.

Welcome back! Now let's get better acquainted wth your ATARI computer console.

Of course, the most obvious feature of the computer is its keyboard. The keyboard of the ATARI 800 looks like this:

This is your means of communicating with your ATARI computer. It is called an *input device,* because you can use the keyboard to put information *into* the computer.

1. The keyboard is the input device that will allow you to communicate with the computer in the computer language called ______________ .

— — — — — — — — — —

BASIC

2. The part of the computer's electronics that actually "computes" is called the CPU or Central Processing Unit. It is located on a single printed circuit board under the ribbed cover at the back of the console.

Also under that ribbed cover of the console is the computer's memory bank. The first section of the memory bank contains the 8K Operating System ROM Module or *R*ead-*O*nly-*M*emory. The ROM Module has a program, a set of instructions, which tells the computer how it is to respond to messages from the outside world. From our point of view, the ROM and its programs are part of the computer itself.

(a) The computing action takes place in the ______________ .

(b) Another of the electronics that contains the Operating System is stored in ROM, which stands for ______________ .

— — — — — — — — — —

(a) CPU (Central Processing Unit)
(b) Read Only Memory

3. We mentioned the "8K Operating System" that helps the computer interpret our instructions to it. The "8K" is a way of measuring the size of computer memory. The K stands for thousands of bytes of memory. Byte is a computer term that refers to units of memory. Each memory byte can store approximately one letter, number, or other character, so 8K can hold around 8 thousand characters.

Therefore, 16K would indicate the capacity to store about ______________ characters.

— — — — — — — — — —

16 thousand

4. Both the 400 and 800 have a second memory section called RAM or *R*andom *A*ccess *M*emory. This is where the computer stores information that you enter through the keyboard. The amount of memory depends on which system you selected. We often refer to RAM memory as our workspace. We can write in it or erase it with just a few keystrokes.

RAM is different from ROM, the Read Only Memory. The computer uses the ROM, but ROM is permanent in that it cannot be erased or changed by you from the keyboard.

Answer the following questions by writing RAM and/or ROM.

(a) Which can be erased? ______________________

(b) Which is permanent? ______________________

(c) Which has a size indicated by such notations as 8K? ______________

(d) Which is used to store information entered from the keyboard? _________

— — — — — — — — — — —

(a) RAM
(b) ROM
(c) RAM and ROM
(d) RAM

5. If you have an ATARI 800 you can purchase extra RAM memory modules to expand the workspace in your computer. You won't need extra memory while you are using this book, but in the future you may find you want to write longer programs which require more RAM for storage.

Make sure you have the ATARI BASIC cartridge in the cartridge slot of your computer (follow the instructions in your Operators Manual). Inserting a cartridge does for the computer what adding an extra piece of already-educated gray matter would do for your brain. It makes the memory bigger and gives it more information. This cartridge contains another preprogrammed 8K ROM; the computer instantly knows how to speak ATARI BASIC when this cartridge is in place. Now you need to learn ATARI BASIC to communicate instructions to the computer. A set of one or more instructions to the computer is called a *program*. Your program, or instructions, must be entered or typed into the computer in BASIC, following the rules for BASIC you will learn in this book. Your instructions to make the computer do what you want it to do,

and following the rules of BASIC, is called a ______________________ .

— — — — — — — — — — —

program

6. Let's pretend you are typing a program into the computer. As soon as the computer receives a character from the keyboard (as you begin typing) it displays that same character on the television screen, thus providing us with a record of what we have typed.

Therefore, the television screen is an *output* device, for it takes what you put in, and puts it back out again. This allows you to make sure that you did, indeed, enter what you thought you did. Later, when the computer follows the instructions in your programs, the results are also displayed on the screen. This is another example of the TV as an ____________________ device.

— — — — — — — — — — —

output

7. Look at the photo of the ATARI 400 computer connected to a television on page 2.

(a) We use the keyboard to type information into the computer. What happens to the information that we type? ______________________________

____

(b) How does the computer communicate with us, the users? ____________

____

— — — — — — — — — — —

(a) It is sent to the computer and then printed on the screen.
(b) It prints information on the screen.

8. After you have learned how to write programs for your ATARI computer, you may want to "store" them someplace. Then you won't have to retype your programs each time you want to use them. Since you can't "store" programs in the computer's memory, you will need an external memory storage device. You can choose to buy either a program recorder (similar to a home cassette recorder) or a disk drive.

Both the program recorder and the disk drive can be used to store or save your computer programs and information (called data) such as mailing lists, recipes, appointments, and budget or accounting figures. Once you have mastered the BASIC computer language, you will find this kind of storage device quite handy and easy to use. However, in this book you need only the three main parts of a computer system we have discussed earlier, which are____________

____

— — — — — — — — — — —

a computer, a keyboard, and a TV screen

9. Think back over frames 1 through 8. We have described the ATARI computer. For our purposes, the important ingredients are:

(1) The computer itself—the central processing unit with its supporting electronic circuitry hidden away inside the console.
(2) An input device—the keyboard, which we use to type information into our computer.
(3) An output device—the TV screen, which displays information typed on the keyboard and/or sent by the computer.
(4) BASIC installed in the computer, ready to go.

In this book, we will show you many programs in ATARI BASIC, and will help you learn to read, understand, and use these programs for your own enjoyment. We will concentrate on applications that we think will be of interest to users of home/school/personal computers. And so . . . for our appetizer, a computer game.

```
100 REMARK *** THIS IS A SIMPLE COMPUTER GAME
110 LET X = INT(100*RND(1))+1
120 PRINT
130 PRINT "I'M THINKING OF A NUMBER FROM 1 TO 100."
140 PRINT "GUESS MY NUMBER!!!"
150 PRINT : PRINT "YOUR GUESS"; : INPUT G
160 IF G<X THEN PRINT "TRY A BIGGER NUMBER." : GOTO 150
170 IF G>X THEN PRINT "TRY A SMALLER NUMBER." : GOTO 150
180 IF G=X THEN PRINT "THAT'S IT!!! YOU GUESSED MY NUMBER." : GOTO 110

RUN
```

These lines, down to the word RUN, are a computer program.

```
I'M THINKING OF A NUMBER FROM 1 TO 100.
GUESS MY NUMBER!!!

YOUR GUESS? 50
TRY A BIGGER NUMBER.

YOUR GUESS? 75
TRY A SMALLER NUMBER.

YOUR GUESS? 65
TRY A SMALLER NUMBER.

YOUR GUESS? 58
TRY A BIGGER NUMBER.

YOUR GUESS? 62
TRY A SMALLER NUMBER.

YOUR GUESS? 60
TRY A BIGGER NUMBER.

YOUR GUESS? 61
THAT'S IT!!! YOU GUESSED MY NUMBER.

I'M THINKING OF A NUMBER FROM 1 TO 100.
GUESS MY NUMBER!!!

YOUR GUESS?
```

And this is what the computer prints on the screen.

The guesses are typed by the computer user.

This part is called a RUN of the program. The computer generates a random number from 1 to 100. The player types in guesses. After each guess, the computer types a clue to help the player make a better guess.

If this sounds confusing, read on! All will be revealed. And it won't be long before you can read and write programs like this in BASIC.

And so on. Chances are that the computer will have a different number this time.

Look again at the program shown in our computer game. The program consists of nine (9) *lines,* each containing one or more BASIC *statements.* Each line begins with a *line number.*

This is a line number.

```
130 PRINT "I'M THINKING OF A NUMBER FROM 1 TO 100."
```

This is a statement.

In our program, each numbered line contains one or more BASIC ________________________ . The numbers, 100 through 180, are called ______ .

— — — — — — — — — — — —

statements; line numbers

10. The program in frame 9 was typed, one line at a time, on the keyboard. As we typed it, the program was stored in the computer's memory and also displayed on the ________________________ .

— — — — — — — — — — — —

TV screen (or video screen)

Note: The TV screen can hold up to 24 lines. So, if the screen is filled, new information typed in will cause old information to be "scrolled up" or "pushed off" the top of the screen.

11. First, we typed in the entire program (lines 100 through 180). At the end of each line we pressed the RETURN key. This process is called "entering the program." This stored the program in the computer's memory. Then we typed RUN. This tells the computer to RUN, or carry out, the program. Computer people also say "to *execute* the program." In other words, after storing the program, we then told the computer to follow the instructions (statements) of the program, or execute the program.

If there is a program in the computer's memory, then typing RUN tells the computer to ____ .

— — — — — — — — — — — —

carry out or execute the instructions in the program.

12. During the RUN, the computer obeyed the instructions (statements) in the program, as follows: First, the computer generated a random number from 1 to 100, inclusive (line 110). This number is an integer—a "whole" number with no fractional part.

```
                  ┌Tells the computer you want numbers to be random.
                  ↓         ┌Tells the computer the lowest number will be 1.
110 LET X = INT(100*RND(1))+1
            ↑    ↑↑─── Multiplication sign
            │    └──── Tells the computer the highest number will be 100
            └───────── Tells the computer you want a "whole" number
```

Next, the computer typed instructions to the player (lines 130 and 140).

```
100 REMARK *** THIS IS A SIMPLE COMPUTER GAME
120 PRINT
130 PRINT "I'M THINKING OF A NUMBER FROM 1 TO 100."
140 PRINT "GUESS MY NUMBER!!!"
```

Then, you told the computer to ask for a guess (line 150).

```
150 PRINT : PRINT "YOUR GUESS"; INPUT G
```

After the player typed a guess, and pressed the RETURN key, the computer compared the guess with its secret number and gave the player the appropriate response (lines 160, 170, and 180).

```
160 IF G<X THEN PRINT "TRY A BIGGER NUMBER." : GOTO 150
170 IF G>X THEN PRINT "TRY A SMALLER NUMBER." : GOTO 150
180 IF G=X THEN PRINT "THAT'S IT!!! YOU GUESSED MY NUMBER." : GOTO 110
```

If the player did *not* guess the computer's number, the computer went back to line 150 and asked for another guess. But, if the lucky player *did* guess the secret number, the computer acknowledged the correct guess and went back to line 110 to "think" of another number.

```
100 REMARK *** THIS IS A SIMPLE COMPUTER GAME
```

Oh yes, line 100 is a REMARK statement. It doesn't tell the computer to *do* anything. It is simply included to tell something *about* the program to us humans who may read the program itself.

What do we type to instruct the computer to execute or carry out a program? ____________________

— — — — — — — — — — —

RUN

Now, to see how much you've learned from this first chapter, try the Self-Test. Then on to Chapter 2 where you'll learn how to actually use the computer.

SELF-TEST

Try this Self-Test, so you can evaluate how much you have learned so far.

1. What does your computer use for an output device? ________________ .
2. What do the following abbreviations stand for?
   (a) CPU ____________________
   (b) RAM ____________________
   (c) ROM ____________________
3. Since a computer doesn't have legs, what do we want a computer to do when we tell it to RUN? ____________________

Answers to Self-Test

The frame numbers in parentheses refer to the frames in the chapter where the topic is discussed. You may wish to refer to these for quick review.

1. A screen or television set (frame 6)
2. (a) Central Processing Unit or computer
   (b) Random Access Memory or user workspace
   (c) Read Only Memory (frames 2, 4)
3. Execute the program (follow the instructions we give it) (frames 11, 12)

CHAPTER TWO

Getting Started

To get you started in computer programming in BASIC, we will now introduce you to some of the statements used to instruct the computer, that is, to tell it what you want accomplished. In this chapter, you will use the *direct,* or immediate, mode of operation. Using direct mode, you tell the computer something to do, and it does it immediately. When you complete this chapter, you will be able to:

- use direct statements to instruct the computer;
- recognize error messages from the computer;
- use the PRINT statement with quotation marks to print strings (messages);
- correct typing errors or delete a statement with errors;
- use direct statements to do arithmetic;
- compute values of simple mathematical expressions using the symbols and rules of BASIC for arithmetic;
- recognize and convert floating point or E notation to ordinary numbers.

1. Now we begin ''talking'' with the computer. We assume that your ATARI computer system is set up and ready to go, with the BASIC language cartridge inserted in the language cartridge slot. You can find directions on how to do this in the *Operators Manual* for your computer. If you own an ATARI 400, you will consult the very friendly and helpful ATARI 400™ OPERATORS MANUAL. If you are using an ATARI 800, you will avidly peruse the ATARI 800™ OPERATORS MANUAL. As you work through this book, you will find your ATARI OPERATORS MANUAL a constant source of know-how and inspiration!

Ready? Turn on the computer.* CLICK! The TV screen will look like this:

The tiny rectangle is called the CURSOR. When you see it, you know that it is your turn to do something.

READY

■

Your ATARI computer is ready for *you* to use. *You* know that it is ready because it typed READY and turned on the tiny rectangle called the

________________________ .

— — — — — — — — — — —

cursor

2. We will, of course, use the keyboard to communicate with the computer.

In the diagram, there is a large black arrow pointing to the key labeled

________________________ .

— — — — — — — — — — —

RETURN

---

*Remember, we assume that *you* know how to hook up the various components of your ATARI system and turn it on. If not, consult your friendly ATARI OPERATORS MANUAL.

3. Your computer is waiting patiently for *you* to do something. So, try this: Type your name and press the RETURN key. The computer will probably print an error message on the screen. Here is what happened when Karl typed his name.

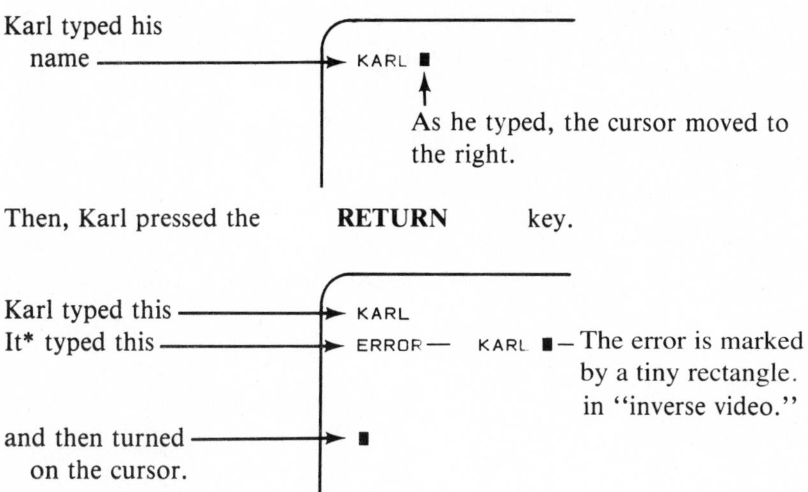

Hmmm . . . Why did that happen? Well, you see, the computer is of quite limited intelligence. It simply did not understand the word, KARL.

(a) If you type something, then press **RETURN,** and the computer types ERROR, what is the computer trying to tell you? ____________________

(b) After typing ERROR— KARL■, what did the computer do? ________

____

— — — — — — — — — —

(a) It does not understand you.
(b) It turned on the cursor.

The cursor is the computer's way to let you know that everything is OK. No damage has been done. The computer is very patient and forgiving. After you make a mistake, it will display the error and then turn on the cursor to let you know it is ready for you to try again.

*By *it,* we mean the computer. Saves space in writing this book!

4. Find the SHIFT key and the CLEAR < key. Press the **SHIFT** key and, while holding it down, press the **CLEAR** key. The screen will now look like this:

Except for the cursor, the screen is blank! Pressing **SHIFT** and **CLEAR** simultaneously erases the screen, leaving only the cursor in its *home position*.

(a) Where is the *home position* of the cursor?______________________________

____

(b) To clear the screen and home the cursor, press__________________________

and ______________________ , together.

— — — — — — — — — —

(a) In the upper left corner of the screen.
(b) **SHIFT; CLEAR**

Another way to clear the screen and home the cursor is to press and hold the **CTRL** key and then press the **CLEAR** key. **CTRL** is an abbreviation for CONTROL. The **CTRL** key is located on the left of the keyboard, directly above the **SHIFT** key. This **CTRL** key is similar to the **SHIFT** key in that you use it only in connection with other keys. If you press it without pressing another key at the same time, nothing happens.

5. To avoid misunderstandings with a computer, we must learn its language. We will start with some simple, one-line statements that the computer *does* understand.

In this chapter we will use *direct statements.* Direct statements do not have line numbers. When you type a direct statement and press **RETURN**, the computer executes the statement immediately, then forgets the statement. We call this BASIC's *direct* mode of operation. Here is another example of a statement that is "executed in direct mode."

Then we press RETURN.

We type: `PRINT "MY HUMAN UNDERSTANDS ME"`

It types: `MY HUMAN UNDERSTANDS ME`

Now you complete the following.

We type: `PRINT "BURGLARS ARE IN THE HOUSE!"`

It types: ____

— — — — — — — — — — — —

`BURGLARS ARE IN THE HOUSE!`

Along with the burglar message, we could also arrange (as we will see later) to have the computer sound an audible alarm. For example, it might play *The Jailhouse Blues* in four part harmony! Hopefully, this might remind the burglar of the possible consequences of crime and thus prevent the attempted theft. More about that later!

6. The statement PRINT "MY HUMAN UNDERSTANDS ME" is called a PRINT statement. It tells the computer to print something on the screen. The computer prints the verbal message following the word PRINT. Note that the message is enclosed in quotation marks. This message, enclosed in quotation marks, is called a *string*.

```
PRINT "MY HUMAN UNDERSTANDS ME"
```

This is a string. It is enclosed in quotation marks. The quotation marks enclose the string, but are not part of the string.

A *string* may include:

Numerals (0, 1, 2, . . .)
Letters (A, B, C, . . .)
Special characters (+, -, *, /,^, comma, period, etc.)

Since quotation marks define the beginning and the end of a string, do you think they can be used as a character in the string? ______________________

____

— — — — — — — — — — — —

No, they cannot. (That would *really* confuse the computer!) However, single quotes (') can be used in a string. For example:

We type: `PRINT "THEY SAID, 'ALL RIGHT.'"`

It types: `THEY SAID, 'ALL RIGHT.'`

Complete the statement so that the computer types what we say it types.

We type: `PRINT` ______________________

It types: `THE ROAST IS DONE. TURN OFF THE OVEN.`

— — — — — — — — — — — —

```
"THE ROAST IS DONE. TURN OFF THE OVEN."
```

Did you remember the quotation marks? Someday, of course, the computer will turn off the oven! Almost anything electric can be controlled by the computer, with the proper electronic connections *and* program, of course.

7. Have you made any typing mistakes yet? In case you should make a typing error, BASIC has a dandy way of fixing it. Watch while we make a typing error.

We type: `PTINT "DENTIST APPOINTMENT TODAY"`

It types: `ERROR -    PTINT "DENTIST APPOINTMENT TODAY"`

We misspelled PRINT, so the computer doesn't know what we want. However, if we had noticed that we hit T when we meant to hit R, we could have corrected our mistake by using the **DELETE BACK S** key. Each time we press this key, the cursor moves back (to the left) one space and erases the character in that space.

We type

Then press **DELETE BACK S**

Press **DELETE BACK S** again

and yet again

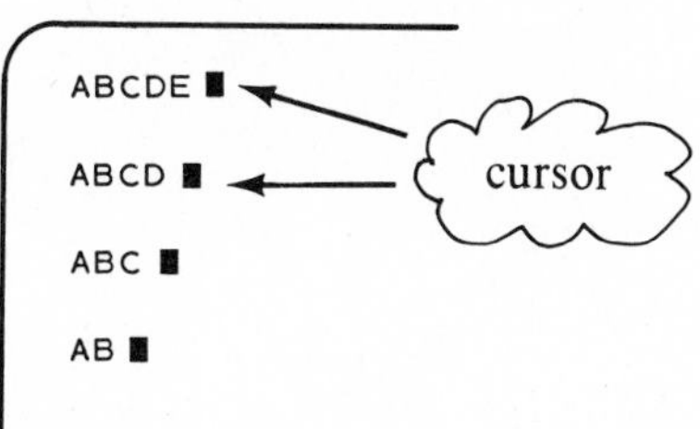

What will happen if we press **DELETE BACK S** two more times?______________

____

— — — — — — — — — — —

The cursor will move two places to the left, erasing A and B.

8. Complete the following so that the computer prints what we want it to print.

We type: `PRIMR` __________ `"TOMORROW IS YOUR MOTHER'S BIRTHDAY!!!"`

It types: `TOMORROW IS YOUR MOTHER'S BIRTHDAY!!!`

— — — — — — — — — — —

DELETE BACK S **DELETE BACK S** NT

Remember: To delete the last character typed, press **DELETE BACK S.** To delete two characters, press **DELETE BACK S** twice. And so on.

9. The **DELETE BACK S** key is great for deleting errors that you have just made. But, suppose you are typing a long line and are almost to the end when, alas, out of the left corner of your left eye, you spot a mistake way back at the beginning. If you complete the line and press **RETURN**, you will probably get an error message. You would *like* to just abort the line—that is, erase it from the beginning.

Well you can! Hold down the **SHIFT** key and press the **DELETE BACK S** key.

We type: `PRIMT "ONCE UPON A TIME THERE WAS A`

The computer erases the entire line and turns on the cursor. Whenever we see the cursor, what is the computer telling us?

— — — — — — — — — —

It is our turn to type.

10. We can also tell the computer to do arithmetic and print the answer. In other words, we can use the computer as a calculator.

We type: `PRINT 7 + 5`

It types: `12`

The statement PRINT 7 + 5 tells the computer to compute the value of 7 + 5 (do the arithmetic) and then print the answer.

Note that calculations are entered to the computer without using quotation marks. Compare the formats below.

We type: `PRINT "13 + 6"`	We type: `PRINT 13 + 6`
It types: `13 + 6`	It types: `19`

`PRINT "13 + 6"`	`PRINT 13 + 6`
This is a string. The computer prints it *exactly* as it appears.	This is a *numerical* expression (no quotation marks). The computer does the arithmetic and prints the result.

Your turn. Complete the following, showing what the computer typed.

We type: `PRINT 23 + 45`

It types: ______________________

We type: `PRINT 1 + 2 + 3 + 4 + 5`

It types: ______________________

We type: `PRINT "1 + 2 + 3 + 4 + 5"`

It types: ______________________

— — — — — — — — — — —

```
68
15
1 + 2 + 3 + 4 + 5
```

11. Subtraction? Of course.

We type: `PRINT 7 - 5`

It types: `2`

We type: `PRINT 25.68 - 37.95`

It types: `-12.27`

Complete the following, showing what the computer typed.

We type: `PRINT 29 - 13`

It types: ______________________

We type: `PRINT 15ØØ - 2ØØØ`

It types: ______________________

We type: `PRINT "15ØØ - 2ØØØ"`

It types: ______________________

— — — — — — — — — — —

```
16
-5ØØ
15ØØ - 2ØØØ
```

12. BASIC uses + for addition and - for subtraction, just as we do with paper and pencil. However, for multiplication, BASIC uses the asterisk (*) instead of the "times" (x) sign.

We type: `PRINT 7 * 5`

It types: `35`

We type: `PRINT 1.23 * 4.567`

It types: `5.61741`

We type: `PRINT 9 * 8`

It types: ____________________

We type: `PRINT 3.14 * 2Ø`

It types: ____________________

— — — — — — — — — —

```
72
62.8
```

13. For division, use the slash (/).

We type: `PRINT 7/5`

It types: `1.4`

We type: `PRINT 13/16`

It types: `Ø.8125`

We type: `PRINT 24/3`

It types: ____________________

We type: `PRINT 3.14/4`

It types: ____________________

— — — — — — — — — —

```
8
Ø.785
```

14. The computer will print up to 9 or 10 digits as the result of an arithmetic operation. If the true result would have more digits, the printed result will be truncated (chopped) to 9 or 10 digits.

We type: `PRINT 1.2345 * 6.78999`

It types: `8.38224265` — Complete answer is 8.382242655 which has 10 digits.

We type: `PRINT 1/3`

It types: `ø.3333333333` — Complete answer cannot be given with a finite number of digits. It goes on forever as a repeating decimal.

We type: `PRINT 2/3`

It types: `ø.6666666666` — Truncated at the 10th digit.

Suppose the complete result of an arithmetic operation is 1.234567898765. What might the computer print? ______________________

Suppose the complete result is 3.14159265359. What might the computer print?

____

— — — — — — — — — —

```
1.23456789 OR 1.234567898
3.14159265 OR 3.141592653
```

15. Write PRINT statements to tell the computer to evaluate each of the following numerical expressions. Also show the result printed by the computer.

Numerical expression	PRINT statement and result
(a) 10 + 6	______________________ ______________________
(b) 15 - 8	______________________ ______________________
(c) 23 ÷ 5	______________________ ______________________
(d) 3 × 13	______________________ ______________________

(e) 8 ÷ 3 ________________
____

(f) 120 ÷ 7 ________________
____

— — — — — — — — — — —

(a)
```
PRINT 1Ø + 6
 16
```
(b)
```
PRINT 15 - 8
 7
```
(c)
```
PRINT 23/5
 4.6
```
(d)
```
PRINT 3*13
 39
```
(e)
```
PRINT 8/3
 2.6666666
```
Truncated to nine digits

(f)
```
PRINT 12Ø/7
 17.14295714
```
Truncated to ten digits (We will also accept 17.1429571)

16. The computer does arithmetic in *left to right* order, with all multiplications (*) and/or divisions (/) performed *before* additions (+) and/or subtractions (–).

$$\left.\begin{matrix} * \\ / \end{matrix}\right\} \text{ before } \left\{\begin{matrix} + \\ - \end{matrix}\right.$$

Shown below are some BASIC expressions in which two or more operations are used. For some of these expressions, we have shown the value computed by the computer after it does the indicated arithmetic. You complete the rest by typing PRINT followed by the expression and pressing RETURN.

Expression	Value computed by computer	How it did the arithmetic
2*3–4	2	2*3–4 = 6 – 4 = 2
2+3*4	14	2+3*4 = 2 + 12 + 14
2*3+4*5	______	________________
2+3*4–5	______	________________
2*3+4*5–6*7	______	________________

— — — — — — — — — — —

26 2*3+4*5 = 6 + 20 = 26
9 2+3*4–5 = 2 + 12 – 5 = 9
–16 2*3+4*5–6*7 = 6 + 20 – 42 = –16

17. Here are more examples and exercises, using division (/). Study the examples and then complete the exercises. Be sure to follow the computer's order described in frame 16.

Expression	Value computed by computer	How it did the arithmetic
3/4+5	5.75	3/4+5 = .75+5 = 5.75
2–3/4	1.25	2–3/4 = 2–.75 = 1.25
2*3+4/5	6.8	2*3+4/5 = 6+.8 = 6.8
3/4+5*6	_______	____________________
2–3/4+5	_______	____________________

— — — — — — — — — — —

30.75 3/4+5*6 = .75+30 = 30.75
6.25 2–3/4+5 = 2–.75+5 = 6.25

18. Following the computer's rules, give the computed value for each of the expressions below. (Remember, do arithmetic in left to right order.)

Expression	Value computed by computer
2*3/4	____________________
3/4*5	____________________
3/4/5	____________________
2*3/4+3/4*5	____________________

— — — — — — — — — — —

1.5 Multiply 2 by 3, then divide result by 4.
3.75 Divide 3 by 4, then multiply result by 5.
0.15 Divide 3 by 4, then divide result by 5.
5.25 First compute 2*3/4, then compute 3/4*5, then add the two results.

19. For each of the following numerical expressions, show the order in which the computer does the arithmetic by putting numbers 1, 2, or 3 in the circles above the operation symbols. We have completed the first three for you.

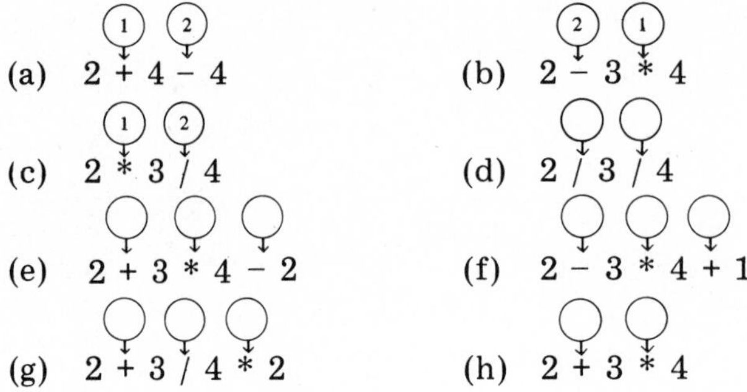

(d) 2 / 3 / 4 — circles: 1, 2

(e) 2 + 3 * 4 − 2 — circles: 2, 1, 3

(f) 2 − 3 * 4 + 1 — circles: 2, 1, 3

(g) 2 + 3 / 4 * 2 — circles: 3, 1, 2

(h) 2 + 3 * 4 — circles: 2, 1

20. If you want to change the order in which operations are done by the computer, use parentheses. Operations in parentheses are done *first.*

Starting with the leftmost inner set of parentheses, the computer does arithmetic within each set of parentheses in *left to right* order, with all multiplications (*) and/or divisions (/) *before* additions (+) and/or subtractions (–).

$$\left.\begin{array}{c} * \\ / \end{array}\right\} \text{ before } \left\{\begin{array}{c} + \\ - \end{array}\right.$$

Look at these examples of how the order of operations can give different results.

	2*3+4 = 10	
but	2*(3+4) = 14	Compute 3 + 4 first because it is inside the parentheses, then multiply the result by 2.
	2+3*4+5 = 19	
but	(2+3)*(4+5) = 45	Compute 2 + 3, then compute 4 + 5, and then multiply these two results.

Complete the following.

Expression	Value computed by computer
(2 + 3)/(4*5)	______________
2 + 3*(4 + 5)	______________
1/(3 + 5)	______________

— — — — — — — — — — —

0.25　(2 + 3)/(4*5) = 5/20 = .25
29　2 + 3*(4 + 5) = 2 + 3*9 = 2 + 27 = 29
0.125　1/(3 + 5) = 1/8 = .125

21. Let's take another look at the order in which arithmetic is done. In the expressions below, the numbers in the circles show the order in which the operations are carried out. Write the final value for each expression. The operations are always done in the innermost set of parentheses first.

Expression	Value computed by computer
2 + 3 * (4 − (5 + 6 * 7)) — order: + ⑤, * ④, − ③, + ②, * ①	________
(3 * 4 + 5 * 6 − 7) / 8 — order: * ①, + ③, * ②, − ④, / ⑤	________

— — — — — — — — — — —

−127
4.375

22. Your next task is to write a proper PRINT statement to tell the computer to compute and print the value of each expression listed below. We have shown the actual value printed by the computer. Remember to indicate all multiplication and division operations with the proper BASIC symbol.

Expression	PRINT statement	Result
$2 \times 3 + 6 \div 7$	____________________	6.85714285
$16(33 - 21)$	____________________	192
$3.14 \times 2 \times 2$	____________________	12.56
$\frac{88 - 52}{18 + 47}$	____________________	0.5538461538

— — — — — — — — — —

```
PRINT 2*3+6/7
PRINT 16*(33-21)
PRINT 3.14*2*2
PRINT (88-52)/(18+47)
```

(Did you remember the asterisk?)

23. For each numerical expression, show the order of operations by putting numbers 1, 2, 3, and so on, in the circles above the operation.

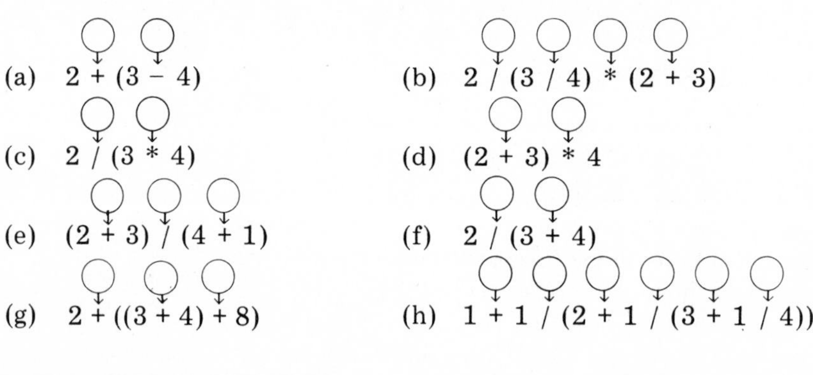

— — — — — — — — — —

(a) 2 + (3 − 4): 2, 1

(b) 2 / (3 / 4) * (2 + 3): 3, 1, 4, 2

(c) 2 / (3 * 4): 2, 1

(d) (2 + 3) * 4: 1, 2

(e) (2 + 3) / (4 + 1): 1, 3, 2

(f) 2 / (3 + 4): 2, 1

(g) 2 + ((3 + 4) + 8): 3, 1, 2

(h) 1 + 1 / (2 + 1 / (3 + 1 / 4)): 6, 5, 4, 3, 2, 1

24. There is a fifth arithmetic symbol in BASIC, which indicates raising a number to a power. This operation is called *exponentiation*.

^ means raise to a power [SHIFT] [→ * ^]

The volume of a cube is a good example of how exponential numbers are used.

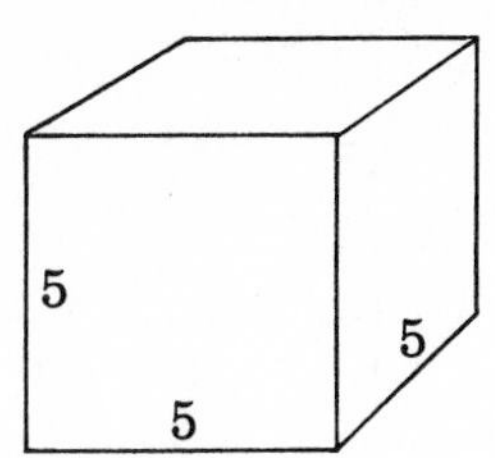

Volume of a cube: $V = S^3$, where S is the length of a side.

If $S = 5$ and $V = 5^3$, then $V = 5^3 = 5 \times 5 \times 5 = 125$.

S^3 This is called a *superscript*

We press the [SHIFT] and [→ * ^] keys together to tell the computer to raise a number to a power.

We type:	`PRINT 5 ^ 3`	(5 ^ 3 means 5^3 or 5×5×5)
It types:	`124.99999998`	Hmmm . . . Call it 125. Since the computer uses the logarithm of a number in computing exponentiation, you will never see it print a "whole" number.

Now complete the following. Give your answers as whole numbers.

We type: `PRINT 2 ^ 3`

It types: ____________

We type: `PRINT 2 ^ 4`

It types: ____________

We type: `PRINT 2 ^ 5`

It types: ____________

We type: `PRINT 7 ^ 2`

It types: ____________

---

8 `2^3` = 2^3 = 2X2X2 = 8 (The computer gave 7.99999986)
16 `2^4` = 2^4 = 2X2X2X2 = 16 (The computer gave 15.9999993)
32 `2^5` = 2^5 = 2X2X2X2X2 = 32 (The computer gave 31.99993444)
49 `7^2` = 7^2 = 7X7 = 49 (The computer gave 48.99999631)

25. Write a PRINT statement to evaluate each expression. We have supplied the results.

Expression	PRINT statement	Result
3^7	____________________	2187
8×8×8×8×8	____________________	32768 (Use ^)
1.06^{10}	____________________	1.79085
$3^2 + 4^2$	____________________	25

— — — — — — — — — — — —

```
PRINT 3 ^ 7
PRINT 8 ^ 5 (PRINT 8*8*8*8*8 will also produce the desired result.)
PRINT 1.Ø6 ^ 1Ø
```

26. Suppose we put $123 into a savings account that pays 6% interest per year, compounded yearly. The amount of money in the account after N years can be computed using the compound interest formula shown below.

$$A = P(1 + R/100)^N$$

where:
P = Principal, or original amount put into the account.
R = Rate of interest per year, in percent.
N = Number of years.
A = Amount in account at the end of N years.

In our problem, P = $123, R = 6%, and we want to know the value of A for N = 2, N = 5, and N = 12 years.

We type: `PRINT 123*(1+6/1ØØ)^2`

It types: `138.2Ø3` ← After 2 years

We type: `PRINT 123*(1+6/1ØØ)^5`

It types: `164.6Ø2` ← After 5 years

Your turn. Write the PRINT statement for N = 12. We have supplied the result printed by the computer.

We type: ____________________

It types: `247.5` ← After 12 years our money doubled.

— — — — — — — — — — — —

```
PRINT 123*(1+6/1ØØ)^12
```

27. Computers use a special notation to indicate very large numbers, or very small decimal fractions. This method of representing numbers is called *floating point notation.* You decipher it in the same way you do the *scientific notation* commonly used in mathematics and science textbooks.

For example, the population of the earth is about 40 billion people.

40 billion = 40,000,000,000

Now let's ask the computer to print the population of the earth.

We type: `PRINT 40000000000` ← No commas. See note below.

It types: `4E+10` ← What's this?

Our ATARI computer printed 40 billion as a *floating point number.* Read it as follows.

4E+10 = four times ten to the tenth power, or
4E+10 = 4×10^{10}

Floating point notation is simply a shorthand way of expressing very large or very small numbers. In floating point notation, a number is represented by a *mantissa* and an *exponent.*

The mantissa and the exponent are separated by the letter __________.

— — — — — — — — — — —

E

NOTE: In typing numbers into the computers, we may *not* use commas as we normally do when writing numerals. Commas have a special use in BASIC PRINT statements. Please be patient. We will get to it soon.

28. Here are some examples showing numbers in good old everyday notation, in floating point notation, and scientific notation.

One trillion
ordinary notation: 1,000,000,000,000
floating point notation: 1E+12
scientific notation: 1×10^{12}

Volume of the earth in bushels
ordinary notation: 31,708,000,000,000,000,000,000
floating point notation: 3.1708E+22
scientific notation: 3.17×10^{22}

Speed of a snail in miles per second
ordinary notation: .0000079
floating point notation: 7.9E–6 (Exponent is *negative.*)
scientific notation: 7.9×10^{-6}

In each floating point number above, underline the mantissa and circle the exponent.

— — — — — — — — — —

1 E + 12

3.1708 E + 22

7.9 E – 6

29. Here are more examples, showing how the ATARI computers print floating point numbers.

We type: `PRINT 123456789`

It types: `12345789`

We type: `PRINT 12345678899`

It types: `1.23456788E+1Ø`

We type: `PRINT 1234567800Ø`

It types: `1.2345678E+1Ø`

Our ATARI computer prints at most nine digits for the mantissa and chops the mantissa at the ninth digit. The mantissa is printed as a nonzero digit to the left of the decimal point and up to eight digits to the right of the decimal point.

We type: `PRINT 333333333333`

It types: ______________________

We type: `PRINT 666666666666`

It types: ______________________

— — — — — — — — — —

`3.33333333E+11`

`6.66666666E+11`

30. It works the same way with very small numbers.

We type: `PRINT .0000001234567889`

It types: `1.23456788E-07` ← Negative exponent

We type: `PRINT .0000001234567884`

It types: `1.23456788E-07` ← Negative exponent

The mantissa is printed with how many digits to the *left* of the decimal point?__________ With how many digits to the *right* of the decimal point?__________

— — — — — — — — — — —

one; eight (See frames 28 and 29 for examples of mantissas with fewer than 8 digits to the right of the decimal point.)

31. Numbers printed in floating point notation can be converted to ordinary notation, as follows. When the exponent is positive, we do the following.

(a) Write the mantissa separately.
(b) Move the decimal point of the mantissa to the *right* the number of places specified by the exponent. If necessary, add zeros.

Example: 6.12345678E+08

(a) 6.12345678 (b) 6.12345678. (Move point 8 places.)

Therefore, 6.12345678E+08 = 612,345,678

Example: 4E+09

(a) 4. (b) 4.000000000. (Move point 9 places and add 9 zeros.)

Therefore, 4E+09 = 4,000,000,000

Now you try it: 1.2345678E+13

(a) __________ (b) __________________

Therefore, 1.2345678E+13 = __________________

— — — — — — — — — — —

(a) 1.2345678 (b) 1.2345678000000 (Move point 13 places.)
12,345,678,000,000

32. When the exponent is negative, we simply change the direction that the decimal point moves.

(a) Write the mantissa separately.
(b) Move the decimal point of the mantissa to the *left* the number of places specified by the exponent. If necessary, add zeros.

Example: 7.9E–06

(a) 7.9 (b) .000007.9 (Move point 6 places and add 5 zeros)

Therefore, 7.9E–06 = .0000079

Your turn. 1.23456E–08

(a) __________ (b) ________________

Therefore, 1.23456E–08 = ________________

— — — — — — — — — —

(a) 1.23456
(b) .00000001.23456

.0000000123456

33. Write each of the following floating point numbers in ordinary notation.

Floating point notation	Ordinary notation
(a) 1.23456E + 06	________________
(b) 1.23456E–06	________________
(c) 1.23456E + 07	________________
(d) 1.23456E–09	________________
(e) 1E + 11	________________
(f) 1E–11	________________

— — — — — — — — — —

(a) 1234560 or 1,234,560
(b) .00000123456
(c) 12345600 or 12,345,600
(d) .00000000123456
(e) 100,000,000,000
(f) .00000000001

34. Write each of the following numbers in ATARI BASIC floating point notation.

Ordinary notation	Floating point notation
(a) 1,234,560,000	__________
(b) .000000123456	__________
(c) 10,000,000,000	__________
(d) .000000001	__________
(e) 1234567888888	__________
(f) .000001234567888888	__________
(g) 6.02×10^{21} (See note.)	__________
(h) 1.67×10^{-11} (See note.)	__________

— — — — — — — — — — —

(a) 1.23456E+09
(b) 1.23456E-07
(c) 1E+10
(d) 1E-09
(e) 1.23456788E+12 Mantissa truncated to 9 digits
(f) 1.23456788E-06 Mantissa truncated to 9 digits
(g) 6.02E+21
(h) 1.67E-11

35. Perhaps you have heard of the ancient story of the wise person who did a great service for a wealthy king. The king asked this person what reward would be appropriate. The person's request was simple. She asked only for grains of wheat, computed as follows. For the first square on a chess board, one grain of wheat; for the second square, 2 grains of wheat; for the third square, 4 grains of wheat and so on, doubling at each square. It goes on as shown below.

Square number	Grains of wheat
1	1
2	2
3	4
4	8
5	16
6	32
7	64

And so on. For square N, there will be 2^{N-1} grains. Let's find out how many grains on square 16.

We type: `PRINT 2 ^ 15`   Since N = 16, N−1 = 15.

It types: `32768`

Your turn. Write a PRINT statement to find out how many grains of wheat for square number 64.

We type: ______________________

It types: `9.2233704E+18`   That's a lot of wheat!

— — — — — — — — — — — —

```
PRINT 2 ^ 63
```

SELF-TEST

Try this Self-Test, so you can evaluate how much you've learned so far.

1. In this chapter, we used direct statements. Direct statements do not have line numbers. When we type a direct statement and press **RETURN**, what does the computer do? ______________________________

   ____

   ____

2. Assume that you are typing a statement into the computer, and you make a typing error. How would you correct the error? ______________

   ____

3. Write the symbols used in ATARI BASIC for the following arithmetic operations.

   addition ______

   subtraction ______

   multiplication ______

   division ______

   exponentiation
   (raising a number to a power) ______

4. Complete the following.

   We type: `PLEASE DO THE HOMEWORK ON PAGE 157`

   It types: ______________________________

5. Complete the following.

   We type: `PRINT "PLEASE DO THE HOMEWORK ON PAGE 157"`

   It types: ______________________________

6. Complete the following.

   We type: `PRINT 9*37/5+32`

   It types: ______________

7. The formula to convert temperature from degrees Fahrenheit to degrees Celsius is shown below.

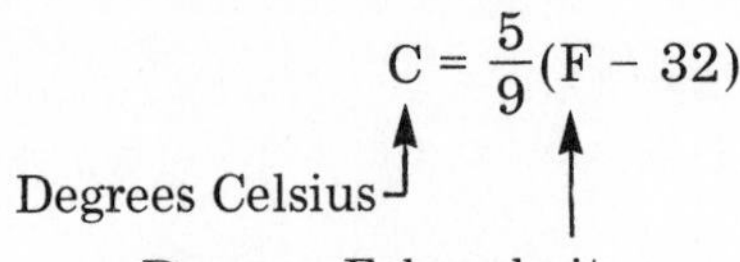

Write a PRINT statement to tell the computer to compute and print the degrees Celsius (value of C) if F = 72 degrees.

____

8. Complete the following.

We type: `PRINY "THE QUICK RED FOX JU` **SHIFT** **DELETE BACK S**

It types: ______________________________

9. What does the following statement tell the computer to do?

PRINT 23 + 45______________________________

10. Indicate which of the following numerical expressions are valid, *as written*, in BASIC.

___ (a) 2*3*4*5

___ (b) 7(8 + 9)

___ (c) 1.23 ÷ 4.567

___ (d) 3 ^ 2 + 4 ^ 2

___ (e) $\frac{1}{37 - 29}$

___ (f) $(1 + 7/100)^3$

___ (g) 2 ^ 2 ^ 2

11. For each invalid numerical expression in problem 10, write a valid BASIC numerical expression.______________________________

____

12. For each of the following numerical expressions, show the order in which the computer does the arithmetic by putting numbers 1, 2, 3, and so on, in the circles above the operation symbols.

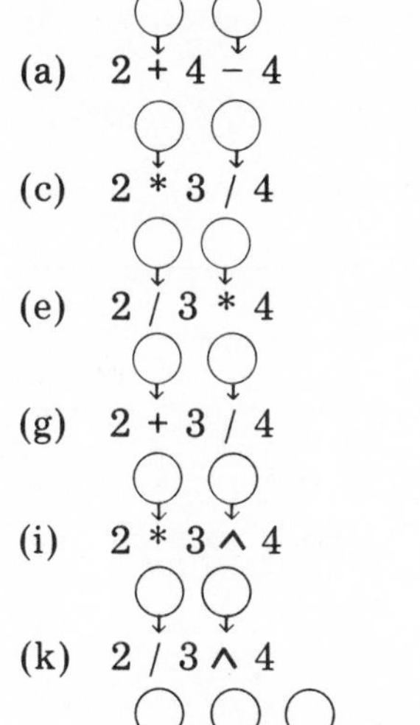

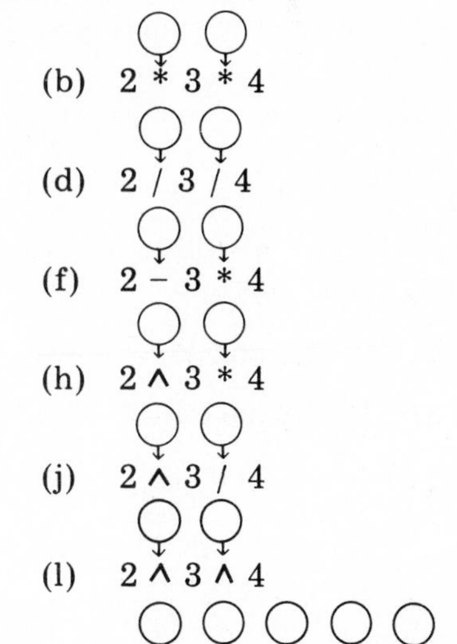

13. For each numerical expression, show the order of operations by putting numbers 1, 2, 3, and so on, in the circles above the operation.

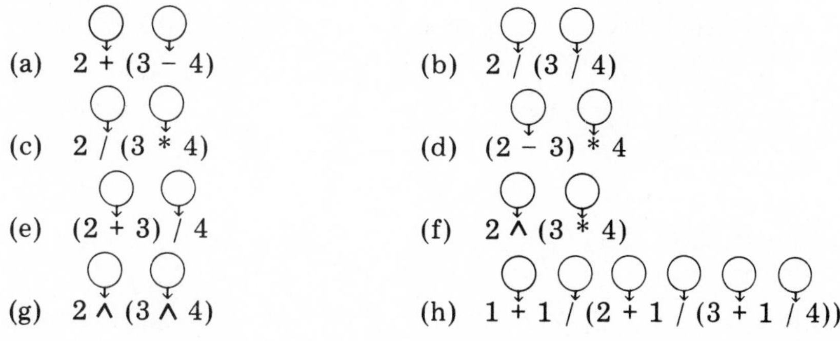

14. Write each of the following floating point numbers in ordinary notation.

Floating point notation	Ordinary notation
(a) 1.23456E+05	______________
(b) 1.23456E−05	______________
(c) 1.23456E+08	______________
(d) 1.23456E−08	______________
(e) 1E+12	______________
(f) 1E−12	______________

15. Write each "ordinary" number in ATARI BASIC floating point notation.

Ordinary notation	Floating point notation.
(a) 1,234,560,000,000	__________
(b) .00000000123456	__________
(c) 10,000,000,000	__________
(d) .0000000001	__________
(e) 12345678999	__________
(f) .00000123456789	__________
(g) 6.02×10^{23} (See note.)	__________
(h) 1.67×10^{-21} (See note.)	__________

Note: The numbers in (g) and (h) are written in scientific notation commonly used in mathematics and science.

Answers to Self-Test

The frame numbers in parentheses refer to the frames in the chapter where the topic is discussed. You may wish to refer to these for quick review.

1. Executes the statement, then "forgets" it (frame 5)
2. Press **DELETE BACK S** to delete the mistake, then type the correct character (frames 7–9)
3. addition +
   subtraction −
   multiplication *
   division /
   exponentiation ^
   (frames 10–24)
4. ERROR – PLEASE DO THE HOMEWORK (The computer does not understand what we want.) (frame 3)
5. PLEASE DO THE HOMEWORK ON PAGE 157 (frames 5–6)
6. 98.6 (frames 16–24)
7. PRINT 5/9*(F–32) or PRINT (5/9)*(F–32) Did you remember the asterisk? By the way, we will also accept PRINT 5*(F–32)/9 (frames 20–23)
8. Only the cursor shows. Entire line deleted. (frame 9)
9. Evaluate the numerical expression 23 + 45 and print the result. The computer will add 23 and 45, getting 68, and print 68. (frame 10)

10. Expressions (a), (d) and (g) are valid. In (g), the computer will evaluate 2^2^2, as follows: 2^2^2 = 4^2 = 16. In other words, the computer will do it left to right, as if it were written (2^2)^2. (frames 24–26)

11. (b) 7*(8+9)
(c) 1.23/4.567
(e) 1/(37–29)
(f) (1+7/100)^3
(frames 16–26)

12. (a) ① ②
2 + 4 − 4

(b) ① ②
2 * 3 * 4

(c) ① ②
2 * 3 / 4

(d) ① ②
2 / 3 / 4

(e) ① ②
2 / 3 * 4

(f) ② ①
2 − 3 * 4

(g) ② ①
2 + 3 / 4

(h) ① ②
2 ↑ 3 * 4

(i) ② ①
2 * 3 ∧ 4

(j) ① ②
2 ∧ 3 / 4

(k) ② ①
2 / 3 ∧ 4

(l) ① ②
2 ∧ 3 ∧ 4

(m) ③ ② ①
1 + 2 * 3 ∧ 4

(n) ③ ④ ① ⑤ ②
2 * 3 − 4 ∧ 3 + 5 ∧ 2

(frames 16-25)

13. (a) ② ①
2 + (3 − 4)

(b) ② ①
2 / (3 / 4)

(c) ② ①
2 / (3 * 4)

(d) ① ②
(2 − 3) * 4

(e) ① ②
(2 + 3) / 4

(f) ② ①
2 ∧ (3 * 4)

(g) ② ①
2 ∧ (3 ∧ 4)

(h) ⑥ ⑤ ④ ③ ② ①
1 + 1 / (2 + 1 / (3 + 1 / 4))

(frames 16-25)

14. (a) 123,456
    (b) .0000123456
    (c) 123,456,000
    (d) .0000000123456
    (e) 1,000,000,000,000
    (f) .000000000001
    (frames 29–34)

15. (a) 1.23456E+12
    (b) 1.23456E–09
    (c) 1E+10
    (d) 1E–10
    (e) 1.23456789E+10
    (f) 1.23456789E–06
    (g) 6.02E+23
    (h) 1.67E–21
    (frames 29–34)

CHAPTER THREE

Assignment Statements, Stored Programs, and Branching

This chapter introduces some of the most useful BASIC statements. From here on, we can work with more interesting programs to illustrate home, school, and personal applications of computers.

In this chapter, you will learn the function and format for the statements and commands listed below.

Statements:	LET, INPUT, GO TO, PRINT, REMARK
Commands:	NEW, RUN, LIST

You will learn how you can store programs for automatic and repetitive execution. You will also learn about *variables* and be able to supply values for variables used in BASIC programs. When you have finished this chapter, you will be able to:

- write programs in which values are assigned to variables by means of LET statements or INPUT statements;
- distinguish between and use numeric variables and string variables;
- write programs in which a value calculated by a BASIC expression is assigned to a numerical variable in a LET statement;
- store a BASIC program in the computer's memory;
- erase an unwanted program from the computer's memory, LIST a program currently in the computer, and RUN (execute) a program;
- edit, correct, and delete statements in a stored program;
- write programs that use the GO TO statement to repeat a portion of a program or to skip over a portion of a program;
- use REMARK statements to make programs more readable and understandable by *humans;*
- write PRINT statements which identify printed results with descriptive messages.

1. To illustrate the concept of *variable* and the function of the LET statement in BASIC, imagine that there are 26 little boxes inside the computer. Each box can contain one number at any one time.

A	7	H		O		V	
B	5	I		P	4E + 09	W	
C		J	4	Q		X	2.5
D		K		R		Y	
E		L		S	-6	Z	
F	2	M		T			
G		N		U			

We have already stored numbers in some of the boxes. For example, 7 is in box A and 5 is in box B.

(a) What number is in box F? ________

(b) In J? ________

(c) -6 is in box ________.

(d) 2.5 is in box ________.

(e) What box contains a floating point number? ________

— — — — — — — — — — —

(a) 2; (b) 4; (c) S; (d) X; (e) P (The floating point number is 4E + 09.)

2. Boxes C and N are shown below. Use a *pencil* to do the following.

(a) Put 8 into box C. In other words, write the numeral "8" in the box labeled "C." Do this before you go on to (b).
(b) Put 12 into N. Do this before you go on to (c).
(c) Put 27 into N. But wait! A box can hold only one number at a time. Before you can enter 27 into N, you must first erase the 12 that you previously entered.

C		N	

Fill in the boxes before you look at the answer.

— — — — — — — — — — —

C	8	N	27

3. When the computer puts a number into a box, it *automatically* erases the previous content of the box, just as you did. In order to put 27 into box N, you first erased the previous content, 12.

We call A, B, C, . . ., Z *variables.* The number in box A is the *value of A;* the number in box B is the *value of B;* the number in box C is the *value of C,* and so on.

We use the LET statement to instruct the computer to "put a number in a box." To say it more technically, we are assigning a numerical *value* to a *variable.*

We type: `LET A = 7` — Put 7 into box A.

We type: `PRINT A` — Prints the contents of box A.

It types: `7`

In the above example, the *variable* is ________ and the *value* assigned to it by the LET statement is ________.

— — — — — — — — — —

A; 7

4. Complete the following.

(a) We type:
```
LET X = 23
PRINT X
```
It types: ________

(b) We type:
```
LET Z = -1
PRINT Z
```
It types: ________

(c) We type:
```
LET A = 1
LET A = 2
PRINT A
```
It types: ________

(d) We type:
```
LET D = 7
LET W = D
PRINT W
```
It types: ________

— — — — — — — — — —

(a) 23
(b) -1
(c) 2 (The statement LET A=2 *replaced* the value previously assigned by LET A=1.)
(d) 7 (LET W=D copies the value in D into W. The value is still in D, also.)

5. Write a LET statement to assign the value 3.14 to P and a PRINT statement to print the value of P.

We type: ____________________

____

It types: ____________________

— — — — — — — — — — —

```
LET P = 3.14
PRINT P
3.14
```

Note: In ATARI BASIC, the word LET can be omitted. For example, we can type P=3.14 instead of LET P=3.14.

6. Once we have assigned a value to a variable, that variable can be used in mathematical expressions.

We type:
```
LET A = 7
LET B = 5
```

A	7
B	5

We now have 7 in box A and 5 in box B.

We type: `PRINT A + B`

It types: `12` Since A=7 and B=5, A+B=7+5=12.

We type: `PRINT A - B`

It types: `2` Since A=7 and B=5, A–B=7–5=2.

Your turn. Complete the following.

We type: `PRINT A*B`

It types: __________

We type: `PRINT A/B`

It types: __________

— — — — — — — — — — —

35
1.4

7. The variables that we have used so far are called *numeric* variables. The value assigned to a numeric variable must be a number.

BASIC has another type of variable, called a *string* variable. The value assigned to a string variable must be a string. A string can contain letters, numbers, spaces and symbols, but you must enclose a string in quotation marks.

Before we use a string variable, we must first tell the computer how long the string might be. That is, we must tell the computer how much memory might be needed to hold the string. We do this with a DIMension statement. For example, the following DIM statement tells the computer to make room for a string of up to 5 characters in length.

We type: `DIM N$(5)`

It types: `READY`

We have told the computer that a string variable called N$ can have as many as 5 characters in length.

We type: `LET N$ = "JERRY"`

This assigns the string JERRY to the string variable N$.

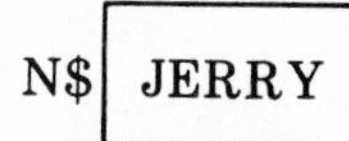

Now, let's print the contents of N$.

We type: `PRINT N$`

It types: `JERRY`

Complete the following.

We type:
```
DIM Z$(100)

LET Z$ = "MY HUMAN UNDERSTANDS ME"
PRINT Z$
```

It types: ____

— — — — — — — — — — —

```
MY HUMAN UNDERSTANDS ME
```

Our DIM statement reserved space for *up to* 100 characters. Our actual string, in this case, is shorter than 100 characters. Chapter 9 will describe strings in much more detail.

8. Let's look at a problem. We have three bicycles with wheels of 16-, 24-, and 26-inch diameters. For each bike, we want to know how far the bike travels during one revolution of the wheel. This distance, of course, is the *circumference* of the wheel. Let's use D to represent the diameter of the wheel and C to represent the circumference.

$$C = \pi D$$

where $\pi = 3.14159 \ldots$

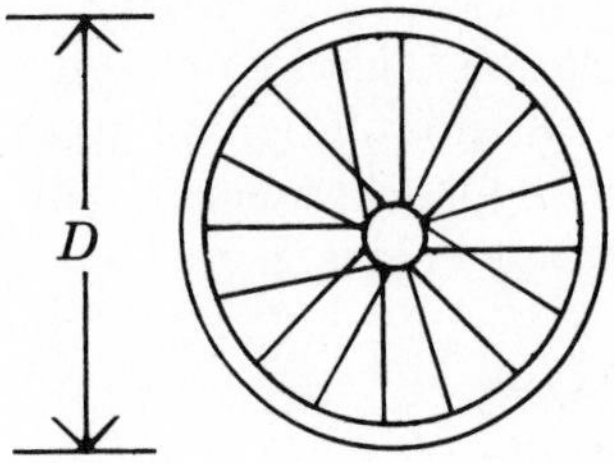

We will use 3.14 as a crude approximation to π. We could do this problem as follows.

We type: `PRINT 3.14 * 16`

It types: `5Ø.24`

We type: `PRINT 3.14 * 24`

It types: `75.36`

We type: `PRINT 3.14 * 26`

It types: `81.64`

Here is another way to do it. Complete the parts we have omitted

We type:
```
LET D = 16
PRINT 3.14 * D
```

It types: `5Ø.24`

We type:
```
LET D = 24
PRINT 3.14 * D
```

It types: ___________

We type: LET ___________

____

It types: `81.64`

```
75.36
D = 26
PRINT 3.14 * D
```

9. Now we are ready to take the big step from one-at-a-time *direct* statements to a *stored program.* We will store this program in the memory of our computer. (Just look at it, then read on.)

```
10 LET D = 16
20 PRINT 3.14 * D
```

The above program has two statements, each on a single line. Each statement begins with a *line number* (in this case, the 10 and 20). A line number can be any integer from 1 to 32767.

When we type statements with line numbers, the statements are *not* executed when you press RETURN. Instead, the statements are stored in the computer's memory for later execution.

As you learned in Chapter 2, statements without line numbers are called *direct statements.* The computer executes a direct statement immediately and then forgets it. However, this does not happen when we type a statement *with* a line number. Instead, what does happen?

____

____

— — — — — — — — — — —

The statement is stored in the computer's memory for later execution. That is, the computer remembers the statement.

10. The line numbers tell the computer the order in which it is to follow statements in the program. It is not necessary for line numbers to be consecutive integers (e.g., 1, 2, 3, 4, 5 . . .). It is common practice to number by tens as we do in the following program. Then, if we wish, we can easily insert or add more statements into the program between existing statements.

```
10 LET D = 16
20 PRINT 3.14 * D
```

How many additional lines could be added betwen line 10 and line 20?

____

— — — — — — — — — — —

9 (lines 11, 12, 13, 14, 15, 16, 17, 18, 19)

Of course, you don't *have* to number by tens. If you prefer numbering by thirteens or fives, help yourself!

11. Before we store a program, we must first remove or erase any old programs that may already be stored in the computer's memory.

____

We type: NEW　　And, of course, press **RETURN.**

It types: READY

The computer has erased the portion of its memory that stores BASIC programs. It is now ready to accept a new program.

How do we erase, remove, or delete an old program from the computer's memory? ______________________________

— — — — — — — — — — —

We type NEW and press **RETURN** key.

Note: If we misspell NEW, we may get an error message. For example:

We type: GNU

It types: ERROR- GNU□

Our computer doesn't appreciate puns, but if we type NEW correctly and press RETURN, all is well.

12. Now we are ready to store our two-line program from frames 9 and 10.

First, we must erase any old program by typing __________ and pressing the RETURN key. To store the program, we type the first line or statement and press the RETURN key, then type the second line and ______________________ ______________________.

— — — — — — — — — — —

NEW; press the RETURN key

13. Let's do it.

We type: NEW

It types: READY

We type:

```
10 LET D = 16
20 PRINT 3.14 * D
```

If we make a typing error, we start over. The program is now stored. The computer is waiting patiently for our next statement or command.

Hmmmm . . . we wonder if the program really *is* stored in the computer's memory. We can find out by typing LIST and pressing the **RETURN** key.

We type: `LIST` And press **RETURN.**

It types:
```
10 LET D=16
20 PRINT 3.14*D
READY
```

The command LIST tells the computer to type all of the program statements that are currently stored in its memory. After listing the program, the computer types READY to let us know it is our turn again. If there is *no* program stored, the computer will simply type READY.

How do we tell the computer to type out the program that is currently stored in its memory? ______________________________

— — — — — — — — — — —

We type LIST and press the **RETURN** key.

14. Listing a BASIC program lets us know whether or not a program is stored in the computer's memory. We may want to add more statements to the program. Or we may wish to see if we have typed the statements correctly. If we want the computer to execute the program, we type ________. If we want the computer to tell us if there is a program stored in its memory, and to type out the program for us, we type ____________.

— — — — — — — — — — —

`RUN; LIST`

15. After you type RUN to tell the computer to execute a program, or after you type LIST to command the computer to tell us "what's on its mind" (that is, what is stored in its memory), what else do you have to do before the computer will respond? ______________________________

— — — — — — — — — — —

press the RETURN key

16. Assume you have typed our little program into the computer.

```
10 LET D = 16
20 PRINT 3.14 * D
```

The program is stored in the computer's memory. Now you want the computer to execute (carry out) the program. Type RUN and press the **RETURN** key.

We type: `RUN` And press RETURN.

It types:

```
50.24
READY
```

The computer has RUN the program. That is, it has executed the statements of the program in line number order. First, the computer was told to assign a value to a variable with this statement: 10 LET D=16. That means that the computer placed the value ________ in the box identified by the variable ________.

— — — — — — — — — —

16; D

17. After following the instruction in the statement with line number 10, the computer went on to the next statement in line number order: 20 PRINT 3.14*D. Part of line 20 tells the computer to multiply two numbers. One number is given in the statement. The other number is stored in a place labeled by the variable D. What are the two values that the computer uses to multiply?

____

— — — — — — — — — —

3.14 and 16 (Because 16 is the value of D.)

18. In the last frame we saw that part of line 20 tells the computer to multiply two values. What else does line 20 tell the computer to do?________________

____

— — — — — — — — — —

PRINT the results of the multiplication

Note: some computers require an END statement as the last statement in the program, as we show below. Our ATARI computer does not need END, but you may use it if you wish.

```
10 LET D = 16
20 PRINT 3.14 * D
30 END
```

19. Let's review what happens when we use our little program that calculates the circumference of a bicycle wheel.

`NEW` `READY`	First, we erase any old program.
`10 LET D = 16` `20 PRINT 3.14 * D`	Then, we type in this program, which consists of two statements.
`LIST`	Next, we tell the computer to LIST the program.
`10 LET D=16` `20 PRINT 3.14*D`	The computer LISTs (types) the program,
`READY`	then types READY and stops.
`RUN`	Finally, we tell the computer to RUN the program.
`50.24`	It executes the program,
`READY`	then types READY and stops.

The program is still stored in the computer's memory. What will happen if we now type RUN ____________________

— — — — — — — — — — —

The computer will execute the program again. Since nothing in the program has changed, the same result (50.24) will be printed.

20. What happens if we make a typing mistake in entering a program?

We type:	`10 LET F = 16` `20 PRINT 3.14 * D`	We typed F instead of D.
We type:	`RUN`	
It types:	`0`	Oops! Something wrong. Let's look at the program.
We type:	`LIST`	
It types:	`10 LET F = 16` `20 PRINT 3.14 * D`	Sure enough, we notice that we mistakenly hit F instead of D in line 10.
We type:	`10 LET D=16`	We retype line 10, correctly. This replaces the old line 10.
We type:	`LIST`	To make sure the new line 10 replaced the old line 10, we LIST the corrected program (and also check to make sure we typed it right this time!)
It types:	`10 LET D=16` `20 PRINT 3.14*D`	

Suppose we had seen the mistake immediately after we had typed it. How could we have corrected it?____________________

— — — — — — — — — — —

We could have pressed the **DELETE BACK S** key, then the correct letter.

21. We assume that our circumference program is still stored in memory. Now we want to change the value assigned to *D*. To do this, we *replace* line 10 with a different line 10. After making this change, we will LIST the modified program.

We type:
```
10 LET D = 24
LIST
```

It types:
```
10 LET D=24
20 PRINT 3.14*D
```

Here is the new line 10, and the old line 20.

How do we *replace* a line in a stored program? ______________________

____

— — — — — — — — — — —

We type a new line with the same line number as the line we wish to replace.

Note: We do *not* type NEW because we want line 20 to remain in the computer while we change *only* line 10. Typing NEW would erase *both* statements from the computer's memory.

22. We will RUN the modified program of frame 23.

We type: `RUN`

It types: `75.36`

Your turn. Complete the following.

We type: `10 LET D = 26`

We type: `LIST`

It types: ______________________

____

We type: `RUN`

It types: ______________________

From now on, we will usually omit the word READY in this book.

— — — — — — — — — — —

```
10 LET D = 26          ← New line 10
20 PRINT 3.14*D        ← Old line 20
 81.64
```

23. How fast does your money grow?

Problem: We put P dollars in a savings account which pays R percent interest, per year, compounded yearly. How much money will we have in the account at the end of N years?

P is the original amount (principal).
R is the interest rate, in percent, per year.
N is the number of years.
A is the amount after N years.

$A = P(1 + R/100)^N$ Formula for A, given P, R, and N

Below is a program to compute A for P = $1000, R = 6%, and N = 3 years. Complete line 40 in correct BASIC notation, using the formula above as a guide.

```
10 LET P = 1000
20 LET R = 6
30 LET N = 3

40 LET A = ____________________
50 PRINT A
```

— — — — — — — — — —

`P*(1+R/100)^N` (Did you remember the asterisk? Did you remember to use ^ to tell the computer to raise to a power?)

24. We will store and RUN the program, then ask *you* to make some changes.

We type:

```
NEW
10 LET P = 1000
20 LET R = 6
30 LET N = 3
40 LET A = P*(1+R/100)^N
50 PRINT A
RUN
```

Don't forget, we are usually omitting the READY typed by the computer. We also will omit reminders to use the RETURN key after entering a statement or a command such as RUN, LIST, or NEW

It types: `1191.01598`

Now, show how to change line 30 so that N = 5.

We type: ____________________

```
RUN
```

It types: `1338.22557` Value of A for P = 1000, R = 6, N = 5.

— — — — — — — — — —

```
30 LET N = 5
```

25. Now change the program so that R=7% and N=8 years.

We type: ______________________

____

```
RUN
```

It types:
```
1718.18617
```

— — — — — — — — — — —

```
2Ø LET R=7
3Ø LET N=8
```

26. Now show how the computer will respond if we type LIST.

We type:
```
LIST
```

It types: ______________________

____

____

____

____

— — — — — — — — — — —

```
1Ø LET P=1ØØØ
2Ø LET R=7
3Ø LET N=8
4Ø LET A=P*(1+R/1ØØ)^N
5Ø PRINT A
```

27. LET statements are all fine and good, but what a hassle to change all those LET statements every time you want to change the values of variables. Ah, but leave it to BASIC to come up with a clever solution—the INPUT statement.

The INPUT statement allows the computer user to assign different values to variables each time a program is RUN *without* modifying the program itself. When the computer comes to an INPUT statement in a program, it types a question mark and waits for the user to enter a value for a variable. Below is an example:

We type:
```
NEW
1Ø INPUT A
2Ø PRINT A
RUN
```

First, we erase any old program, then enter this program.
Then we tell the computer to RUN the program.

It types:
```
?■
```

The computer types a question mark, turns on the cursor, then waits.

When we typed RUN, what did the computer do? ______________________

____

— — — — — — — — — — —

It typed a question mark and waited for us to do something.

Note: The question mark is an example of a *prompt*. The computer types a prompt to tell you it is *your* turn to do something. The message READY is another example of a prompt.

28. The INPUT statement causes the computer to type a question mark, then stop and wait. It is waiting for a value to assign the variable which appears in the INPUT statement. Computers are very patient. If we don't cooperate by typing a value, the computer will simply wait, and wait, and wait.

So let's cooperate with our ever-patient computer and type in a numeric value for A. We will enter 3 as a value to be assigned to A, then press RETURN. The computer will put our numeric value into box A, then continue running the program.

```
NEW
10 INPUT A
20 PRINT A

RUN
?3
 3
```

After we typed 3 as the value for A and then pressed RETURN, the computer went on to line 20 and printed our numeric value.

After we typed RUN and pressed the RETURN key, the computer typed a ______________________. We then typed 3, which is our value for the INPUT variable ________. The computer then executed the PRINT A statement (line 20) and printed the ______________________ of A.

— — — — — — — — — — —

question mark; A; numeric value

29. The program can be RUN again with a different numeric value of A supplied by the user. Pretend you are the computer, and show how a RUN would look if your human computer user typed 23 as the value of A.

```
RUN

________

________

_ _ _ _ _ _ _ _ _ _ _

?23
 23
```

30. Now let's use an INPUT statement to enter (type in) data for our familiar bicycle wheel problem. *Data* is the name for information used by a computer program.

We type:
```
NEW
10 INPUT D
20 PRINT 3.14*D

RUN
```
It types:
```
?
```

The computer wants a value for D, the diameter of our bicycle wheel. It will then compute the distance traveled in one revolution, and print it. Let's do it for D = 16, D = 24, and D = 26.

```
RUN

?16
 50.24
```

First, we RUN the program for D = 16. When the computer typed a question mark, we entered 16 as the value of D. The computer computed and printed 3.14*D, then stopped.

```
RUN

?24
 75.36
```

We typed RUN again and, when the computer typed the question mark, we supplied 24 as the value of D. The computer zapped out the answer, and stopped.

```
RUN
```

Your turn. Complete the third RUN.

```
________

________

_ _ _ _ _ _ _ _ _ _ _

?26
 81.64
```

31. One INPUT statement can be used to assign values to *two or more* variables.

```
1Ø INPUT A,B          Two variables, A and B.
2Ø PRINT A+B
RUN
? 7,5                 Two values, 7 and 5.
 12
```

When the computer typed a question mark, we typed *two* numbers separated by a comma, then pressed the RETURN key. The computer assigned the first number as the value of A and the second number as the value of B. Note the following.

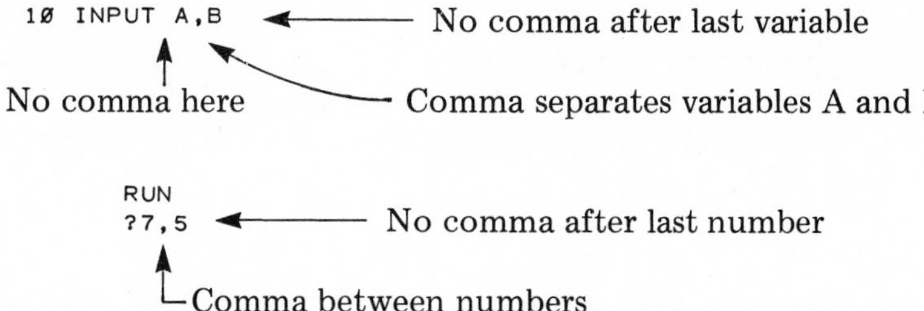

The value 7 is assigned to the variable A, and the value 5 is assigned to the variable B.

Here is the summary; you fill in the blanks. When a program containing an INPUT statement with multiple variables is RUN, the first value typed in by the user after the INPUT question mark will be assigned to the ________________ variable that appears in the INPUT statement; the ______________ value typed in by the user will be assigned to the second variable appearing in the INPUT statement, and so on. Both the variables in the INPUT statement in the program, and the values typed in by the user when the program is RUN, must be separated by ________________________.

— — — — — — — — — —

first; second; commas

32. Here is another RUN of the program in frame 31. We want to enter 73 as the value of A and 59 as the value of B.

```
RUN
? 73          Oops! We absentmindedly hit the RETURN key.
?■
```

The computer typed another question mark and turned on the cursor. This means "Didn't you forget something?"

We then completed the RUN by entering the *second* number, the value of B.

```
RUN
? 73
? 59
 132
```

What happens if we don't enter a numerical value for *every* variable in an INPUT statement? ______________________________

____

— — — — — — — — — — — —

The computer types another question mark.

Note: If you enter *more* numbers than there are variables, the computer will ignore the extra values.

33. Suppose you and a bunch of friends, all bicycle aficionados, are gathered about your computer, and they are marveling at your newly acquired computer programming skills. You decide to demonstrate how the computer works by using the program to compute the distance traveled in one turn of the wheel. However, you have to do a separate RUN of the program for each friend. But wait—first add a new statement to the program.

```
10 INPUT D
20 PRINT 3.14*D
30 GO TO 10          ←——— Something new—a GO TO statement.
```

In BASIC, a GO TO statement tells the computer to jump to or branch to the line number following the words GO TO, and then to continue following the instructions in the program in the usual line number order.

In the above program, the GO TO statement tells the computer to jump to line __________ and start the program over again.

— — — — — — — — — — — —

10

34. Let's see what happens when we RUN the program. (Assume that you, or someone, has typed NEW, then entered the program.)

```
RUN
?16
 5Ø.24
?24
 75.36
?26
 81.64
?■
```

Following each question mark, we typed the value of D. The computer then computed the value of 3.14*D, printed the result, and typed another question mark.

Well, we are finished, but the computer doesn't know that we are finished. It is hung up on line 10, waiting for INPUT data. How do we get out of this situation? Easy! Just press the **BREAK** key.

```
?                        ← We press the BREAK key.
STOPPED AT LINE 1Ø       ← It types the line number where the BREAK occurred
■                          and turns on the cursor
```

Suppose the computer is executing an INPUT statement and has typed a question mark. If we press the BREAK key, what does the computer do? ____________

____

— — — — — — — — — — —

It "escapes" from the INPUT statement, types STOPPED AT ℓ (where ℓ is the line number where the BREAK occurred) and turns on the cursor.

35. Remember: BASIC statements are executed in line number order, unless a GO TO statement changes the order. In the program from frame 33, the statements are executed in the order shown below by the arrows. Instead of executing the PRINT statement at line 40, the GO TO statement in line 30 sends the computer back to line 10.

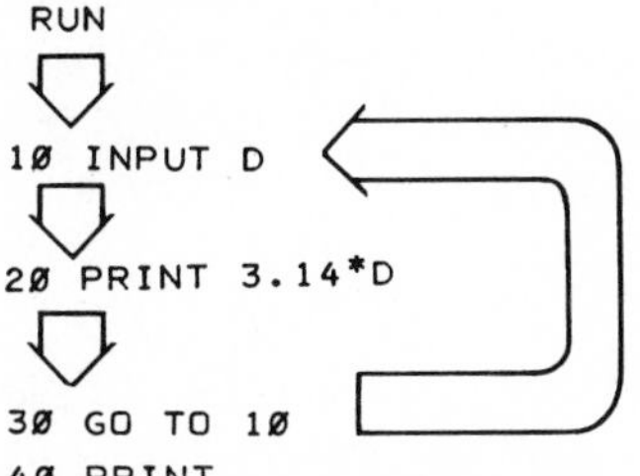

Around and around and around—until you quit by pressing the **BREAK** key.

In this program, the computer never gets to execute line 40.

The above program is an example of a *loop*. The GO TO statement causes the computer to "loop back" to the beginning. In this program, the computer loops back to an INPUT statement and then stops. Watch out! We can write programs with nonstop loops. Here is an example. Type NEW before you enter the program.

```
13 PRINT "TO STOP ME, PRESS THE 'BREAK' KEY"
27 GO TO 13
```

Do *not* RUN this program yet! Instead, draw arrows as we did on the previous page to show how the computer executes the program.

```
RUN

13 PRINT "TO STOP ME, PRESS THE 'BREAK' KEY"

27 GO TO 13
```

— — — — — — — — — — — —

```
RUN

13 PRINT "TO STOP ME, PRESS THE 'BREAK' KEY"

27 GO TO 13
```

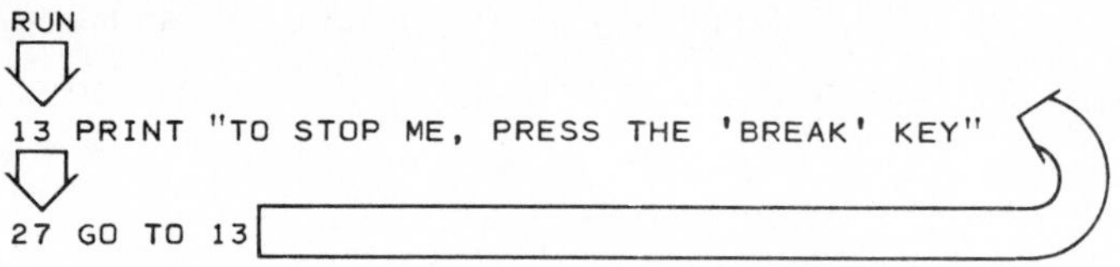

We have used line numbers 13 and 27 to remind you that you don't have to number by 10, although we usually do.

36. Now let's enter the program of frame 35 and RUN it. Remember, to stop the computer, press the **BREAK** key.

```
13 PRINT "TO STOP ME, PRESS THE 'BREAK' KEY"
27 GO TO 13

RUN
TO STOP ME, PRESS THE 'BREAK' KEY
TO STOP ME, PRESS THE 'BREAK' KEY
TO STOP ME, PRESS THE 'BREAK' KEY
TO STOP ME, PRESS THE 'BREAK' KEY
TO STOP ME, PRESS THE 'BREAK' KEY

STOPPED AT LINE 13  ←—— We pressed the BREAK key!
```

The computer executed line 13 over and over again, because the GO TO statement in line 27 repeatedly told the computer to go back to line 13. This is a "forever" loop—it just keeps going around and around until someone interrupts it. Sometimes this is referred to as an "infinite" loop, because it does not stop automatically.

How do we interrupt, or stop, the computer when it is running a program?

____

— — — — — — — — — — — —

We press the BREAK key.

37. Now that you know how to stop a runaway computer by pressing the BREAK key, let's write a "Happy Computer" program. This program will quickly fill the screen with laughter! Remember: before entering the program, type NEW to erase any old program. Then, enter the following program. The program contains some old statements, such as PRINT and GO TO, and a new statement called REMARK. We use the REMARK statement to tell something about the program to a *human* who may be reading the program. The computer simply ignores REMARK statements.

```
1ØØ REMARK FILL THE SCREEN WITH 'LAUGHTER'

11Ø PRINT "HA HA ";        <-- Include this semicolon

12Ø GO TO 11Ø
```

Be sure to put a space betwen the 2nd HA and the quotation mark.

OK, run this program. Did the screen fill with laughter? ___________

— — — — — — — — — — —

We think you answered YES. When we did it, the entire screen quickly filled with HA HA.

38. Try the above program with line 110 modified as follows:

Run the modified program. Did only the left portion of the screen fill with HA HA? ___________

— — — — — — — — — — —

Again, we think you answered YES. The semicolon causes the computer to print *across* the screen from left to right. When the computer gets to the right edge, it simply continues on the next line. Without the semicolon, the computer starts a new line after each PRINT statement.

39. The REMARK statement has a short form that you can use. The short form is simple, the first three letters in REMark. When executing a program, the computer only "looks" at the first three letters, and if those three letters are REM, then the computer will skip on to the next statement in line number order without considering the rest of the statement. Therefore, you could use the word REMEMBER instead of REMark and the effect would be the same.

Rewrite line 100 in frame 37 using the short form of the REMark statement ______________________________

— — — — — — — — — —

```
100 REM FILL THE SCREEN WITH 'LAUGHTER'
```

40. When the computer executes a PRINT statement that has only the word PRINT following the line number and nothing else in the statement, it does the same thing that happens when you press the **RETURN** key. It spaces down one line on the screen. This has the effect of leaving a blank or "empty" line on the screen. An "empty" PRINT statement is very handy for making the printout of a program easier to read.

Here is a RUN from our bicycle wheel program from Frames 33 and 34.

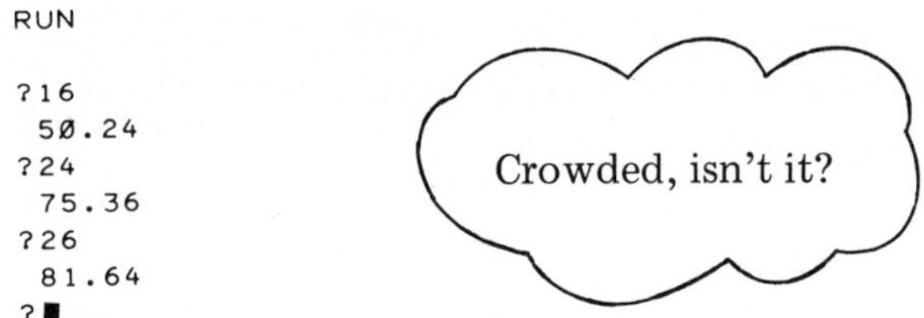

Well, let's make it less crowded! We will add the following empty PRINT statement to the program.

```
25 PRINT
```

We type:

```
10 INPUT D
20 PRINT 3.14*D
25 PRINT
30 GOTO 10
```

Let's RUN it and see what happens.

```
RUN

?16
 50.24
                ←——— Note the line space. The "empty" line is provided by line 25.
?24
 75.36
                ←——— Another line space.
?26
 81.64
                ←——— Still another line space.

?■                   and so on.
```

Compare the two RUNs. What does 25 PRINT tell the computer to do?

____

____

— — — — — — — — — —

Print a line space ("empty" line) after printing the value of 3.14*D. This happens *before* the computer executes GO TO 10.

41. Now, to make things clear to other humans dealing with INPUT statements, we need a way to inform the user what the INPUT statement is asking for. Let's add this statement to the bicycle program:

```
5 PRINT "WHEEL DIAMETER" ;
```

See the semicolon at the end of the PRINT statement? When a semicolon is used at the end of a PRINT statement, the computer stays on the same line of the screen *instead of* going to the beginning of the next line. Here is our revised program. We changed line 30 so that the program loops back to line 5 and prints WHEEL DIAMETER each time.

```
 5 PRINT "WHEEL DIAMETER" ;
10 INPUT D
20 PRINT 3.14*D
25 PRINT
30 GOTC 5
```

Let's RUN the modified program.

We type: RUN
It types: WHEEL DIAMETER? ■ ← cursor

This is from line 5. (WHEEL DIAMETER)

The question mark is from the INPUT statement in line 10.

Aha! Now we know exactly what the computer wants. It wants a value for WHEEL DIAMETER. OK, we type 16 as the value of WHEEL DIAMETER and press RETURN. Show what happens next.

```
WHEEL DIAMETER? 16
```

____

____

— — — — — — — — — — —

```
5Ø.24
WHEEL DIAMETER? ■
```

42. Now what the computer wants is clearly identified by the string enclosed in quotation marks in the PRINT statement. We use the same approach in a PRINT statement to identify the calculation performed by the computer for that statement (see line 20).

```
 5 PRINT "WHEEL DIAMETER" ;
1Ø INPUT D
2Ø PRINT "DISTANCE IN ONE TURN IS " ; 3.14*D
25 PRINT
3Ø GOTO 5
```

Note semicolon

The statement 20 PRINT "DISTANCE IN ONE TURN IS " ; 3.14*D tells the computer to:

(1) print the string DISTANCE IN ONE TURN IS, then
(2) compute and print the value of 3.14*D.

Let's try it. Complete the RUN.

```
RUN

WHEEL DIAMETER? 16
DISTANCE IN ONE TURN IS 5Ø.24

WHEEL DIAMETER? 24
DISTANCE IN ONE TURN IS ____________________

WHEEL DIAMETER? 26
```

____

____

— — — — — — — — — — —

```
75.36
DISTANCE IN ONE TURN IS 81.64
WHEEL DIAMETER? ■
```

← Our ever-friendly cursor.

43. Rewrite the program in frame 42 so that a RUN looks like the one shown below.

```
RUN

IF YOU ENTER THE DIAMETER OF A BICYCLE
WHEEL, THEN I WILL TYPE THE DISTANCE
TRAVELED IN ONE TURN OF THE WHEEL.

WHEEL DIAMETER?16
DISTANCE IN ONE TURN IS 50.24

WHEEL DIAMETER?24
DISTANCE IN ONE TURN IS 75.36

WHEEL DIAMETER?
```

. . . and so on. To stop, press BREAK.

Write the program below.

```
10 REMARKABLE* BICYCLE PROGRAM
20 PRINT "IF YOU ENTER THE DIAMETER OF A BICYCLE"
30 PRINT "WHEEL, THEN I WILL TYPE THE DISTANCE"
40 PRINT "TRAVELED IN ONE TURN OF THE WHEEL"
50 PRINT
60 PRINT "WHEEL DIAMETER";
70 INPUT D
80 PRINT "DISTANCE IN ONE TURN IS" ;3.13*D
90 GO TO 50
```

*(The computer ignores everything following REM. See frame 39.)

44. The INPUT statement, like the LET statement, belongs to the class of BASIC instructions called assignment statements. The value we type in response to a question mark is assigned to the variable in the INPUT statement. If the INPUT variable is a string variable, we can type in a string as the value and it will be assigned to the string variable. Here is a simple example. *You* do the parts that we omit.

```
 5 DIM N$(1ØØ)
1Ø PRINT "WHAT IS YOUR NAME";
2Ø INPUT N$
3Ø PRINT N$
4Ø PRINT
5Ø GO TO 1Ø
RUN
WHAT IS YOUR NAME? JERALD R. BROWN
JERALD R. BROWN
WHAT IS YOUR NAME? LEROY FINKEL
```

Remember! N$ is a *string* variable. See frame 7.

____

```
WHAT IS YOUR NAME? FIREDRAKE, THE DRAGON
```

____

— — — — — — — — — —

```
LEROY FINKEL
FIREDRAKE, THE DRAGON
```

In Chapter 9, we will discuss strings in much detail.

45. Here's a program that lets you use the computer as an adding machine, by repeating an "adding routine" with a GO TO loop. A "routine" is one or more statements to complete a computing task.

```
100 REM ** WORLD'S MOST EXPENSIVE ADDING MACHINE
110 PRINT "I'M THE WORLD'S MOST EXPENSIVE ADDING"
120 PRINT "MACHINE. EACH TIME I TYPE 'X=?', YOU"
130 PRINT "TYPE A NUMBER AND PRESS THE RETURN KEY. "
140 PRINT "I WILL THEN TYPE THE TOTAL OF ALL THE"
150 PRINT "NUMBERS YOU HAVE ENTERED. "
160 LET T=0
170 PRINT
180 PRINT "X=";
190 INPUT X
200 LET T=T+X
210 PRINT "TOTAL SO FAR IS"; T
220 GOTO 170
```

Lines 170 through 220 are a GO TO loop. These lines are done for each number entered by the user.

Notice the LET statements using the variable T in lines 160 and 200. Line 160 is *outside* the GO TO loop. It is executed *once* before the loop begins, setting T equal to zero. This is called *initializing,* giving an initial or starting value to a variable.

Line 200 is *inside* the GO TO loop. Therefore line 200 will be executed *each time* through the loop. In line 200, a *new* value of T is computed by adding the old value stored in box T to the INPUT value of X entered by the computer user.

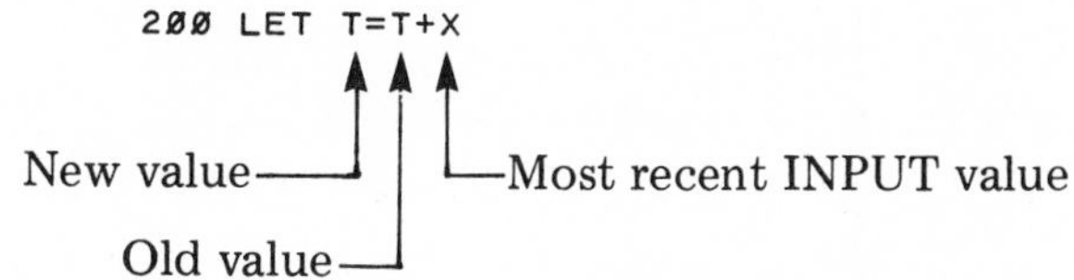

(a) Suppose the *old* value of T is zero and the INPUT value of X is 12.

What is the *new* value of T? ___________

(b) Suppose the *old* value of T is 12 and the INPUT value of X is 43. What is the *new* value of T? ___________

— — — — — — — — — —

(a) 12; (b) 55

46. Note how the PRINT statements (lines 110—150) are used to provide the user with an explanation and instructions for using the program. Are the PRINT statements inside or outside the GO TO loop? ______________________

— — — — — — — — — — — —

outside

Therefore, lines 110—150 will be done *once,* when you first type RUN. Of course, if you interrupt the computer (by pressing BREAK) and RUN the program again, lines 110—150 will be done again.

47. It's RUN time. Let's see how the progam works.

```
RUN

I'M THE WORLD'S MOST EXPENSIVE ADDING
MACHINE. EACH TIME I TYPE 'X+?' YOU
TYPE A NUMBER AND PRESS THE RETURN KEY.
I WILL THEN TYPE THE TOTAL OF ALL THE
NUMBERS YOU HAVE ENTERED.

X=? 12
TOTAL SO FAR IS 12

X=? 43
TOTAL SO FAR IS 55

X=? 33
TOTAL SO FAR IS 88

X=? 92
TOTAL SO FAR IS 18Ø

X=? 76.25
TOTAL SO FAR IS 256.25

X=? ▮ ←
```

Do you remember how to get out of this? If not, check frame 34.

From the listing in frame 45, let's focus on the statement in line 200. For the RUN above, the *first* time through the program the values of the variables to the right of the = symbol in 200 LET T=T+X will be:

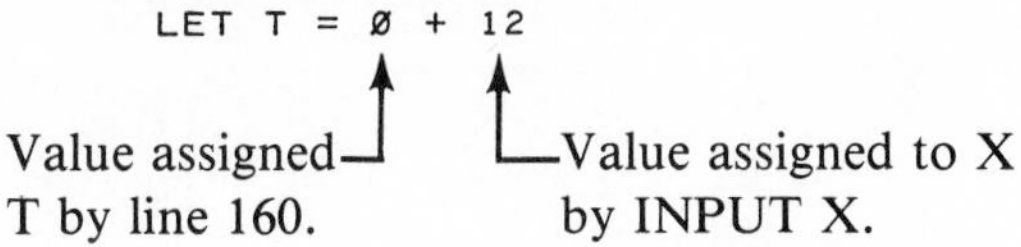

So the *new* value for T is 12. The value is printed. Notice that the computer substitutes the current values in the boxes for the variables to the right of the = sign each time it executes line 200.

For the *second* time through the "loop" section of the program show the values:

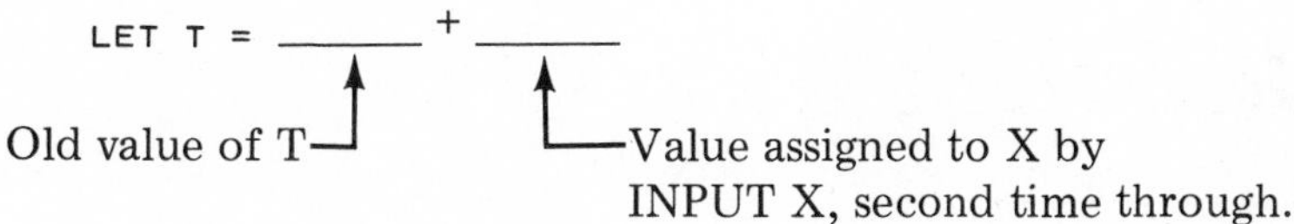

The *new* value of T is ________.

```
LET T = 12 + 43
55
```

48. Now that you know how to stop a "runaway" computer, try this program, which causes the computer to print counting numbers, 1, 2, 3, 4, 5, and so on, until you press **BREAK**.

```
10 LET N=1
20 PRINT N
30 LET N=N+1
40 GO TO 20

RUN

 1
 2
 3
 4
 5
 6
 7

STOPPED AT LINE 20
```

How does it work? Follow the arrows.

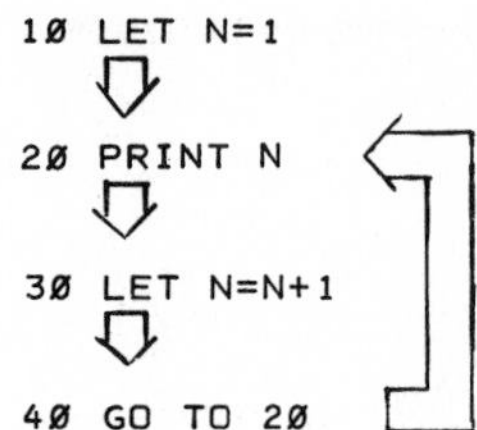

This program is another example of a *loop.* Line 10 is outside the loop. Lines 20, 30, and 40 comprise the loop; they are repeated over and over and over. Line 10 is done *once,* initializing N equal to one.

Line 30 is *inside* the loop. It will be done each time through the loop. In line 30, a new value of N is computed by adding 1 to the old value of N.

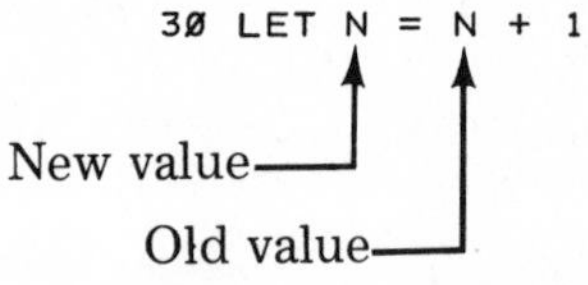

(a) Suppose the old value of N is 1. What will the new value of N be? ________

(b) Suppose the old value of N is 2. What will the new value of N be? ________

— — — — — — — — — — — —

(a) 2; (b) 3 (Line 20 will print the new value next time around the loop.)

49. With a counting loop and a few other statements, we can write a program to show how our money grows, year by year. Here it is.

```
1ØØ REM***WATCH YOUR MONEY GROW

11Ø PRINT "IF YOU TYPE THE AMOUNT OF PRINCIPAL"
12Ø PRINT "AND THE INTEREST RATE PER YEAR, I WILL"
13Ø PRINT "SHOW YOU HOW YOUR MONEY GROWS, YEAR BY"
14Ø PRINT "YEAR. TO STOP ME, PRESS THE BREAK KEY."

15Ø PRINT
16Ø PRINT "PRINCIPAL";
165 INPUT P
17Ø PRINT "INTEREST RATE";
175 INPUT R

18Ø LET N=1          <---- Start year (N) at 1.

19Ø PRINT
2ØØ LET A=P*(1+R/1ØØ)^N  ]
21Ø PRINT "YEAR =";N      ] Compute and print results for year N.
22Ø PRINT "AMOUNT =";A    ]
23Ø LET N=N+1        <---- Increase year (N) by 1 and go around again.
24Ø GOTO 19Ø

RUN

IF YOU TYPE THE AMOUNT OF PRINCIPAL
AND THE INTEREST RATE PER YEAR, I WILL
SHOW YOU HOW YOUR MONEY GROWS, YEAR BY
YEAR. TO STOP ME, PRESS THE BREAK KEY.

PRINCIPAL? 1ØØØ
INTEREST RATE? 6

YEAR = 1
AMOUNT = 1Ø59.99999

YEAR = 2
AMOUNT = 1123.59997

YEAR = 3
AMOUNT = 1191.Ø1596
```

In Chapter 4, we will show you how to round off to the nearest penny.

And so on, until someone presses **BREAK.** Which statements are part of the loop? Give the line numbers. ______________________________

— — — — — — — — — — —

19Ø,2ØØ,21Ø,22Ø,23Ø,AND24Ø

We suggest that you also draw a box around the loop with a felt tip pen. Note that lines 100 through 180 are outside the loop. They are done once during a RUN, while lines 190 through 240 are repeated over and over until you press **BREAK.**

SELF-TEST

Try this Self-Test, so you can evaluate how much you have learned in this chapter.

1. Before entering a program, we usually first type NEW and press **RETURN.** Why?____

   ____

2. How do we tell the computer to type a complete listing of a program stored in its memory?________________________________

3. Assume that we have just stored a program in the computer's memory. How do we tell the computer to execute the program? ________________

   ____

4. Assume that the following program is stored in the computer's memory.

```
10 PRINT "MY COMPUTER UNDERSTANDS ME"
20 PRINT "MY COMPUTER CONFUSES ME"
```

   Describe how to replace the second statement (line 20) without erasing the entire program. ____________________________________

   ____

5. What is the difference between direct statements and statements to be stored in the computer's memory for later execution?________________

   ____

6. We store the following program and RUN it.

```
100 PRINT "I PROMISE NOT TO CHEW BUBBLE GUM IN CLASS"
200 GO TO 100
```

   How do we stop the computer? ______________________________

   ____

7. Each of the following statements contains an error. Mark the error and show the statement in correct BASIC format (syntax, that is).

(a) `20 PRINT DISTANCE IN ONE TURN IS;3.14*D`

(b) `20 "DISTANCE IN ONE TURN IS";3.14*D`

(c) `20 LET P*(1 + R/100)^N = A`

(d) `20 TYPE "X=";X`

8. Describe what is wrong with each statement.

(a) `99999 LET A = 7`

(b) `30 GO TO 3.14`

(c) `30 GO TO - 100`

(d) `10 INPUT, Z`

(e) `10 INPUT Z,`

9. Describe what is wrong with each program.

(a)
```
10 INPUT A
20 INPUT B
30 PRINT A+B
40 GO TO 12
```

(b)
```
10 LET A = 7
20 LET B = 5
30 PRINT X + Y
```

10. Complete the RUN on the line provided.

```
10 PRINT "A=";
15 INPUT A
20 PRINT "B=";
25 INPUT B
30 PRINT "A + B =";A+B

RUN

A=? 7
B=? 5
```

____

11. Write a program to convert temperatures, given in degrees Celsius, to degrees Fahrenheit, using the following formula.

$$F = \frac{9}{5}C + 32$$

A RUN of your program should look like this.

```
RUN
YOU ENTER DEGREES CELSIUS.
I WILL TYPE DEGREES FAHRENHEIT.

DEGREES CELSIUS? 0
DEGREES FAHRENHEIT = 32

DEGREES CELSIUS? 100
DEGREES FAHRENHEIT = 212

DEGREES CELSIUS? 37
DEGREES FAHRENHEIT = 98.6

DEGREES CELSIUS?
```

And so on.

12. Congratulations! You are the big winner on a TV show. Your prize is selected as follows.

A number from 1 to 1000 is chosen at random. Call it N. You then select one, and only one, of the following prizes. You have 60 seconds to make your selection.

PRIZE NO. 1: You receive N dollars
PRIZE NO. 2: You receive D dollars, where $D = 1.01^N$

Perhaps you recognize the formula for D. It is the amount you would receive if you invested $1 at 1% interest per day, compounded daily for N days.

The question, of course, is: For a given value of N, which prize do you take, PRIZE NO. 1 or PRIZE NO. 2? Write a program to help you decide. A RUN might look like this.

```
RUN

N=? 100
PRIZE NO. 1 = 100                    Take PRIZE NO. 1
PRIZE NO. 2 = 2.704781277

N=? 500
PRIZE NO. 1 = 500                    Take PRIZE NO. 1
PRIZE NO. 2 = 144.772491

N=? 1000
PRIZE NO. 1 = 1000                   Take PRIZE NO. 2
PRIZE NO. 2 = 20959.0741

N=?                                  And so on.
```

13. Write this program to assist you in performing that tiresome task called "balancing the checkbook." Here is a RUN of our program.

```
RUN
I WILL HELP YOU BALANCE YOUR CHECKBOOK.
ENTER CHECKS AS NEGATIVE NUMBERS AND
DEPOSITS AS POSITIVE NUMBERS.

OLD BALANCE? 123.45

CHECK OR DEPOSIT? -3.95              Remember to enter checks as negative
NEW BALANCE: 119.5                   numbers.

CHECK OR DEPOSIT? -25
NEW BALANCE: 94.5

CHECK OR DEPOSIT? -73.69
NEW BALANCE: 20.81

CHECK OR DEPOSIT? -8.24
NEW BALANCE: 12.57

CHECK OR DEPOSIT? 50                 At last! A deposit, and just in time!
NEW BALANCE: 62.57

CHECK OR DEPOSIT?                    And so on. Do you remember how to
                                     get out of this? If not, see frame 36.
```

14. Suppose we enter this program and then type RUN. Show the first seven numbers printed by the computer.

```
10 LET N = 1
20 PRINT N
30 LET N = N + 1
50 GO TO 20

RUN
```

____

____

____

____

____

____

____

How do we stop the computer from continuing to print numbers? ________

____

15. The U.S. is going metric, so here is a metric problem. Write a program to convert feet and inches to centimeters, as indicated by the following RUN.

```
RUN

FEET =? 5
INCHES =? 11
CENTIMETERS =180.34

FEET =? 3
INCHES =? 0
CENTIMETERS =91.44

FEET =?
```

We enter, as requested, the number of feet, and the number of inches. The computer computes and prints the number of centimeters.

And so on.

Answers to Self-Test

The frame numbers in parentheses refer to the frames in the chapter where the topic is discussed. You may wish to refer to these for quick review.

1. This erases, or removes, any old program that might be in the computer's memory. If we *don't* do this, statements of an old program might be intermingled with statements of the new program, thus causing mysterious and unpredictable behavior when we try to RUN the new program. (frames 11, 12)
2. Type LIST and press the **RETURN** key. (frames 13, 14)
3. Type RUN and press the **RETURN** key. (frames 14, 16)
4. Type a new line numbered 20 and press the **RETURN** key. The old statement 20 is automatically erased and we may now replace it. If we type the line number (and only the line number) of a statement and press **RETURN**, the computer deletes from its memory the statement (if any) with that line number. (frame 21)
5. Direct statements do *not* have line numbers and are executed immediately after we press **RETURN.** A statement to be stored must have a line number; the computer "remembers" it for later execution (at "RUN time" as we sometimes say). (frame 9)
6. Press the **BREAK** key. (frames 34–36)
7. (a) `20 PRINT DISTANCE IN ONE TURN IS ;3.14*D` Quotation marks missing

   `20 PRINT "DISTANCE IN ONE TURN IS " ;3.14*D` frames (42, 43)

   (b) `20 "DISTANCE IN ONE TURN IS " ;3.14*D` PRINT is missing.

   `20 PRINT "DISTANCE IN ONE TURN IS " ;3.14*D` (frame 42)

   (c) `20 LET P*(1 + R/100)^N = A` Left side of = must be *only* a variable. (frames 1–4)

   `20 LET A = P*(1 + R/100)^N`

   (d) `20 TYPE "X=";X` Computer doesn't know what TYPE means.

   `20 PRINT "X=";X`

8. (a) line number too big (frame 9)

   (b) 3.14 is not a valid line number because it is not an *integer* in the range 1 to 32767 (frame 9)

   (c) -100 is not a valid line number (frame 9)

   (d) should not be a comma following the word INPUT (frame 31)

   (e) should not be a comma at the end of the INPUT statement (INPUT statements with two or more variables have commas *between* variables.) (frame 31)

9. (a) The program does not have a line number 12. Therefore, the computer cannot execute the statement 40 GO TO 12. Instead, it will type ERROR— 12 AT LINE 40. (frames 33, 35, 36)

   (b) The PRINT statement does not use the same variables assigned values in the first two statements. (In ATARI BASIC, the computer would print a 0 (zero) for the PRINT statement.) We probably should have done one of the following.

```
10 LET A = 7            10 LET X = 7
20 LET B = 5            20 LET Y = 5
30 PRINT A + B          30 PRINT X + Y
```

(frames 1–6)

10. Here is the complete RUN.

```
RUN
A=? 7
B=? 5
A+B = 12
```

This statement: `30 PRINT "A+B= " ;A+B`
Caused this: `A+B = 12`
(frame 42)

11.

```
100 REM***CONVERT CELSUIS TO FAHRENHEIT
110 PRINT "YOU ENTER DEGREES CELSUIS,"
120 PRINT "I WILL TYPE DEGREES FAHRENHEIT."
130 PRINT
140 PRINT "DEGREES CELSUIS";
150 INPUT C
160 PRINT "DEGREES FAHRENHEIT = "  ;(9/5)*C + 32
170 GOTO 130
```

(frames 42, 43)

12.
```
100 REM***TV SHOW PRIZE PROBLEM
110 PRINT
120 PRINT "N=";
125 INPUT N
130 PRINT "PRIZE NO. 1 = " ;N
140 PRINT "PRIZE NO. 2 = " ;1.01^N
150 GOTO 110
```

(frames 42, 43)

13.
```
100 REM***CHECKBOOK BALANCING PROGRAM
110 PRINT "I WILL HELP YOU BALANCE YOUR CHECKBOOK."
120 PRINT "ENTER CHECKS AS NEGATIVE NUMBERS AND"
130 PRINT "DEPOSITS AS POSITIVE NUMBERS."
140 PRINT
150 PRINT "OLD BALANCE";
155 INPUT B
160 PRINT
170 PRINT "CHECK OR DEPOSIT";
175 INPUT X
180 LET B=B+X   <---- Compute new balance as shown below.
190 PRINT "NEW BALANCE: ";B
200 GOTO 160
```

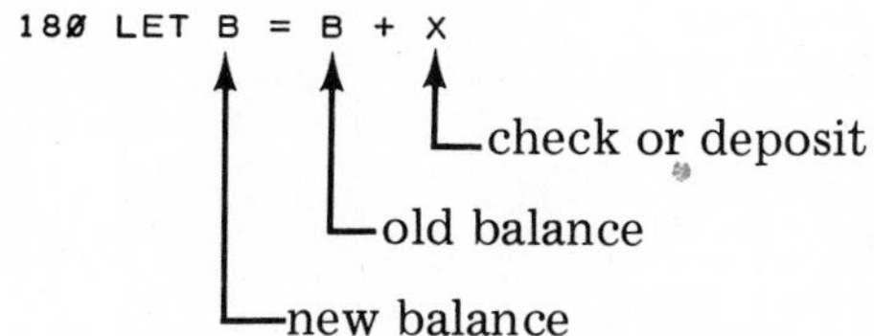

(frames 47–49)

14.
```
RUN
 1
 2
 3
 4
 5
 6
 7 AND SO ON.
```

This program illustrates a *counting loop.* Once you type RUN, the computer will begin counting. It will count and count and count and keep on counting until the power fails or the computer breaks down or you press **BREAK** to stop the computer. (frames 47–49)

15.
```
100 REM***CONVERT FEET AND INCHES TO CENTIMETERS
110 PRINT
120 PRINT "FEET = " ;
125 INPUT F
130 PRINT "INCHES = " ;
135 INPUT I
140 LET T = 12*F+I
150 LET C = 2.54*T
160 PRINT "CENTIMETERS = " ;C
170 GO TO 110
```

T is total number of inches in F'I".
C is total of centimeters in T".

(frame 42)

CHAPTER FOUR

Decisions Using IF-THEN Statements

By now you have probably gotten the idea that a computer only does what you very specifically tell it to do. So how can a computer ever decide anything on its own? Well, it can't decide "on its own," but it can make certain comparisons that you instruct it to make, and then either execute or skip other statements in the program according to whether the comparison you specified is true or false. The statement that you use to set up such comparisons is the IF-THEN statement. (As you will see, IF-THEN is actually a whole family of statements.) When you finish this chapter, you will be able to:

- use the IF-THEN statement;
- use the following comparisons in an IF-THEN statement:

Symbol	*Meaning*
<	less than
>	greater than
=	equal to
< >	not equal to
> =	greater than or equal to
< =	less than or equal to

- use the RND function to generate random numbers;
- use the INT function to "drop" the fractional part of a number;
- use the INT and RND functions together to generate random digits;
- use the ON-GOTO statement to selectively branch to various statements in a program;
- use a colon (:) to separate multiple statements in the same line as a means to organize your programs and to save computer memory space;
- use multiple statements per line to increase the usefulness of IF- THEN statements.

1. In this chapter, we present a very important capability of BASIC—the ability to compare and decide. We will begin with the IF-THEN statement, which tells the computer to carry out a specified operation IF a given condition is TRUE. However, if the condition is FALSE (not true), the operation will not be done. An IF-THEN statement is shown below.

```
150 IF X > 0 THEN PRINT "YOUR NUMBER IS POSITIVE"
```

This IF-THEN statement tells the computer: If the value of X is greater than zero, then print the message, YOUR NUMBER IS POSITIVE, and go on to the next statement in line number order. The symbol > means "is greater than."

If the value of X *is less than zero* or *equal to zero,* the computer does *not* print the message. Instead it simply continues executing the program in the line number order.

Here is another way to look at it. Follow the arrows.

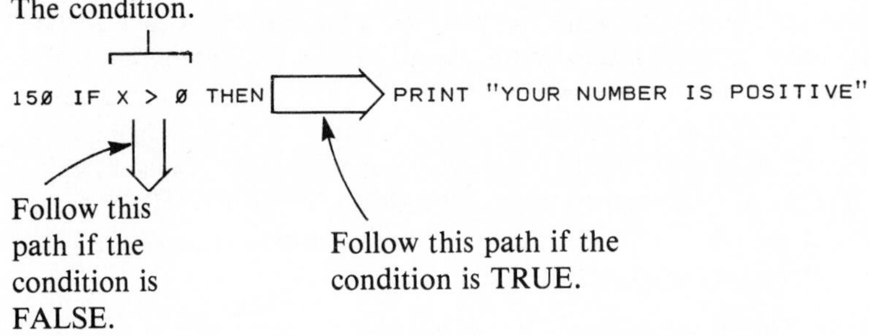

What is the *condition* in the above IF-THEN statement? ______________

X > 0 or X is greater than zero

2. Using our sample statement from frame 1:

(a) Suppose X = 3. Is the condition TRUE or FALSE? ______________

(b) Suppose X = -7. Is the condition TRUE or FALSE? ______________

(c) Suppose X = 0. Is the condition TRUE or FALSE? ______________

(a) TRUE. The computer *will* print the message: YOUR NUMBER IS POSITIVE.
(b) FALSE. The computer will *not* print the message.
(c) FALSE. The computer will *not* print the message.

3. The symbol > in an IF-THEN comparison means "is greater than." The symbol = means "is equal to." You can guess that the symbol < used in an IF-THEN comparison means ________________________ .

— — — — — — — — — — —

"is less than"

4. Here is a simple program illustrating the use of the IF-THEN statement. This program has three IF-THEN statements that tell the computer to "compare and decide." Remember, the message in an IF-THEN PRINT statement will be printed only if the comparison is true.

```
100 REM***DETERMINE IF X IS POSITIVE, NEGATIVE OR ZERO
110 PRINT "WHEN I ASK, YOU ENTER A NUMBER AND I"
120 PRINT "WILL TELL YOU WHETHER YOUR NUMBER IS"
130 PRINT "POSITIVE, NEGATIVE OR ZERO"
135 PRINT
140 PRINT "WHAT IS YOUR NUMBER";
145 INPUT X
150 IF X>0 THEN PRINT "YOUR NUMBER IS POSITIVE"
160 IF X<0 THEN PRINT "YOUR NUMBER IS NEGATIVE"
170 IF X=0 THEN PRINT "YOUR NUMBER IS ZERO"
180 GOTO 135
```

```
RUN
WHEN I ASK, YOU ENTER A NUMBER AND I
WILL TELL YOU WHETHER YOUR NUMBER IS
POSITIVE, NEGATIVE OR ZERO
WHAT IS YOUR NUMBER? -7   <———— This message printed by line 160.
YOUR NUMBER IS NEGATIVE

WHAT IS YOUR NUMBER? 3    <———— This message courtesy of line 150.
YOUR NUMBER IS POSITIVE

WHAT IS YOUR NUMBER? 0    <———— Thank you, line 170.
YOUR NUMBER IS ZERO

WHAT IS YOUR NUMBER? ■    <———— And so on. (Do you remember how to
                                stop a program waiting at the INPUT
                                question mark?)
```

(a) What is the condition in line 150? ______________________________

(b) What is the condition in 160? ______________________________

(c) What is the condition in line 170? ______________________________

— — — — — — — — — — —

(a) X > 0 or X is greater than zero
(b) X < 0 or X is less than zero
(c) X = 0 or X is equal to zero

5. In running the program from frame 4, the computer executes lines 100 through 130 once, since they are "outside the loop." Lines 135 through 180 are included in the loop and are executed for each value of X supplied by the user after an INPUT question mark. Suppose the user runs the program and types 13 after the INPUT question mark, then presses **RETURN.** This assigns the value 13 to the variable X. Now look back at the program. Since X = 13 (13 is the value of X), the condition in line 150 is TRUE and the conditions in lines 160 and 170 are FALSE. So, the computer will print the message in line 150, but will *not* print the messages in lines 160 and 170.

(a) Suppose X = -7. The condition in line 160 is (TRUE or FALSE) ______________________ and the conditions in lines 150 and 170 are (TRUE or FALSE) ______________________ .

(b) Suppose X = 0. Which condition is TRUE? (Give line number.) __________ Which conditions are FALSE? (Give line numbers.) ______________________

— — — — — — — — — — —

(a) TRUE; FALSE. The computer will print the message in line 160, but will *not* print the messages in lines 150 and 170.
(b) line 170; lines 150 and 160. The computer will print the message in line 170, but will *not* print the messages in lines 150 and 160.

6. The program on the following page compares two numbers, A and B, and prints an appropriate message. Complete lines 160 and 170 so that the program will RUN as shown.

```
100 REM***COMPARE TWO NUMBERS, A AND B
110 PRINT "WHEN I ASK, ENTER VALUES FOR A AND B."
120 PRINT
130 PRINT "A = ";
135 INPUT A
140 PRINT "B = ";
145 INPUT B
150 IF A>B THEN PRINT "A IS GREATER THAN B"

160 IF A<B ______________________________

170 _____________________________________
180 GOTO 120

RUN
WHEN I ASK, ENTER VALUES FOR A AND B.

A =? 1
B =? 2
A IS LESS THAN B

A =? 7
B =? 2
A IS GREATER THAN B

A =? 55
B =? 55
A IS EQUAL TO B

A =?
```

— — — — — — — — — —

```
160 IF A<B THEN PRINT "A IS LESS THAN B"
170 IF A=B THEN PRINT "A IS EQUAL TO B"
```

7. Let's look at another IF-THEN statement.

This statement:	`190 IF X=-1 THEN GO TO 230`
Tells the computer;	If the value of X is equal to -1, then go to line 230. If the value of X is *not* equal to -1, the computer continues in usual line number order.

In general, the IF-THEN statement has the following form.

IF *condition* THEN *statement*

The statement could be almost any BASIC statement. The condition is usually a comparison between a variable and a number, between two variables, or between two BASIC expressions. On the following page is a handy table of comparison symbols.

BASIC symbol	*Comparison*	*Math symbol*
=	is equal to	$=$
<	is less than	$<$
>	is greater than	$>$
< =	is less than or equal to	$\leq$
> =	is greater than or equal to	$\geq$
< >	is not equal to	$\neq$

Write each of the following conditions in proper BASIC.

(a) M is greater than 10. ______________________

(b) Z is less than or equal to A squared. ______________________

(c) X is not equal to Y. ______________________

(d) 3 times P is equal to Z times Q. ______________________

— — — — — — — — — —

(a) M > 10
(b) Z < = A^2 or Z < = A * A
(c) X < > Y
(d) 3 * P = Z * Q

8. So far you have seen two members of the IF-THEN family of statements.

```
IF-THEN PRINT
IF-THEN GOTO
```

IF-THEN PRINT (message in quotes)
IF-THEN GOTO (line number)

The second IF-THEN statement shown above tells the computer to branch or GOTO the line number given, if the comparison is true. You may omit the instruction GOTO following THEN, and just specify the line number. Show how you could write the following statement in shorter form.

```
19Ø IF X = -1 THEN GOTO 23Ø
```
____

— — — — — — — — — —

```
19Ø IF X = -1 THEN 23Ø
```

9. Remember, the basic form of the IF-THEN statement is as follows.
IF (condition) THEN (almost any BASIC statement)

Since almost any BASIC statement can follow THEN, we could have the computer assign a value or ask for an INPUT (provided that the condition or comparison is true) in an IF-THEN statement.

```
IF Y = 3 THEN LET X = 1
IF X*X + Y*Y<25 THEN PRINT "YOUR GUESS IS INSIDE THE CIRCLE"
```

10. It's your turn to practice writing the IF-THEN statements that will assign values if the comparison is true. From the following descriptions, write an IF-THEN statement.

(a) If A does not equal B then assign the new value 10 to variable B.

____

(b) IF H is more than 100, have the computer say "OOPS! TOO MANY HOURS."

— — — — — — — — — —

(a) `IF A<>B THEN B = 10` (Remember, you can omit the LET in an assignment statement.)

(b) `IF H>100 THEN PRINT "OOPS! TOO MANY HOURS."`

10. For each description, write an IF-THEN statement.

(a) If the value of A is less than or equal to 10, go to line 100.

____

(b) If A is less than 2*B, then increase the old value of T by 1.

____

(c) If X is greater than 2 times Y, then print the message X IS MORE THAN Y DOUBLED. ______________________________

(d) If Z does not equal -1, then INPUT a new value for X.

____

— — — — — — — — — —

(a) `IF A <= 10 THEN 100` (The GOTO is optional and usually omitted).

(b) `IF A < 2*B THEN T = T+1` or
`IF A < 2*B THEN LET T = T+1`

(The LET may be included or omitted.)

(c) `IF X>2*Y THEN PRINT "X IS MORE THAN Y DOUBLED"`

(d) `IF Z<>-1 THEN INPUT X`

11. One common use of the IF-THEN statement is to recognize a signal called a "flag" that terminates one process and begins another. Here is another version

of the "World's Most Expensive Adding Machine" which you first encountered in Chapter 3, frame 45. You may wish to review that frame before plunging onward.

```
100 REM ** WORLD'S MOST EXPENSIVE ADDING MACHINE
110 PRINT "I'M THE WORLD'S MOST EXPENSIVE ADDING"
120 PRINT "MACHINE. EACH TIME I TYPE 'X=?', YOU"
130 PRINT "TYPE A NUMBER. WHEN YOU ARE FINISHED, "
140 PRINT "TYPE -1 AND I WILL TYPE THE TOTAL"
150 PRINT "OF YOUR PREVIOUS NUMBERS. "
160 T=0
170 PRINT
180 PRINT "X=";
190 INPUT X
200 IF X = -1 THEN 230
210 T=T+X
220 GOTO 170
```

Lines 170 through 220 are a GOTO loop. However, if someone types -1 for the value of X, line 200 will cause the computer to jump out of the loop and go to line 230.

```
230 PRINT
240 PRINT "TOTAL = "; T
250 PRINT
260 GOTO 110
```

This section of the program tells the computer to print a line space, the total of the numbers, and then another line space, then go back to line 110 and start over.

```
RUN
I AM THE WORLD'S MOST EXPENSIVE ADDING
MACHINE. EACH TIME I TYPE 'X=?'. YOU
TYPE A NUMBER. WHEN YOU ARE FINISHED,
TYPE -1 AND I WILL TYPE THE TOTAL
OF YOUR PREVIOUS INPUTS.


X =? 6.95

X =? .47

X =? 8.49

X =? 3.06

X =? -1
```

← Aha! Here is our flag saying "that's all folks."

```
TOTAL=18.97

I AM THE WORLD'S MOST EXPENSIVE ADDING
```

And so on.

The flag used in our program is -1; statement 200 checks each and every input value of X and, if it is -1, causes the computer to jump out of the loop to line 230. Lines 230 through 260 print the total (T) and then cause the computer to jump back to line 110 and start over.

Any unusual number that will not be used as a normal INPUT value could be used as a flag.

Modify the program so that, instead of using -1 as the flag, we use 999999 as the flag. You will have to change lines 140 and 200

140 ______________________________

200 ______________________________

— — — — — — — — — — — —

```
140 PRINT "TYPE 999999 AND I WILL TYPE THE TOTAL"
200 IF X=999999 THEN 230
```

12. In our program in frame 11 we first used -1 as the flag. This may not be a good idea if some of the values we wish to use are negative. For example, here are temperatures recorded during one cold week in Minneapolis, Minnesota.

S	M	T	W	T	F	S
10	3	−9	−15	−23	−25	−30

In this case, using 999999 as the flag would prevent confusion between a temperature of -1 and an end-of-data flag of -1.

With a few changes, we can modify the program in frame 11 and obtain a program to compute the mean, or average, of a set of numbers. The formula for determining the mean of a set of N numbers is as follows.

$$\text{Mean} = \frac{\text{Sum or total of the Numbers}}{\text{Number of Numbers}} = \frac{T}{N}$$

In the Friendly "Mean" Progam, we use the variable T for the total (sum) of the numbers, and N for the number of numbers. Complete the program.

```
100 REM***A FRIENDLY 'MEAN' PROGRAM
110 PRINT "I WILL COMPUTE THE MEAN OF NUMBERS."
120 PRINT "WHEN I TYPE 'X=? TYPE A NUMBER. WHEN"
130 PRINT "FINISHED ENTERING NUMBERS, TYPE 999999"

140 LET T=0

150 LET N= ____________ <-------- We will use N to count the
                                  numbers.
160 PRINT
170 PRINT "X = ";
175 INPUT X
180 IF X=999999 THEN 220
190 LET T=T+X

200 LET N= ____________ <-------- Increase the count by one.
210 GOTO 160
220 PRINT
230 PRINT "N = "; ____________ <-------- First, print the number of
240 PRINT "TOTAL = "; T                  numbers.

250 PRINT "MEAN = "; ____________ <-------- Compute and print the
260 PRINT                                   mean.
270 GOTO 110
```

The RUN is on the next page.

```
RUN
I WILL COMPUTE THE MEAN OF NUMBERS.
WHEN I TYPE 'X =?' TYPE A NUMBER. WHEN
FINISHED ENTERING NUMBERS, TYPE 999999.

X =? 10

X =? 3

X =? -9

X =? -15

X =? -23

X =? -25

X =? -30

X =? 999999
```

← The flag!

```
N = 7
TOTAL =-89
MEAN =-12.71428571
```

N is the number of numbers. One week's worth. That was the cold week that was, or yes, that was a *mean* week.

— — — — — — — — — — —

```
150 LET N=0
200 LET N=N+1
230 PRINT "N = "; N
250 PRINT "MEAN = "; T/N
```

13. For temperatures in Minneapolis, 999999 is a good flag. We assume, of course, that the temperature *never* reaches 999999 degrees, even in the summer. For other types of data, 999999 may not be a good flag. One of the most outrageous and least likely BASIC numbers we can think of is the floating point number, 1E97. For most data, 1E97 would be a good flag. So, modify lines 130 and 180 in the program of frame 12 so that the flag is 1E97.

130 ______________________________

180 ______________________________

— — — — — — — — — — —

```
130 PRINT "FINISHED ENTERING NUMBERS, TYPE 1E97."
180 IF X=1E97 THEN 220
```

14. You have helped us write several computer programs using IF-THEN comparisons. Now it is time for you to do a solo flight and write a program on your own. Think carefully about the use of IF-THEN comparisons, and what the computer will do if the conditions are TRUE or if they are FALSE. On the following page is a RUN of the program we want you to write.

```
RUN
INPUT A NUMBER AND I WILL TELL YOU IF
IT IS 100 OR LESS, OR OVER 100.

YOUR NUMBER? 99
YOUR NUMBER IS 100 OR LESS.

YOUR NUMBER? 101
YOUR NUMBER IS OVER 100.

YOUR NUMBER? 100
YOUR NUMBER IS 100 OR LESS.

YOUR NUMBER?
```

Now you write the program.

— — — — — — — — — —

```
100 REM**NUMBER SIZE PROGRAM
110 PRINT "INPUT A NUMBER AND I WILL TELL YOU IF"
120 PRINT "IT IS 100 OR LESS, OR OVER 100. "
130 PRINT
140 PRINT "YOUR NUMBER";
145 INPUT N
150 IF N<=100 THEN PRINT "YOUR NUMBER IS 100 OR LESS. "
160 IF N> 100 THEN PRINT "YOUR NUMBER IS OVER 100. "
170 GOTO 130
```

15. Soon we will enter the fun-filled realm of computer games. But first, you should learn about random numbers and the unpredictable BASIC function known as RND.

Random numbers are those chosen at random (by chance) from a given set of numbers. Many games come with dice or a spinner or some other device for generating random numbers. Roll the dice; they total 8. You move 8 spaces.

Functions are automatic features of BASIC that you use to perform special operations. These functions are like built-in programs; most of them could be replaced by a program or a segment of a program. But, you will use these functions often enough that it would be very time-consuming to type in the routine to perform the operations each time. Therefore, it is worthwhile to "build them into" a computer language.

BASIC provides, as one of its "built in" functions, the RND function that allows the computer to generate numbers that seem to be chosen at random. The format of this random function is RND (dummy variable) where the dummy variable can be any positive number. In most cases, we use 1 as the dummy variable. The following program shows the use of the RND function. We first show you the program (enclosed in a box) and two different executions of that program. We interrupted the first RUN by pressing BREAK, then typed RUN again.

```
10 PRINT RND(1)
20 GOTO 10
```

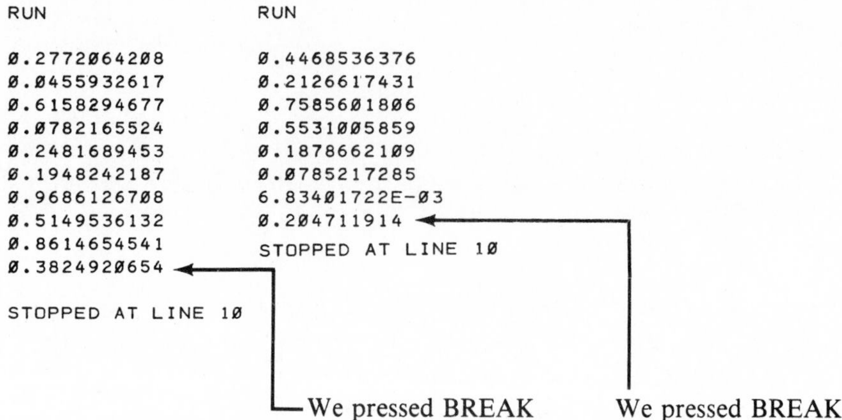

```
RUN                        RUN

0.2772064208               0.4468536376
0.0455932617               0.2126617431
0.6158294677               0.7585601806
0.0782165524               0.5531005859
0.2481689453               0.1878662109
0.1948242187               0.0785217285
0.9686126708               6.83401722E-03
0.5149536132               0.204711914
0.8614654541               STOPPED AT LINE 10
0.3824920654

STOPPED AT LINE 10
```


Two runs of the program are shown. Are the lists of random numbers in the two runs the same? ___________

— — — — — — — — — — —

No. In fact, *don't* expect to enter our program into your computer, type RUN, and get either list. That's the idea of random numbers. They are, well, random!

16. The statement 10 PRINT AND (1) causes the computer to produce a different list of random numbers each time the program is executed. Although we used a 1 as the dummy variable, we could also have used 0, .25, 5, or even 100. The numbers that the computer generates will still be between 0 and 1 even though you get different numbers each time you run the program.

We use the number 1 in parentheses. However, *any* positive number is OK, even numbers with decimal fractions! On our computer, a positive number in parentheses following RND will cause the computer to produce a different list of random numbers each time.

Examine the random numbers in frame 15.

(a) Is any number less than zero (negative)? ___________

(b) Is any number equal to zero? ___________

(c) Is any number greater than one? ___________

(d) Is any number equal to one? ___________

(e) From the evidence, it appears that random numbers produced by the RND function are _______________ zero and _______________ one.

— — — — — — — — — — —

(a) no
(b) no
(c) no
(d) no
(e) greater than; less than. However, we haven't shown much evidence—only a few random numbers. We suggest you run off a bunch of random numbers on your computer in order to get more evidence. (But remember! Evidence is not proof.)

17. It's true that random numbers produced by the RND function *are* greater than zero and less than one. Another way to say it: random numbers produced by the RND function are *between* 0 and 1. Or, in still another way: 0 < RND(1) < 1.

However, random numbers between 0 and 1 are not always convenient. Sometimes we would like random *digits* (the numbers 0, 1, 2, 3, 4, 5, 6, 7, 8, and 9) or random integers (whole numbers) from 1 to 100. Below is a RUN in which the computer acts as a teaching machine to teach *one-digit* addition to children.

```
RUN

 1 + 4 =? 5                  <---- Computer typed:1 + 4 = ?
RIGHT ON...GOOD WORK!!!            Student typed the answer, 5,
                                   and pressed RETURN.
 9 + 6 =? 14
HMMM...I GET A DIFFERENT ANSWER. <---- Student missed this one.

 9 + 6 =? 15                 <---- Computer repeats problem.
RIGHT ON...GOOD WORK!!!            This time student gets it correct.

 7 + 2 =? 9
RIGHT ON...GOOD WORK!!!
                                   New problem. . . . And so on.
 8 + Ø =?
```

Let's build this program, piece by piece. First, how do we generate *random digits?*

The random numbers produced by the RND function are *uniformly distributed* between 0 and 1. That is, they are "spread evenly" between 0 and 1. Each random number is about as likely (or unlikely) to occur as any other random number.

RND(1) is *between* 0 and 1, but is never 0 or 1. Therefore, 10*RND(1) is between 0 and ___________ .

— — — — — — — — — — —

BUT 10*RND(1) is never *equal* to zero or ten.

18. Below is a program to print random numbers between 0 and 10. We show you two RUNs to remind you that you get a different list each time.

```
1Ø PRINT 1Ø*RND(1)
2Ø GOTO 1Ø
```

```
RUN                     RUN

7.ØØ8Ø5664              1.17Ø19653
8.1372Ø7Ø3              5.948Ø2856
2.74749755              1.483612Ø6
6.Ø7574462              3.89282225
3.9ØØ299Ø7              9.85137939
1.66ØØØ366              4.83612Ø61
4.94537259              2.Ø3781128
Ø.382461547
6.671295166
4.277496337             STOPPED AT LINE 1Ø

STOPPED AT LINE 1Ø
```

Each random number in the runs is greater than zero and less than ten. Each random number can be thought of as having an *integer* part to the left of the decimal point and a fractional part to the right of the decimal point.

The integer part of 7.00805664 is 7 and the fractional part is .00805664.

The integer part of 0.382461547 is zero (0). The fractional part is .382461547.

(a) What is the integer part of 1.66000366? ____________________

The fractional part? ____________________

(b) What is the integer part of 4.83612061? ____________________

The fractional part? ____________________

— — — — — — — — — — —

(a) 1; .66000366
(b) 4; .83612061

19. Now you write three short programs to print random numbers in the ranges specified.

(a) between 0 and 100

(b) between 0 and 50

(c) between 0 and 6

— — — — — — — — — — —

(a)

```
10 PRINT 100*RND(1)
20 GOTO 10

RUN
73.3308125
12.7318066
37.9114539
87.8885027
2.10936001
20.1256433
69.5790702
4.26022968
```

(b)

```
10 PRINT 50*RND(1)
20 GOTO 10

RUN
28.9513492
35.5718117
44.6059096
11.4345026
6.48894357
15.2396004
```

(c)

```
10 PRINT 6*RND(1)
20 GOTO 10

RUN
2.60018182
1.31444039
3.24057255
0.1153584267
0.02287558154
2.90792334
5.72100528
2.03216904
```

20. For each random number *between* 0 and 10, the integer (whole number) part is a *single digit.* Wouldn't it be nice if we could direct the computer to delete the fractional part and keep the integer part?

Well, as you may suspect, we can. BASIC has another clever and useful function called INT. Here are some examples.

INT (3) = 3	INT (7) = 7
INT (3.14159) = 3	INT (7.99999) = 7
INT (1.23456) = 1	INT (.999999) = 0

(Say it like this: "The integer part of 3.14159 is 3.")

In general, if X is any positive number, INT(X) is the *integer* part of X. Now, you apply INT to some of the random numbers from frame 18.

(a) INT(7.00805664) = __________ (b) INT(0.382461547) = __________

(c) INT (2.74749755) = __________ (d) INT (9.85137939) = __________

— — — — — — — — — — —

(a) 7
(b) 0
(c) 2
(d) 9

21. Caution. INT works as shown in frame 20 only for *positive* numbers or zero. In general, INT(X) computes *the greatest integer less than or equal to X.* For example:

INT (3.14) = 3	but	INT (–3.14) = –4
INT (7) = 7	and	INT (–7) = –7
INT (.999) = 0	but	INT (–.999) = –1

For positive numbers, or zero, INT (X) computes the integer part of X. In a program, the *value* assigned to X will be substituted for X in the INT parentheses when the program is RUN. The computer then performs the INT function on the numerical value. Of course, any variable could be used instead of the letter X, as long as it has been assigned a value earlier in the program.

You be the computer and show what you will print when your human tells you to RUN the following programs.

(a)
```
10 X=15.77
20 PRINT INT(X)
RUN
```
____

(b)
```
10 A=99.999
20 PRINT INT(A)
RUN
```
____

(c)
```
10 F=98.6
20 PRINT INT(F)
RUN
```
____

— — — — — — — — — — —

(a; 15; (b) 99; (c) 98

22. Instead of a number, we can write a variable, a function, or any BASIC expression in the parentheses that follow the word INT.

INT(   )
↑
Any BASIC number, variable, function or expression here

You should be able to distinguish between *values, variables, expressions, functions,* and *strings.* To show that you can, identify each of the following with one of the words given above in italics.

(a) X __________________________

(b) X*2 __________________________

(c) RND(1) ______________________

(d) "A+B IS AN EXPRESSION" ______________________

(e) 22 ______________________

(f) 1+1 ______________________

(g) INT(52.88) ______________________

(h) "=" ______________________

(i) 4*(3+X) ______________________

(j) Which of the above could be used in the parentheses of a function such as INT or RND? ______________________

— — — — — — — — — —

(a) variable
(b) expression
(c) function
(d) string
(e) value
(f) expression
(g) function
(h) string
(i) expression
(j) a, b, c, e, f, g, and i

23. Remember, the general form for the INT function is as follows.

```
INT(    )
    ↑
    └──Any BASIC number, variable, function or expression here
```

So, it is OK to write INT(10*RND(1)). This is an expression containing a function as part of the expression.

RND(1) is a random number between 0 and 1.

10*RND(1) is a random number between 0 and 10.

INT(10*RND(1)) is a *random digit* (whole number) between 0 and 10.

The program on the following page causes the computer to generate and print random digits. Digits are the numbers 0, 1, 2, 3, 4, 5, 6, 7, 8, and 9, or 0 to 9, inclusive. Note the "inclusive" means it includes both 0 and 9, as well as the digits between 0 and 9.

```
10 PRINT INT(10*RND(1))
20 GOTO 10
```

```
RUN                          RUN
 5                            4
 3                            6
 2                            3
 Ø                            9
 6                            4
 3                            Ø
 4                            1
 1                            2
 7

STOPPED AT LINE 1Ø           STOPPED AT LINE 1Ø
```

This program prints random digits, which are integers from ________ to ________, inclusive.

— — — — — — — — — —

0; 9

24. Now write a short program to print random integers (whole numbers) from 0 to 19, inclusive. Our RUN looks like this.

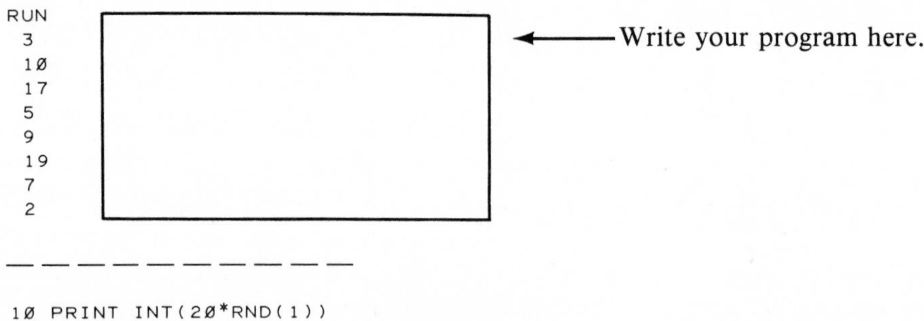

— — — — — — — — — —

```
1Ø PRINT INT(2Ø*RND(1))
2Ø GOTO 1Ø
```

Be sure to match the parentheses. There must be a right, or closing, parenthesis for every left, or opening, parenthesis; if not, the computer will give you an error message when you RUN the program.

25. What if we want random integers from 1 to 20, inclusive, instead of from 0 to 19? Well, that's easy. Simply add a 1 to the random integer. You could do it in two ways.

```
1Ø PRINT INT(2Ø*RND(1)+1)
2Ø GOTO 1Ø
```

or

```
10 PRINT INT(20*RND(1))+1
20 GOTO 10

RUN
 14
 20
 20
 16
 19
 7
 20
 2
 15
```

The "+1" can be added to the random number either before or after taking the integer part of 20*RND(1). The resulting random integer will be the same in either case.

Now you write three simple programs to print a list of random integers.

(a) from 1 to 10, inclusive

(b) from 1 to 100, inclusive

(c) from 1 to 12, inclusive

(a)

```
10 PRINT INT(10*RND(1))+1
20 GOTO 10
```

or

```
10 PRINT INT(10*RND(1)+1)
20 GOTO 10
```

(b)

```
10 PRINT INT(100*RND(1))+1
20 GOTO 10
```

or

```
10 PRINT INT(100*RND(1)+1)
20 GOTO 10
```

(c)

```
10 PRINT INT(12*RND(1))+1
20 GOTO 10
```

or

```
10 PRINT INT(12*RND(1)+1)
20 GOTO 10
```

26. What if we want random integers from 5 to 10 inclusive? Here is a hint: to get random integers from 1 to 10 instead of 0 to 9, we added a +1. Look at it like this.

$$\begin{array}{c} 0 \text{ to } 9 \\ +1 \quad +1 \\ \hline 1 \text{ to } 10 \end{array}$$

(a) The function INT (6*RND(1)) will generate what random digits? ________

____

(b) What should we add to this expression INT(6*RND(1)) in order to generate integers from 5 to 10 inclusive? ________

(c) What should we add in order to generate integers from 11 to 16 inclusive?

____

— — — — — — — — — — —

(a) 0 to 5 inclusive, that is, 0, 1, 2, 3, 4, and 5, a total of 6 digits.

(b) +5

```
 0 to  5
+5    +5
 5    10
```

(c) +11

```
  0 to  5
+11   +11
 11    16
```

27. Look back at the RUN in frame 17 before we continue. Now we are ready to build the addition practice program. Here is the first section of the program that produced the RUN.

```
100 REM***ADDITION PRACTICE PROGRAM
200 REM***GENERATE RANDOM NUMBERS, A AND B
210 LET A=INT(10*RND(1))
220 LET B=INT(10*RND(1))
```

The values of A and B will be ________________________________

— — — — — — — — — — —

random digits (0, 1, 2, 3, 4, 5, 6, 7, 8, or 9)

28. Ready for the next piece? Here we go.

```
300 REM***PRINT PROBLEM AND ASK FOR ANSWER
310 PRINT
320 PRINT A; " + " ; B; " = " ;
330 INPUT C
```

Line 320 is something new. The statement PRINT A; " + "; B; " = "; tells the computer to print the *value* of A, then print +, then print the *value* of B, then print =. These items are separated by semicolons. The fourth semicolon, at the very end, tells the computer *not* to go to the next line down on the CRT. In other words, it tells the computer to stay where it stopped printing.

Do you remember? The INPUT statement causes the computer to print a *question mark*. This question mark will be printed on the same line as the information from the PRINT statement, because of that semicolon at the end of line 320.

For example, if A = 7 and B = 5, then lines 320 and 330 will cause the computer to print the following.

```
            7 + 5 = ?
from line 320 ┘     └ from line 330 (INPUT question mark)
```

If A = 3 and B = 4, what will be printed by lines 320 and 330? ________

____

— — — — — — — — — — —

3 + 4 = ? (This, of course, is the *random problem* which helps the eager young learner practice addition.)

29. After the learner types an answer and presses the RETURN key, the computer assigns the answer value to variable C and continues.

Note how we are using REM (REMARK) statements to tell something about each piece of the program. This doesn't help the computer, but it does help *people* read and understand how the program works.

```
400 REM***IS THE ANSWER CORRECT?
410 IF C=A+B THEN 610
```

If the student's answer (C) is correct, the computer will go to line________

— — — — — — — — — — —

610 (If the answer is not correct, the computer continues in regular line number order.)

30. If the student's answer is not correct, then the IF-THEN condition is false. The computer next does the following as it continues on in the program in line number order.

```
500 REM***ANSWER IS NOT CORRECT
510 PRINT "HMMM...I GET A DIFFERENT ANSWER."
520 GOTO 310
```

Assume an incorrect answer. The computer prints HMMM . . . I GET A DIFFERENT ANSWER, then goes to line 310. From there (check previous frames if necessary), what happens next?________________________

— — — — — — — — — — —

The computer repeats the problem.

31. Review frame 29, which shows lines 400 and 410 of the program. If the learner's answer is correct, line 410 causes the computer to go to line 610.

```
600 REM***ANSWER IS CORRECT
610 PRINT "RIGHT ON...GOOD WORK!!!"
620 GOTO 210
```

Assume a correct answer. The computer prints RIGHT ON . . . GOOD WORK!!! and then goes to line 210. What happens next? ____________________

____

— — — — — — — — — —

The computer generates a new problem (new values for A and B) and prints the new problem.

32. Below is a listing of the complete ADDITION PRACTICE PROGRAM.

```
100 REM***ADDITION PRACTICE PROGRAM
200 REM***GENERATE RANDOM NUMBERS, A AND B
210 LET A=INT(10*RND(1))
220 LET B=INT(10*RND(1))
300 REM***PRINT PROBLEM AND ASK FOR ANSWER
310 PRINT
320 PRINT A; " + " ; B; " = ";
330 INPUT C
400 REM***IS THE ANSWER CORRECT?
410 IF C=A+B THEN 610
500 REM***ANSWER IS NOT CORRECT
510 PRINT "HMMM...I GET A DIFFERENT ANSWER."
520 GOTO 310
600 REM***ANSWER IS CORRECT
610 PRINT "RIGHT ON...GOOD WORK!!!"
620 GOTO 210
```

Change line 210 so that the value of A is a random integer from 0 to 19, inclusive, instead of 0 to 9.

```
210 LET A = ______________________
```

— — — — — — — — — —

```
210 LET A=INT(20*RND(1))
```

33. Careful on this one! Change line 220 so that the value of B is a random in-reger from 10 to 20, inclusive.

```
220 LET B = ____________________
```

— — — — — — — — — — —

```
220 LET B=INT(11*RND(1))+10
```

That gives us 10 to 20 inclusive, eleven numbers in all.

```
  0 to 10
+10   +10
---------
 10 to 20
```

We changed lines 210 and 220 of the program in frame 32 to look like the answer to frame 32, and ran the modified program. Remember, a RUN on your computer will probably show different numbers in the problems. These are random numbers, after all.

```
RUN

 16 + 14 =? 30
RIGHT ON...GOOD WORK!!!

 16 + 15 =? 31
RIGHT ON...GOOD WORK!!!

 4 + 10 =? 15
HMMM...I GET A DIFFERENT ANSWER.

 4 + 10 =? 14
RIGHT ON...GOOD WORK!!!

 6 + 16 =?
```

And so on.

34. When the learner's answer is correct, the computer always prints: RIGHT ON . . . GOOD WORK!!! To relieve the monotony, let's modify the program so that the computer selects at random from three possible replies to a correct answer. The changes are in the portion of the program beginning at line 600.

```
600 REM***ANSWER IS CORRECT
610 LET R=INT(3*RND(1))+1      <---- Note the +1.
620 IF R=1 THEN 630
621 IF R=2 THEN 650
622 IF R=3 THEN 670
630 PRINT "RIGHT ON...GOOD WORK!!!"
640 GOTO 210
650 PRINT "YOU GOT IT! TRY ANOTHER."
660 GOTO 210
670 PRINT "THAT'S GREAT! KEEP IT UP!"
680 GOTO 210
```

The possible values of R are ________, ________, and ________.

— — — — — — — — — — —

1, 2, and 3 (Not 0, 1, and 2, because we added +1 at the end of line 610.)

35. So, we see, R can be 1 or 2 or 3.

(a) If R = 1, the computer will print ______________________

(b) If R = 3, the computer will print ______________________

(c) If R = 2, the computer will print ______________________

— — — — — — — — — — —

(a) `RIGHT ON...GOOD WORK!!!`
(b) `THAT'S GREAT! KEEP IT UP!`
(c) `YOU GOT IT! TRY ANOTHER.`

36. We made the changes in response (frame 34) from the original program (frame 32) and ran the modified program. Here is what happened.

```
RUN
 9 + 7 =? 16
THAT'S GREAT! KEEP IT UP!

 6 + 3 =? 9
YOU GOT IT! TRY ANOTHER.

 8 + 2 =? 1Ø
THAT'S GREAT! KEEP IT UP!

 5 + 9 =? 14
RIGHT ON...GOOD WORK!!!

 0 + 7 =? 7
RIGHT ON...GOOD WORK!!!

 8 + 5 =? 14
HMMM...I GET A DIFFERENT ANSWER.

 8 + 5 =?
```

If the learner's answer is incorrect, the computer always prints: HMMM . . . I GET A DIFFERENT ANSWER. Modify the program in frame 32 so that, for an incorrect response, the computer selects randomly one of the two following responses.

```
HMMM...I GET A DIFFERENT ANSWER
TRY A DIFFERENT ANSWER. GOOD LUCK!
```

```
5ØØ REM***ANSWER IS NOT CORRECT

51Ø LET R=    ______________________________

52Ø IF    ______________________________
```

```
530 IF ______________________________________________

540 PRINT ___________________________________________

550 GOTO 310

560 _________________________________________________

570 GOTO 310
```

— — — — — — — — — —

```
500 REM***ANSWER IS NOT CORRECT
510 LET R=INT(2*RND(1))+1
520 IF R=1 THEN 540
530 IF R=2 THEN 560
540 PRINT "HMMM...I GET A DIFFERENT ANSWER."
550 GOTO 310
560 PRINT "TRY A DIFFERENT ANSWER.  GOOD LUCK!"
570 GOTO 310
```

37. The three statements:

```
620 IF R=1 THEN 630
621 IF R=2 THEN 650
622 IF R=3 THEN 670
```

can be replaced by a single statement.

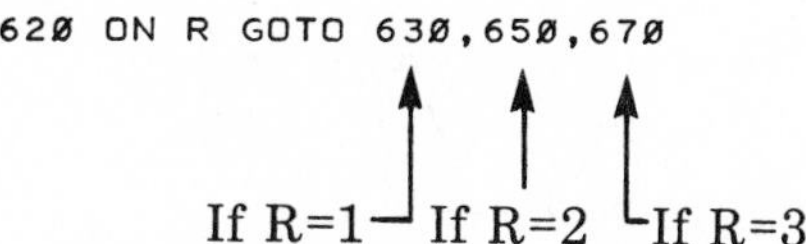

With this change, the program segment in frame 34 can be rewritten as follows.

```
600 REM***ANSWER IS CORRECT
610 LET R=INT(3*RND(1))+1
620 ON R GOTO 630,650,670
630 PRINT "RIGHT ON...GOOD WORK!"
640 GOTO 210
650 PRINT "YOU GOT IT! TRY ANOTHER."
660 GOTO 210
670 PRINT "THAT'S GREAT! KEEP IT UP!"
680 GOTO 210
```

(a) Look at line 610. What are the *possible* values of R? ____________

(b) Suppose, during a RUN, the random number generated by RND (1) in line 610 is .34319. What value will R have? ____________

(c) In this case, which line will the ON R GOTO statement send the computer to? ____________

— — — — — — — — — — —

(a) 1, 2, 3
(b) 2, INT(3*.34319) + 1 = INT(1.02957) + 1 = 1 + 1 = 2
(c) line 650

38. In general, the ON . . . GOTO statement has the following form.

ON *e* GOTO ℓ_1, ℓ_2, ℓ_3, . . ., ℓ_n

Where *e* can be any BASIC expression and ℓ_1,ℓ_2, ℓ_3, . . .,ℓ_n are line numbers. Valid values for *e* are integers 1, 2, 3 . . ., *n*. If *e* = 1, the computer goes to line ℓ_1. If *e* = 2, the computer goes toℓ_2. And so on.

Use an ON . . . GOTO to replace the two IF statements (lines 520 and 530) in our solution to frame 36.

```
500 REM***ANSWER IS NOT CORRECT
510 LET R=INT(2*RND(1))+1

520 ON ______________________________
540 PRINT "HMMM...I GET A DIFFERENT ANSWER."
550 GOTO 310
560 PRINT "TRY A DIFFERENT ANSWER.  GOOD LUCK!"
570 GOTO 310
```

— — — — — — — — — — —

```
520 ON R GOTO 540,560
```

39. And now, a wonderful space saving method! Here is the first part of our addition practice program, featuring *multiple statements per line.*

```
100 REM***ADDITION PRACTICE PROGRAM
200 REM***GENERATE RANDOM NUMBERS, A AND B
210 LET A=INT(20*RND(1))
220 LET B=INT(11*RND(1))+10
300 REM***PRINT PROBLEM AND ASK FOR ANSWER
310 PRINT : PRINT A; " + " ; B; " = " ; : INPUT C
400 REM***IS THE ANSWER CORRECT?
410 IF C=A+B THEN 600
500 REM***ANSWER IS NOT CORRECT
510 LET R=INT(2*RND(1))+1
520 ON R GOTO 540,560
540 PRINT "HMMM...I GET A DIFFERENT ANSWER." : GOTO 310
560 PRINT "TRY A DIFFERENT ANSWER. GOOD LUCK!" : GOTO 310
```

Line 310 has 3 statements.

Lines 540 and 560 each have 2 statements per line.

In the program, line 310 contains three statements, and lines 540 and 560 each contain two statements. In a line that contains more than one statement, what symbol, or character, is used between statements? ____________

— — — — — — — — — —

a colon (:)

```
              ┌─colon          colon──┐
              ↓                       ↓
310 PRINT :PRINT A; " + " ;B; " = ";:INPUT C

                                        colon──┐
                                               ↓
540 PRINT "HMMM...I GET A DIFFERENT ANSWER." : GOTO 310
```

40. For readability, we usually put a space on each side of the colon. However, this is not necessary. For example, we could have typed line 310 as shown below.

```
310 PRINT :PRINT A; " + "; B; " = ";:INPUT C
```

However, we will include spaces to make the statements easier to read. The computer understands either way.

We didn't show you the entire program in the last frame, because we want you to rewrite the part of the program beginning with line 600 as shown in frame 37, using multiple statements in those lines where it makes sense to group statements to work together.

```
600 REM***ANSWER IS CORRECT
610 LET R=INT(3*RND(1))+1
620 ON R GOTO 630,640,650

630 ____________________________________________

640 ____________________________________________

650 ____________________________________________
```

— — — — — — — — — —

```
630 PRINT "RIGHT ON...GOOD WORK!!!" : GOTO 210
640 PRINT "YOU GOT IT! TRY ANOTHER." : GOTO 210
650 PRINT "THAT'S GREAT! KEEP IT UP!" : GOTO 210
```

41. Here is the computer game we promised you earlier in the chapter. Note the use of multiple statements per line in lines 150, 160, 170, and 180.

```
100 REM**GUESS MY NUMBER - A COMPUTER GAME
110 LET X=INT(100*RND(1))+1
120 PRINT
130 PRINT "I'M THINKING OF A NUMBER FROM 1 TO 100."
140 PRINT "GUESS MY NUMBER!"
150 PRINT : PRINT "YOUR GUESS";:INPUT G
160 IF G < X THEN PRINT "TRY A BIGGER NUMBER.":GOTO 150
170 IF G > X THEN PRINT "TRY A SMALLER NUMBER.":GOTO 150
180 IF G = X THEN PRINT "THAT'S IT! YOU GUESSED MY NUMBER"
    :GOTO 110

RUN

I'M THINKING OF A NUMBER FROM 1 TO 100.
GUESS MY NUMBER!

YOUR GUESS? 50
TRY A BIGGER NUMBER.

YOUR GUESS? 75
TRY A SMALLER NUMBER.

YOUR GUESS? 68
TRY A BIGGER NUMBER.

YOUR GUESS? 72
TRY A BIGGER NUMBER.

YOUR GUESS? 73
THAT'S IT! YOU GUESSED MY NUMBER!

I'M THINKING OF A NUMBER FROM 1 TO 100.
GUESS MY NUMBER!

YOUR GUESS?
```

And so on.

Line 110 tells the computer to generate a random number and store it in variable X. This number will be a(n) ________________ from __________ to __________.

— — — — — — — — — — —

integer (or whole number); 1; 100

42. Multiple statements per line give us another nice shortcut. You'll recall that if the comparison in an IF-THEN statement is false, the computer skips the rest of the statement and goes on to the next line in the program in line number order. The nice thing is that the computer will also skip any statements that follow a false IF-THEN comparison if they are on the same multiple statement line. The rest of the statements on a line will be executed if the IF-THEN comparison is true. Therefore, in one line, you can have the computer do more than one thing if an IF-THEN comparison is true. Consider line 170 as it is shown on the following page. The computer will both PRINT and GOTO if the condition

is true, but it won't do either if the condition is false.

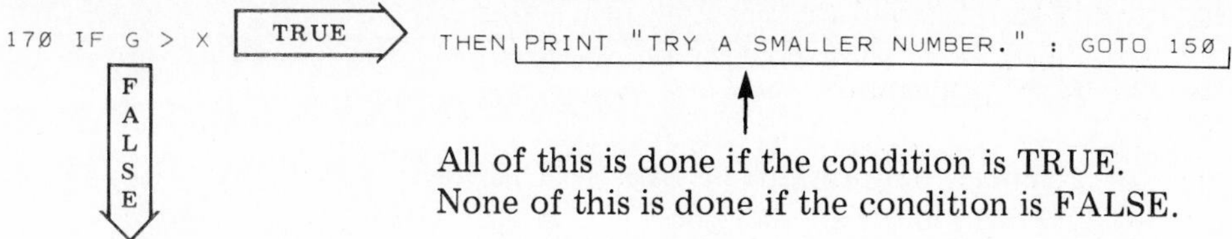

The *condition* is: G> X

(a) Suppose G = 90 and X = 73. Is the condition TRUE or FALSE? _______

(b) Suppose G = 70 and X = 73. Is the condition TRUE or FALSE? _______

(c) Suppose G = 73 and X = 73. Is the condition TRUE or FALSE? _______

— — — — — — — — — —

(a) TRUE; (b) FALSE; (c) FALSE

43. Line 150 causes the computer to print YOUR GUESS? When the player types a guess, the computer stores it in variable G. Lines 160, 170, and 180 compare the guess G with the random number X. Let's look at line 160.

```
160 IF G < X THEN PRINT "TRY A BIGGER NUMBER." : GOTO 150
```

If the guess G is less than the number X, the computer will print the message TRY A BIGGER NUMBER and will then GOTO line 150 to ask for another guess. However, if G is greater than X or equal to X, *neither* the PRINT *nor* the GOTO will be done. Here is another way to "picture" that idea.

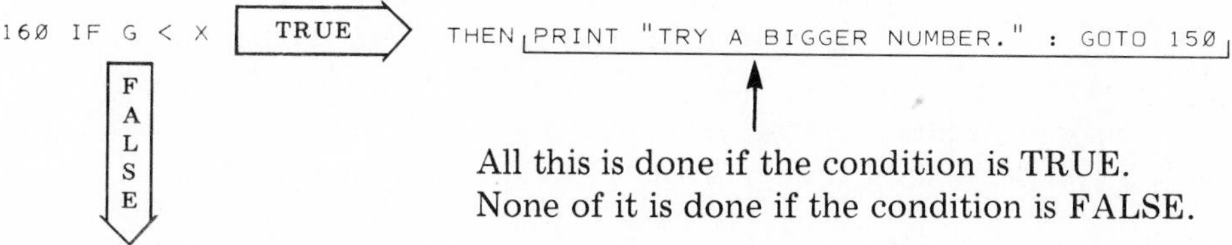

So, if G < X is FALSE, the computer goes on to line 170. Describe what happens when the computer executes line 170.

```
170 IF G > X THEN PRINT "TRY A SMALLER NUMBER." : GOTO 150
```

(a) If G *is* greater than X (G > X is TRUE), then ______________________

____.

(b) However, if G is *not* greater than X (G>X is FALSE), then ______________

____.

— — — — — — — — — —

(a) the computer will print the message TRY A SMALLER NUMBER and then GOTO line 150 for another guess
(b) neither the PRINT nor the GOTO will be done

44. If G<X is FALSE *and* G>X is FALSE, the computer will finally arrive at line 180. Here is a picture of the entire process of arriving at line 180.

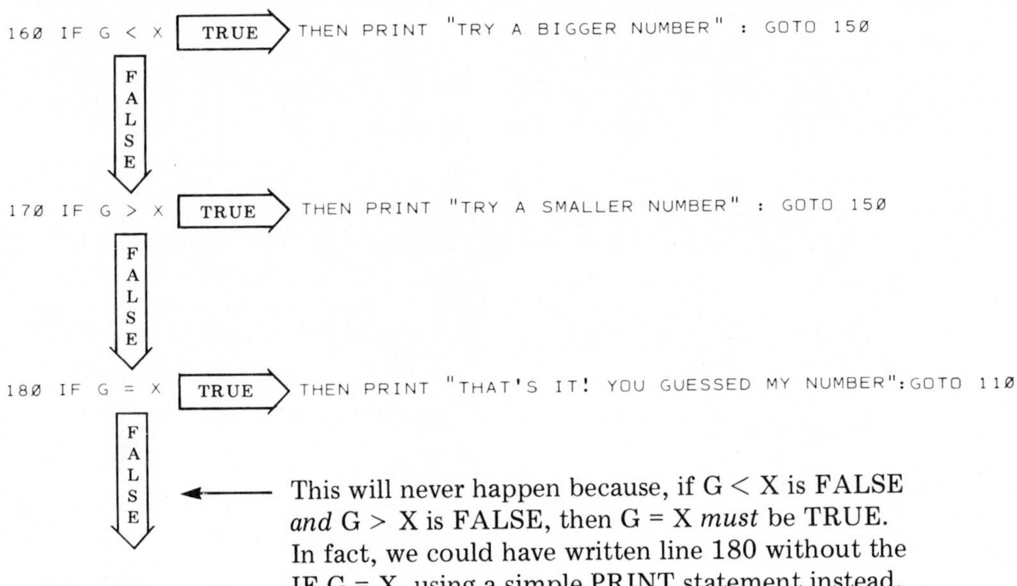

Suppose the player has guessed the number. Therefore, G<X is FALSE, G>X is FALSE, and, of course, G=X is TRUE. What happens?

____

____

____

— — — — — — — — — —

The computer prints the message THAT'S IT! YOU GUESSED MY NUMBER, then goes to line 110, where it is directed to "think of" a new number and start the game again.

45. For very young children, we may wish to reduce the range of integers generated by the statement that uses the RND functions (line 110). For example, instead of generating a number from 1 to 100, we may wish a number from 1 to 25. Conversely, advanced players may prefer a larger range, say 1 to 1000.

(a) Modify lines 110 and 130 so that the range is 1 to 25.

110____

130____

(b) Modify lines 110 and 130 so that the range is 1 to 1000.

110____

130____

— — — — — — — — — — —

(a)
```
110 LET X=INT(25*RND(1))+1
130 PRINT "I'M THINKING OF A NUMBER FROM 1 TO 25"
```

(b)
```
110 LET X=INT(1000*RND(1))+1
130 PRINT "I'M THINKING OF A NUMBER FROM 1 TO 1000."
```

46. Here is a convenient way to make it easy to change the range.

```
100 REM***GUESS MY NUMBER - A COMPUTER GAME
105 LET R=100
110 LET X=INT(R*RND(1))+1
120 PRINT
130 PRINT "I'M THINKING OF A NUMBER FROM 1 TO " ; R
```

Now the range is 1 to R, where R is assigned a value in line 105, then used in lines 110 and 130. So, to change the range, you simply change line 105. Suppose you want the range to be 1 to 500. What do you write for line 105?

105 ____

— — — — — — — — — — —

`105 LET R=500` or simply `105 R=500`

47. Using IF-THEN statements and multiple statements per line, modify and rewrite your NUMBER SIZE PROGRAM from frame 14 so that it will RUN like the one on the following page.

```
RUN
INPUT A NUMBER AND I WILL TELL YOU IF
IT IS LESS THAN 100, BETWEEN 100 AND
1000, OR OVER 1000.

YOUR NUMBER? 99
YOUR NO. IS LESS THAN 100.

YOUR NUMBER? 100
YOUR NO. IS BETWEEN 100 AND 1000.

YOUR NUMBER? 999
YOUR NO. IS BETWEEN 100 AND 1000.

YOUR NUMBER? 1000
YOUR NO. IS BETWEEN 100 AND 1000.

YOUR NUMBER? 1001
YOUR NO. IS OVER 1000.

YOUR NUMBER?
```

```
100 REM***NEW NUMBER SIZE PROGRAM
110 PRINT "INPUT A NUMBER AND I WILL TELL YOU IF"
120 PRINT "IT IS LESS THAN 100, BETWEEN 100 AND"
125 PRINT "1000, OR OVER 1000."
130 PRINT : PRINT "YOUR NUMBER"; : INPUT N
140 IF N<100 THEN PRINT "YOUR NO. IS LESS THAN 100." : GOTO 130
150 IF N<=1000 THEN PRINT "YOUR NO. IS BETWEEN 100 AND 1000." : GOTO 130
160 IF N>1000 THEN PRINT "YOUR NO. IS OVER 1000." : GOTO 130
```

48. Now we want you to put your accumulated knowledge of BASIC to work and write a program to provide practice for a person learning or reviewing the "times table," that is, multiplication from 0 times 0 to 12 times 12. Of course, we are calling this program COMPASSIONATE MULTIPLICATION PRACTICE. Study the RUN and our notes, then build your program. If you have a computer handy to use, check your own program before looking at our way of doing it.

Generate a problem, using random numbers from 0 to 12. Print the problem and ask for an answer. Compare the player's answer with the correct answer.

> If the answer is smaller than the correct answer, print TRY A BIGGER NUMBER and repeat the problem. •

If the answer is bigger than the correct answer, print TRY A SMALLER NUMBER and repeat the problem.

If the answer is correct, tell the player that she or he has typed the correct answer.

Our program uses three different replies to a correct answer. These are chosen at random from the following three possibilities.

THAT'S IT!
CORRECT ANSWER
GOOD WORK! KEEP IT UP

```
RUN

 2 × 4 =? 8
GOOD WORK! KEEP IT UP!

 2 × 2 =? 4
GOOD WORK! KEEP IT UP!

 2 × 8 =? 15
TRY A BIGGER NUMBER.

 2 × 8 =? 16
CORRECT ANSWER!

 1Ø × 1 =? 1Ø
CORRECT ANSWER!

 1Ø × 9 =? 1ØØ
TRY A SMALLER NUMBER.

 1Ø × 9 =? 9Ø
GOOD WORK! KEEP IT UP!

 11 × 7 =?
```

```
1ØØ REM***COMPASSIONATE MULTIPLICATION PRACTICE
11Ø LET A=INT(12*RND(1))+1 : LET B=INT(12*RND(1))+1
12Ø PRINT:PRINT A; " X " ; B; " = " ; : INPUT C
13Ø IF C<A*B THEN PRINT "TRY A BIGGER NUMBER." : GOTO 12Ø
14Ø IF C>A*B THEN PRINT "TRY A SMALLER NUMBER." : GOTO 12Ø
15Ø LET R=INT(3*RND(1))+1 : ON R GOTO 16Ø,17Ø,18Ø
16Ø PRINT "THAT'S IT!" : GOTO 11Ø
17Ø PRINT "CORRECT ANSWER!" : GOTO 11Ø
18Ø PRINT "GOOD WORK! KEEP IT UP!" : GOTO 11Ø
```

49. We mentioned in Chapter 2 that some of the older versions of BASIC required an END statement as the last statement in a program. Most versions of BASIC for home computers do not need this final END. However, the END statement, and its relative, the STOP statement, can be handy for terminating a program in some place other than the last line-numbered statement.

It is often handy to be able to end or stop a program as a result of an IF-THEN decision. END or STOP can be the condition to fulfill after THEN if the condition is TRUE. Examples:

```
20 IF X = 10 THEN STOP
20 IF X = 10 THEN END
```

With ATARI BASIC, using STOP will cause the computer to type a message, as shown below, giving the line number where the STOP statement was encountered and the RUN ended.

```
STOPPED AT 20
■
```

However, a RUN that ends when an END statement is encountered just gives the standard READY.

In a multiple-statement line with IF-THEN, END or STOP could be used as below:

```
120 IF Y * Q = 100 THEN PRINT "THAT'S ALL, FOLKS" : END
120 IF Y * Q = 100 THEN PRINT "THAT'S ALL, FOLKS" : STOP
```

At the end of a math drill or game playing program, you could use the following approach.

```
310 PRINT "ANOTHER GAME (YES OR NO)"; : INPUT A$
320 IF A$ = "NO" THEN END
330 GOTO 100
```

In a counting loop program, insert a line to tell the computer to quit counting when F is greater than 6.

```
10 LET F = 1

20 ____________________
30 PRINT "F ="; F
40 LET F = F + 1
50 GOTO 20
```

```
20 IF F>6 THEN END
20 IF F>6 THEN STOP
```

SELF-TEST

Try this Self-Test, so you can evaluate how much you have learned in Chapter 4.

1. Give the BASIC symbols for each of the following comparisons.

   __________ is equal to

   __________ is less than

   __________ is greater than

   __________ is less than or equal to

   __________ is greater than or equal to

   __________ is not equal to

2. Describe each IF-THEN statement in words. That is, describe what the statement tells the computer to do.

   (a) `IF G = X THEN 2ØØ` __________

   (b) `IF X>=Ø THEN C = C+1` __________

   (c) `IF N <> INT(N) THEN PRINT "N IS NOT AN INTEGER." : GOTO 21Ø`

   ____

   (d) `IF A^2+B^2=C^2 THEN PRINT "YES, IT IS A RIGHT TRIANGLE."`

   ____

3. For each description, write an IF-THEN statement.

   (a) If the value of N is less than or equal to 7, go to line 15.

   ____

(b) If A is less than 2*P, then increase the value of N by 1 and go to line 180. ______________________

(c) If M/N is equal to INT(M/N), then print the message M IS EVENLY DIVISIBLE BY N. ______________________

____

4. Complete the following program to tell how many years are needed to "double your money." Use multiple statements in line 190.

```
100 REM**HOW MANY YEARS TO DOUBLE YOUR MONEY
110 PRINT "IF YOU TYPE THE AMOUNT OF PRINCIPAL"
120 PRINT "AND THE INTEREST RATE PER YEAR, I"
130 PRINT "WILL SHOW YOU HOW MANY YEARS TO"
140 PRINT "DOUBLE YOUR MONEY. "
135 PRINT
150 PRINT "PRINCIPAL";: INPUT P
160 PRINT "INTEREST RATE";: INPUT R
170 LET N=1
180 LET A=P*(1+R/100)^N
190 ______________________          (This is a loop)
200 PRINT
210 PRINT "YEARS TO DOUBLE YOUR MONEY: ";N
220 PRINT "THE ACTUAL AMOUNT WILL BE $";A

RUN
IF YOU TYPE THE AMOUNT OF PRINCIPAL AND THE
INTEREST RATE PER YEAR, I WILL SHOW YOU HOW
MANY YEARS TO DOUBLE YOUR MONEY.

PRINCIPAL? 1000      ]
INTEREST RATE? 6     ]-------- 1000 at 6% per year.

YEARS TO DOUBLE YOUR MONEY: 12
THE ACTUAL AMOUNT WILL BE $2012.2
                          2012.19638
```

5. What will be the result of running the following program? Show the RUN.

```
10 LET K=1
20 PRINT K
30 LET K=K+1
40 IF K<=5 THEN 20
RUN
```

____

6. What will the RUN look like for this program?

```
10 LET K=1
20 IF K<5 THEN K=K+1 : GOTO 20
30 PRINT K
```

7. Describe the random numbers generated by each of the following expressions.

(a) RND(1) ______________________

____

(b) 2*RND(1) ______________________

____

(c) INT(2*RND(1)) ______________________

____

(d) INT(2*RND(1)) + 1 ______________________

____

(e) INT(3*RND(1))–1 ______________________

____

(f) 3.14159*RND(1) ______________________

____

8. Here is an incomplete program to simulate (imitate) flipping a coin. Please complete the program. (Hint: C should be 0 or 1, at random.)

```
1ØØ REM***COIN FLIPPER

11Ø LET C = ________________________________
12Ø IF C=Ø THEN PRINT "TAILS" : GOTO 11Ø
13Ø IF C=1 THEN PRINT "HEADS" : GOTO 11Ø

RUN
HEADS
HEADS
TAILS
TAILS
HEADS
HEADS
HEADS
HEADS
TAILS
HEADS
TAILS
TAILS
HEADS
HEADS
```

Answers to Self-Test

The frame numbers in parentheses refer to the frames in the chapter where the topic is discussed. You may wish to refer to these for quick review.

1. = is equal to
   < is less than
   > is greater than
   <= is less than or equal to
   >= is greater than or equal to
   <> is not equal to
   (frame 7)

2. (a) If the value of G is equal to the value of X, go to line 200. Otherwise (G=X is FALSE), continue in the usual line number order. (frames 1–8)
   (b) If the value of X is greater than or equal to zero, increase the value of C by 1. Otherwise (X>=0 is FALSE), do not execute the LET portion. In either case, continue in regular line number order. (frame 10)
   (c) If N<>INT(N) is TRUE, this means that the value of N is not an integer. In this case, print the string N IS NOT AN INTEGER and then go to line 210. However, if N *is an integer,* N<>INT(N) will be FALSE. In this case, neither the PRINT nor the GOTO will be executed and the computer will simply continue in regular line number order. (frames 1–8, 20–23, 42)
   (d) If the value of A squared plus B squared is equal to the value of C squared, print the string YES, IT IS A RIGHT TRIANGLE.

Otherwise (A^2+B^2=C^2 is FALSE), *don't* print the string. In either case, continue in regular line number order. (frames 1-8)

3. (a) `IF N<=7 THEN GOTO 15`
   (b) `IF A<2*P THEN LET N=N+1 : GOTO 18Ø`
   (c) `IF M/N = INT(M/N) THEN PRINT "M IS EVENLY DIVISIBLE BY N"`

   (frames 1–10)

4. `19Ø IF A<2*P THEN LET N = N + 1 : GOTO 18Ø`
   In other words, if the newly computed amount A is still less than twice the original principal P, increase the year N by 1, and go back to line 180 to compute a new amount A. (frames 9–10)

5.
```
RUN
 1
 2
 3
 4
 5
```
   The PRINT statement is *inside* the loop. Therefore, it is done every time.

   (frame 8)

6.
```
RUN
 5
```
   This time, the PRINT statement is *outside* the loop. It is done only once, after the loop has been completed. (frame 8)

7. (a) Numbers between 0 and 1. Each random number is greater than zero, but less than one. This answer is also acceptable: 0<RND(1)<1. (frames 16, 17)
   (b) Numbers between 0 and 2. Each random number will be greater than 0, but less than 2. Also: 0<2*RND(1)<2. (frames 17–19)
   (c) 0 or 1 No other values are possible. (frames 20, 23–26)
   (d) 1 or 2 (frames 20, 23–26)
   (e) -1, 0, or 1 (frames 20, 23–26)
   (f) Numbers between 0 and 3.14159. Each random number is greater than 0, but less than 3.14159. Also: 0<3.14159*RND(1)<3.14159. Since 3.14159 is an approximation to π, we might also say, although somewhat imprecisely, that these numbers are between 0 and π. (frames 20, 23–26)

8. `11Ø LET C = INT(2*RND(1))` (frames 26, 27)

CHAPTER FIVE

READ and DATA Work Together

This chapter is designed to give you practice using the BASIC statements and programming skills you have learned so far and to add to your bag of programming tricks. You will be able to extend your understanding of the capabilities of the PRINT statement, in order to better control the output of your programs and write more efficient instructions or programming code. In addition, you will learn two frequently used statements that always work together to assign values to variables: the READ and DATA statements. When you finish this chapter, you will be able to:

- use READ statements to assign values or strings to one or more variables at a time, from items in DATA statements;
- control the spacing of output through the use of commas and semicolons separating items in PRINT statements;
- identify the standard print positions in printout and write PRINT statements using comma spacing;

1. You've seen how LET statements and INPUT statements can be used to assign values to variables. (We hope that you have used them on your computer, too.) A third method uses two statements in combination, READ and DATA, to assign values to variables.

```
10 READ X
20 PRINT "THIS TIME THROUGH THE LOOP, X = " ; X
30 GOTO 10
40 DATA 10, 15, 7, 3.25, 11
```

```
RUN
THIS TIME THROUGH THE LOOP, X = 10
THIS TIME THROUGH THE LOOP, X = 15
THIS TIME THROUGH THE LOOP, X = 7
THIS TIME THROUGH THE LOOP, X = 3.25
THIS TIME THROUGH THE LOOP, X = 11
ERROR-   6 AT LINE 10
```

This statement 10 READ X tells the computer to READ one value from the DATA statement, and assign the value to the variable X. Every time the READ statement is executed (each time through the loop), the computer reads the next value from the DATA statement, and assigns the new value to the variable X. The computer keeps track of each value as it is read out, in effect, moving a pointer across the items in the DATA statement, one notch at a time.

How many values are in the DATA statement? ________

— — — — — — — — — —

5

2. As the computer executed the program, it read and printed one value from the DATA statement each time it went through the loop. Then on the sixth trip through the loop, it tried to find still another number. Since it couldn't find another number to read from the DATA statement, the computer printed ERROR-6 IN LINE 10. An Error 6 simply lets you know that the computer program has read through all the values you listed in the DATA statement. It really is not an error. However, to keep it from messing up your screen, you can change your program slightly so that the error message won't appear. Add the following line to your program:

25 IF X = 9999 then END

and change your DATA statement to include 9999 as the last number.

40 DATA 10, 15, 7, 3, 25, 11, 9999

Now when you RUN the program, you will not get the ERROR-6 message.

When you RUN this program, how many times was a new value assigned to the READ variable? ________________________________

— — — — — — — — — —

5 values were assigned

3. Look at the format for DATA statements.

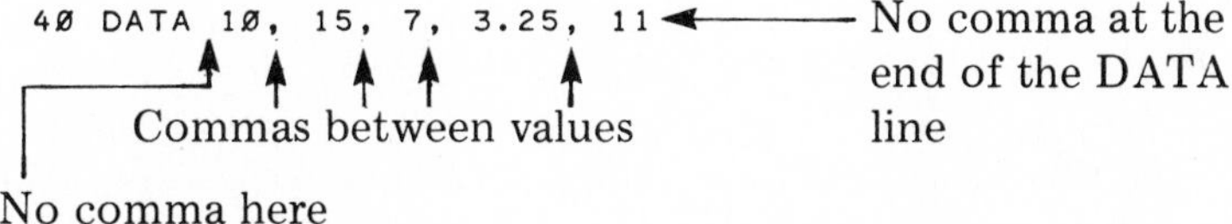

DATA statements may contain whole numbers, numbers with decimal fractions (such as 3.25 above), numbers in floating point or "E" notation, or negative numbers.

DATA statements may *not* contain variables, arithmetic operations, other functions, or fractions.

This is OK: `90 DATA 3, 8, 2.5`
This is NOT OK: `95 DATA 2+3, 1/4, 2/5, 7*8`

Write a DATA statement for these values.

```
342       60.25
1256      -412
205       2.05E8
```

— — — — — — — — — —

```
60 DATA 342,1256,205,60.25,-412,2.05E8
```

Your line number may be different. And remember, no commas can be used in large numbers, such as 1256 above. However, floating point or "E" notation may be used.

4. Data statements may be placed anywhere in the program.

```
10 READ N              10 DATA 123
20 PRINT N             20 READ N
30 DATA 123            30 PRINT N
RUN                    RUN
 123                    123
```

Can the DATA statement be placed as shown in the following program?

____

```
10 READ N
20 DATA 123
30 PRINT N
```

— — — — — — — — — —

yes

5. These DATA statements are not written in correct BASIC. Tell what is wrong with each one.

(a) `20 DATA, 15, 32, 85, 66` ____________________

(b) `30 DATA 22.3; 81.1; 66.66; 43.22` ______________________________

— — — — — — — — — — —

(a) should not have comma after DATA
(b) should use commas instead of semicolons to separate values in a DATA statement

6. This program converts inches to centimeters. One inch = 2.54 centimeters. When the program is RUN, the computer prints the value in inches on one line, and the equivalent in centimeters on the next. Fill in the missing statement (line 20).

```
10 REM***CONVERT INCHES TO CENTIMETERS

20 ______________________________
30 PRINT
40 PRINT "INCHES = ";I
50 PRINT "CENTIMETERS = ";2.54*I
60 GOTO 20
90 DATA 1, 8, 12

RUN

INCHES = 1
CENTIMETERS = 2.54

INCHES = 8
CENTIMETERS = 20.32

INCHES = 12
CENTIMETERS = 30.48
ERROR- 6 AT LINE 20
```

— — — — — — — — — — —

```
20 READ I
```

7. Now you write a program to convert ounces to grams. One ounce = 28.35 grams (rounded to two decimal places). Use a DATA statement to hold the values in ounces that you want converted to grams. Here is what your program should print when it is RUN.

```
RUN

OUNCES = 1
GRAMS = 28.35

OUNCES = 13
GRAMS = 368.55

OUNCES = 16
GRAMS = 453.6
ERROR-  6 AT LINE 2Ø
```

```
1Ø REM***CONVERT OUNCES TO GRAMS
2Ø READ Z
3Ø PRINT
4Ø PRINT "OUNCES = " ; Z
5Ø PRINT "GRAMS = " ; 28.35*Z
6Ø GOTO 2Ø
9Ø DATA 1, 13, 16
```

We used Z to represent ounces because O (oh) can be confused with 0 (zero).

8. Write a "World's Most Expensive Adding Machine" program (from Chapter 3, frame 45) using READ and DATA statements instead of an INPUT statement so that a RUN of the program will look like the one below. Examine the RUN to determine the values in the DATA statement.

```
RUN
X = 12
TOTAL SO FAR IS 12

X = 43
TOTAL SO FAR IS 55

X = 33
TOTAL SO FAR IS 88

X = 92
TOTAL SO FAR IS 18Ø

X = 76.25
TOTAL SO FAR IS 256.25
ERROR-  6 AT LINE 12Ø
```

```
100 REM***WORLD'S MOST EXPENSIVE ADDING MACHINE
110 LET T=0
120 READ X
130 LET T=T+X
140 PRINT "X = " ; X
150 PRINT "TOTAL SO FAR IS " ; T
160 PRINT
170 GOTO 120
180 DATA 12,43,33,92,76.25
```

Your line numbers may be different.

9. Do you remember our program to compute the mean, or average, of a group of numbers? If not, review Chapter 4, frame 12. Below is a rewrite of that program, using READ and DATA statements. We use lots of REMs (REMARKS) to explain what is happening.

```
100 REM***A FRIENDLY 'MEAN' PROGRAM
110 REM***INITIALIZE T (FOR TOTAL) AND N (FOR NUMBER OF NUMBERS)
120 T=0 : N=0
130 REM***READ A NUMBER, X. IF IT IS THE FLAG 1E97
140 REM***GOTO PRINTOUT. OTHERWISE, UPDATE T AND X
150 READ X : IF X=1E97 THEN 180
160 T=T+X : N=N+1 : GOTO 150
170 REM***PRINT ANSWERS
180 PRINT "N = " ; N
190 PRINT "TOTAL = " ; T
200 PRINT "MEAN = " ; T/N
900 REM***DATA FOLLOWS
910 DATA 10,3,-9,-15,-23,-25,-30,1E97 <------ The flag
```

```
RUN
N = 7
TOTAL = -89
MEAN = -12.71428571
```

To RUN this program for a different set of data, simply replace line 910 by one or more DATA statements containing the new data and the flag 1E97. (You'll recall from Chapter 3 that to replace a statement, just type the new statement using the old line number.) For example, suppose we wish to use this data: 63, 72, 50, 55, 75, 67, 59, 61, 64. Write the DATA statement.

```
910 DATA ______________________________
```

— — — — — — — — — — —

```
910 DATA 63,72,50,55,75,67,59,61,64,1E97
```

Did you remember the flag?

10. The following program causes the computer to read numbers from a DATA statement and print only the numbers that are *positive* (greater than zero). Numbers that are less than zero or equal to zero are not printed.

```
10 READ X
20 IF X>0 THEN PRINT "X = " ; X
30 GOTO 10
40 DATA 3,7,0,-2,5,-1,7,8,0,-3
RUN
X = 3
X = 7
X = 5
X = 7
X = 8
ERROR-   6 AT LINE 10
```

Note: 7 is printed *twice* because it occurs twice in the DATA statement.

Look at the numbers in the DATA statement.

(a) For which numbers is the condition X > 0 TRUE? ____________

(b) When X > 0 is TRUE, what does line 20 cause the computer to do?

____

(c) For which numbers is the condition X > 0 FALSE? ____________

(d) When X > 0 is FALSE, what happens in line 20? ____________

— — — — — — — — — — —

(a) 3, 7, 5, 7, 8
(b) print the message X= followed by the value of X
(c) 0, −2, −1, 0, −3
(d) Nothing. The PRINT portion of line 20 is not executed and the computer goes on to line 30.

11. What will the RUN look like for this program?

```
10 READ X
20 IF X<0 THEN PRINT "X = " ;X
30 GOTO 10
40 DATA 3,7,0,-2,5,-1,7,8,0,-3
RUN
```

— — — — — — — — — — —

```
RUN
X = -2
X = -1
X = -3
ERROR-   6 AT LINE 1Ø
```
← Did you remember this?

12. Complete the following program so that the RUN will occur as shown.

```
1Ø READ X

2Ø ______________________________________
3Ø GOTO 1Ø
4Ø DATA 3, 7, Ø, -2, 5, -1, 7, 8, Ø, -3

RUN
X = Ø
X = Ø
ERROR-   6 AT LINE 1Ø
```

Two zeros are printed because there are two zeros in the DATA statement.

— — — — — — — — — —

```
2Ø IF X=Ø THEN PRINT "X = " ;X
```

13. For more practice, do each of the following. If possible, try each one on your computer.

(a) Complete line 20 so that only *nonzero* numbers are printed.

```
2Ø IF ______________ THEN PRINT "X = " ;X
```

(b) Complete line 20 so that the computer prints numbers that are greater than or equal to zero.

```
2Ø IF ______________ THEN PRINT "X = " ;X
```

(c) Complete line 20 so that the computer prints numbers that are less than or equal to 3.

```
2Ø IF ______________ THEN PRINT "X = " ;X
```

— — — — — — — — — —

(a) `X <> Ø (THE COMPUTER WILL PRINT 3,7,-2,5,-1,7,8, AND -3.)`
(b) `X >= Ø (THE COMPUTER WILL PRINT 3,7,0,5,7,8, AND 0.)`
(c) `X <= 3 (THE COMPUTER WILL PRINT 3,0,-2,-1,0, AND -3.)`

If you need review, see Chapter 4, frame 7.

14. In BASIC you may have more than one variable following a READ instruction. On the following page is an example. Use commas to separate the variables.

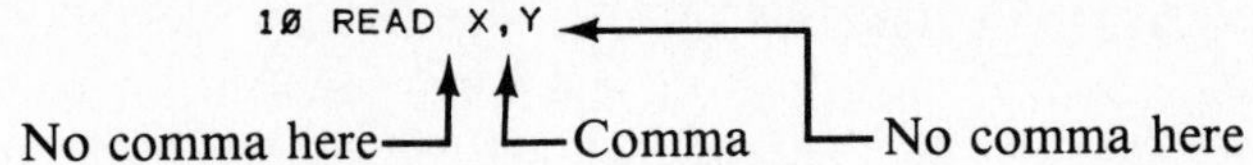

This will cause the computer to take two values from the DATA statement and assign them in order to the three READ variables.

Complete the RUN of this program (fill in blanks).

```
10 READ X,Y
20 PRINT X,Y
30 GOTO 10
40 DATA 10, 20, 30, 40
RUN
   10              20

________      ________

ERROR-   6 AT LINE 10
```

```
   30              40
```

The second time through the loop, these values were assigned to X and Y and printed by line 20. (We'll discuss the spacing of items in PRINT statements later on.)

15. Fill in the blank spaces in the program and in the RUN.

```
10 ______________________________
20 PRINT A + B
30 GOTO 10
40 DATA 3,5,6,4,7,9

RUN
 8

________________

________________

ERROR-   6 AT LINE 10
```

```
10 READ A,B

RUN
 8
 10
 16
```

16. You may have more than one READ statement in a program. However, all READ statements assign values to their variable(s) from the same DATA statement. An item from DATA is assigned to a READ variable in the order that the computer comes to READ statements when the program is RUN.

```
10 READ P
20 READ Q
30 PRINT P
40 PRINT Q
50 GOTO 10
60 DATA 3,5,6,4,7,9
RUN
 3 }—First data item assigned to P, second assigned to Q.
 5
 6 }— Second trip through the loop: third data item is assigned to P, fourth
 4     to Q.
 7
 9
ERROR-  6 AT LINE
```

For the third trip through the loop, what value is assigned to P? _________

What value is assigned to Q? __________

— — — — — — — — — — —

7; 9

17. Write a program that:

> uses three READ statements to assign values to three different READ variables X, Y, and Z;
>
> then prints the *sum* of X + Y + Z;
>
> then loops back to repeat the process until the data are all used up.

Show what the computer will print when your program is RUN. Here are the data for the DATA statement: 3, 5, 6, 4, 7, 9, 2, 5, 2.

— — — — — — — — — — —

```
10 READ X
20 READ Y
30 READ Z
40 PRINT X + Y + Z
50 GOTO 10
60 DATA 3,5,6,4,7,9,2,5,2
RUN
 14
 20
 9
ERROR-   6 AT LINE 10
```

18. Here is a questionnaire we gave to 50 people.

DOES YOUR COMPUTER UNDERSTAND YOU?

1. YES
2. NO

Each of the 50 responses was either 1 (YES) or 2 (NO). The responses are shown below in five DATA statements. The last response is followed by -1, the flag signalling end of data.

```
900 REM***DATA* 1=YES, 2=NO, -1=END OF DATA
910 DATA 1,2,2,2,1,2,1,2,1,2
920 DATA 2,1,1,1,2,1,2,2,2,1
930 DATA 2,2,2,1,2,1,2,2,1,2
940 DATA 1,1,1,1,2,1,2,2,1,1
950 DATA 2,2,2,2,1,1,1,2,1,2,-1
```

How many YES answers? ________

How many NO answers? ________

Write the number of YES answers in the box labeled "Y" and the number of NO answers in the box labeled "N."

Y [ ]

N [ ]

— — — — — — — — — — —

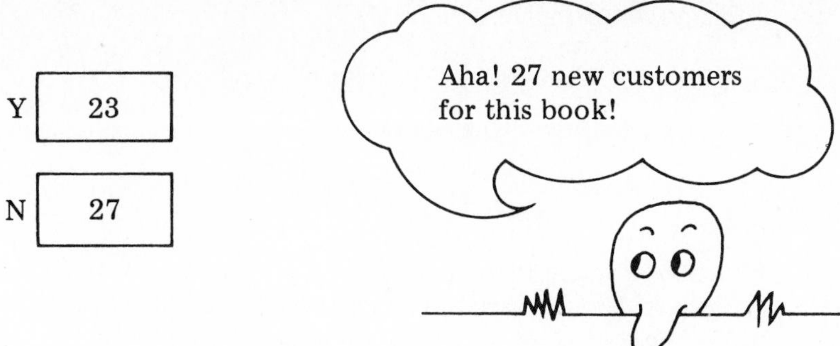

19. Here is a program to read the answers from the DATA statements and count the number of YES answers and NO answers. The variable Y is used to count YES answers. The variable N is used to count NO answers.

```
100 REM***QUESTIONNAIRE ANALYSIS PROGRAM
110 REM***INITIALIZE:  SET COUNTING VARIABLES TO ZERO
120 Y=0 : N=0
200 REM***READ AND COUNT VOTES
210 READ A : IF A=-1 THEN 410
220 IF A=1 THEN LET Y=Y+1 : GOTO 210
230 IF A=2 THEN LET N=N+1 : GOTO 210
400 REM***PRINT THE RESULTS
410 PRINT
420 PRINT "YES: " ; Y
430 PRINT " NO: " ; N
900 REM***DATA*  1=YES, 2=NO, -1=END OF DATA
910 DATA 1,2,2,2,1,2,1,2,1,2
920 DATA 2,1,1,1,2,1,2,2,2,1
930 DATA 2,2,2,1,2,1,2,2,1,2
940 DATA 1,1,1,1,2,1,2,2,1,1
950 DATA 2,2,2,2,1,1,1,2,1,2,-1

RUN
YES: 23
 NO: 27
```

The flag of -1 tells the computer there is no more data and to go to line 410 to start talleying the results.

Note the multiple statements in lines 120, 210, 220, and 230.

(a) Which section of the program is a loop that is repeated for each value in the DATA statements? Lines __________ to __________.

(b) Which statement reads a value corresponding to one vote and puts it into box A? ______________________

(c) Which line determines whether a vote is YES and, if it is, increases the YES count by one? __________

(d) Which line determines whether a vote is NO and, if it is, increases the NO count by one? __________

— — — — — — — — — — — —

(a) lines 210 to 230; (b) line 210; (c) line 220; (d) line 230

20. Now look at this new questionnaire.

DOES YOUR COMPUTER UNDERSTAND YOU?

1. YES
2. NO
3. SOMETIMES

Modify the program in frame 19 so that the computer counts the YES, NO, and SOMETIMES answers. Use the variable Y to count YES answers. Use the variable N to count NO answers. Use the variable S to count SOMETIMES answers. Use the following data.

2, 1, 3, 2, 3, 3, 1, 3, 3, 2, 1, 2, 1, 2, 1, 1, 3, 3, -1

Using this data, the results when the program is RUN should be printed as follows.

```
YES: 6
 NO: 5
SOMETIMES: 7
```

— — — — — — — — — —

Here are our changes.

```
12Ø Y=Ø : N=Ø : S=Ø
24Ø IF A=3 THEN LET S=S+1 : GOTO 21Ø
44Ø PRINT "SOMETIMES: " ; S
9ØØ REM***DATA: 1=YES, 2=NO, 3=SOMETIMES, -1=END OF DATA
91Ø DATA 2,1,3,2,3,3,1,3,3,2,1,2,1,2,1,1,3,3,-1
92Ø
93Ø
94Ø
95Ø
```

We deleted lines 920, 930, 940, and 950 from the program of frame 19. If the program is in the computer, we can do this by typing the line number and pressing **RETURN.** If you have a computer handy, LIST the program to show the modifications and to prove that the deleted lines have disappeared from the computer's memory. On the following page is our listing.

```
LIST

100 REM***QUESTIONNAIRE ANALYSIS PROGRAM
110 REM***INITIALIZE: SET COUNTING VARIABLES TO ZERO
120 Y=0 : N=0 : S=0
200  REM***READ AND COUNT VOTES
210 READ A : IF A=-1 THEN 410
220 IF A=1 THEN LET Y=Y+1 : GOTO 210
230 IF A=2 THEN LET N=N+1 : GOTO 210
240 IF A=3 THEN LET S=S+1 : GOTO 210
400 REM***PRINT THE RESULTS
410 PRINT
420 PRINT "YES : " ; Y
430 PRINT " NO : " ; N
440 PRINT "SOMETIMES : " ; S
900 REM***DATA: 1=YES, 2=NO, 3=SOMETIMES, -1=END OF DATA
910 DATA 2,1,3,2,3,3,1,3,3,2,1,2,1,2,1,1,3,3,-1
```

21. Back in Chapter 2, we used PRINT statements in the following form.

PRINT *e*

where *e* is a numerical expression

For example:

PRINT 7+5

numerical expression

A PRINT statement of this form tells the computer to compute and evalute (do the arithmetic of) the numerical expression and then print the result.

The following PRINT statement tells the computer to evaluate *four* numerical expressions and print the four results.

We type: `PRINT 7 + 5, 7 - 5, 7 * 5, 7 / 5`

It types: `12    2    35    1.4`

In the above, draw arrows connecting each numerical expression with its computed and printed value. We have drawn the first arrow, connecting the expression, 7+5, with its printed result, 12.

```
PRINT 7 + 5, 7 - 5, 7 * 5, 7 / 5
 12         2         35        1.4
```

22. If a PRINT statement has more than one expression, then the expressions are separated by commas.

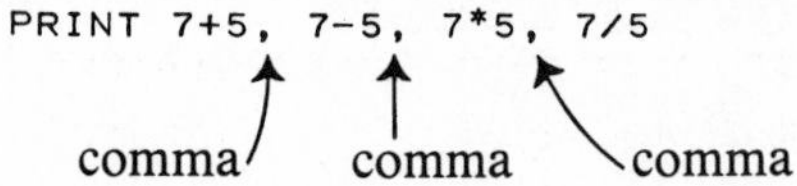

The following PRINT statement directs the computer to compute and print the values of 2+3, 2-3, 2*3, and 2/3. However, we forgot to put in commas. Please insert commas in the correct BASIC form.

```
PRINT 2+3 2-3 2*3 2/3
```

— — — — — — — — — — —

```
PRINT 2+3,2-3,2*3,2/3
```

Note: *No* comma following PRINT and no comma following 2/3. A comma following PRINT will cause an ERROR message. A comma following 2/3 (at the very end of the PRINT statement) has a special purpose which we will discuss later.

23. Complete the following. (Remember, for direct statements, you do not need a line number and you only have to press **RETURN** to have the computer execute the statement.)

We type: `PRINT 3*3, 5*5, 7*7`

It types: _______ _______ _______

We type: `PRINT 2*3+4*5, (2+3)*(4+5)`

It types: _______ _______

— — — — — — — — — — —

```
9         25        49
26        45
```

24. Your turn. Let's go back to our three bicycles, with wheels of 20-, 24- and 26-inch diameters. You want to find out, for each bike, how far it travels during *one turn* of the wheel. In other words, you want to evaluate the following three expressions.

20-inch wheel:	3.14*20	First expression
24-inch wheel:	3.14*24	Second expression
26-inch wheel:	3.14*26	Third expression

Write a PRINT statement to tell the computer to evaluate the three expressions and PRINT the results.

You type: ______________________________

It types: `62.8      75.36      81.64`

— — — — — — — — — — —

```
PRINT 3.14*2Ø, 3.14*24, 3.14*26
```

25. ATARI BASIC has four standard print positions. A comma in a PRINT statement causes the cursor to move to the next available standard print position. Look at the example below and fill in the blanks.

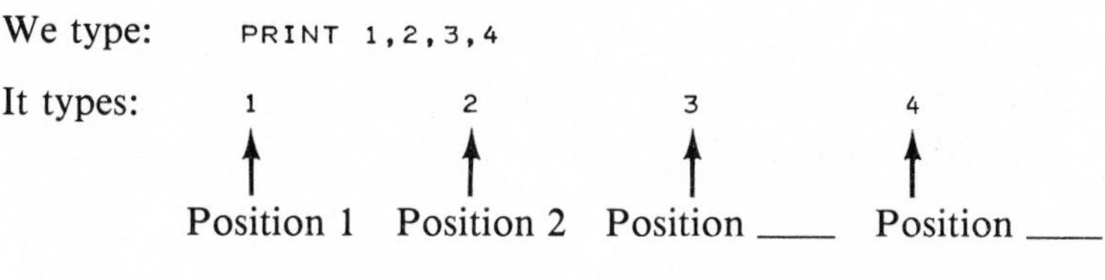

— — — — — — — — — — —

3; 4

26. Positive numbers, or zero, are printed *without* an explicit plus sign (+). Watch what happens when *negative* numbers are printed.

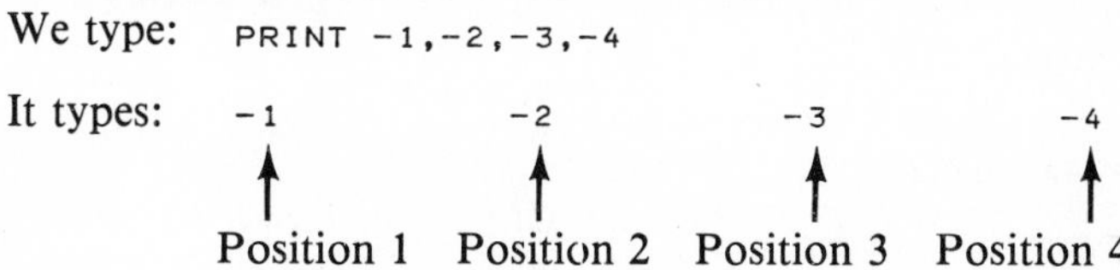

How does the printing of negative numbers differ from that of positive numbers? ______________________________

— — — — — — — — — — —

Negative numbers are printed with a minus sign (–) followed by the digits of the number.

27. What happens if there are *more than* four items in a PRINT statement? Look at the direct statement below and also at how the computer executed it.

We type: `PRINT 1,2,3,4,5,6,7`

It types:

```
1          2          3          4
  5          6          7
```

Describe what happened.____________________________________

____

— — — — — — — — — —

The computer printed the 7 numbers on 2 lines, with 4 numbers on the first line and 3 numbers on the second line.

28. Following the rules for items or expressions separated by commas, show what the computer will print in response to the following PRINT statement.

We type: `PRINT 1,2,3,4,5,6,7,8,9,10`

It types:

— — — — — — — — — —

```
1          2          3          4
  5          6          7          8
    9          10
```

29. Instead of commas, we can also use *semicolons* as separators in a PRINT statement. Watch what happens.

We type: `PRINT-1;-2;-3;-4;-5;-6;-7`

It types: `-1-2-3-4-5-6-7`

We type: `PRINT 1;2;3;4;5`

It types: `12345`

Semicolon spacing *catenates* numbers. That is, it directs the computer to print numbers close together, in a linked series. Comma spacing causes numbers to be printed in predetermined print positions. So, to print results close together, use ____________________.

— — — — — — — — — —

semicolons

30. The screen can hold up to 38 characters on each line. That is, it has 38 *character positions,* numbered from 0 on the left to 37 on the right. Complete the following diagram of character positions on the screen.

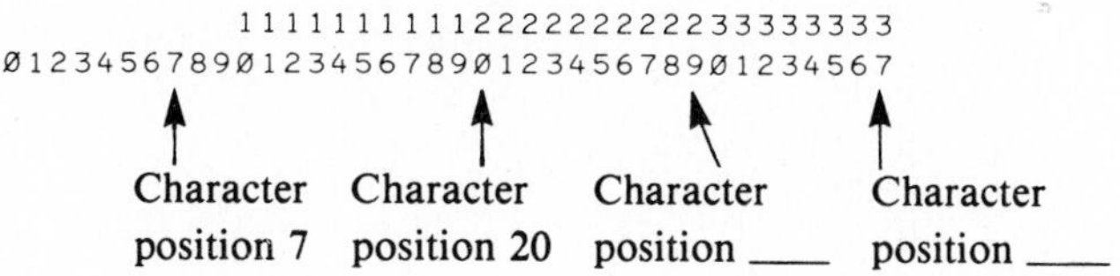

— — — — — — — — — — —

29: 37

31. The four standard print positions, used in *comma* spacing, begin at character position 0. We've marked print positions 1 and 2; you circle print positions 3 and 4 on the following diagram.

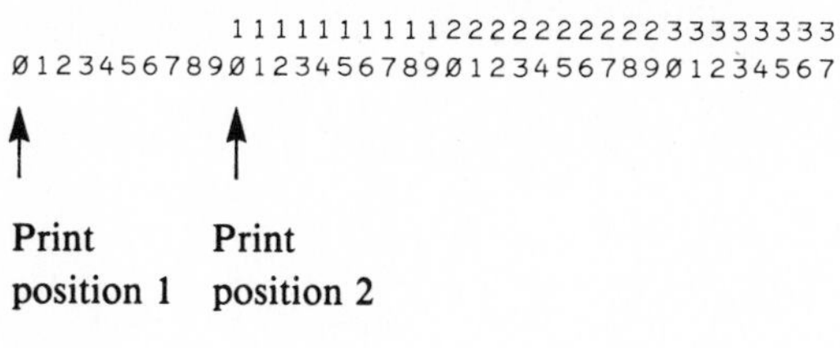

— — — — — — — — — — —

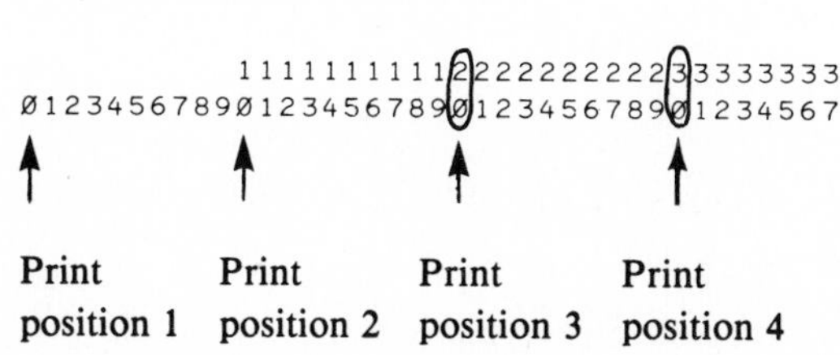

Note: A standard print position is 10 character positions wide. For example, print position 1 occupies character positions 0 through 9, or 10 character positions in all. Print position 2 occupies character positions 10 through 19, and so on.

32. Now watch what happens when we put a comma at the *end* of a PRINT statement.

```
10 LET N=1
20 PRINT N,  <-------- Comma
30 LET N=N+1
40 GOTO 20

RUN
1           2           3         4
  5           6           7         8
    9           10          11
STOPPED AT LINE 20
```

We pressed BREAK here to terminate the RUN.

Remember what the comma does. It tells the computer to move to the next standard print position. So, after printing number 1, the computer moves to print position 2; after print 2, the computer moves to standard print position 3, and so on. After printing something in standard print position 4, it continues printing on the next line.

Show the first 7 items printed by the following program.

```
10 LET N=1
20 PRINT N,
30 LET N=N+2
40 GOTO 20

RUN
```

- - - - - - - - - - - -

```
1           3           5         7
  9           11          13
```

33. Now, what do you suppose happens if we put a semicolon at the end of a PRINT statement? As always with computers, if we don't know, we EXPERIMENT. Let's try it.

```
10 LET N=1
20 PRINT N;
30 LET N=N+1
40 GOTO 20
RUN
12345678910111213141516171819
STOPPED AT LINE 20
```

We pressed BREAK. (Bet you weren't this quick!)

Rewrite line 20 so that the computer puts a space *after* each number it prints.

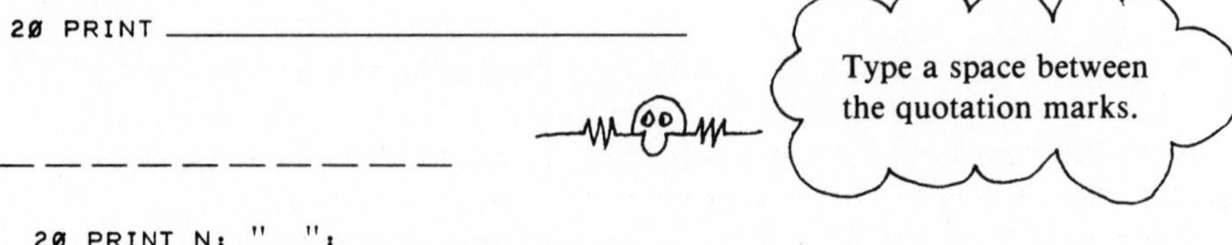

- - - - - - - - - - - -

```
20 PRINT N; " ";
```

It you want to put a space *before* each number, do it like this:

```
20 PRINT " "; N;
```

The space between quotes, is *before* the number (N).

34. We have spent some time with comma spacing and semicolon spacing with *numbers.* Next, let's try *strings.*

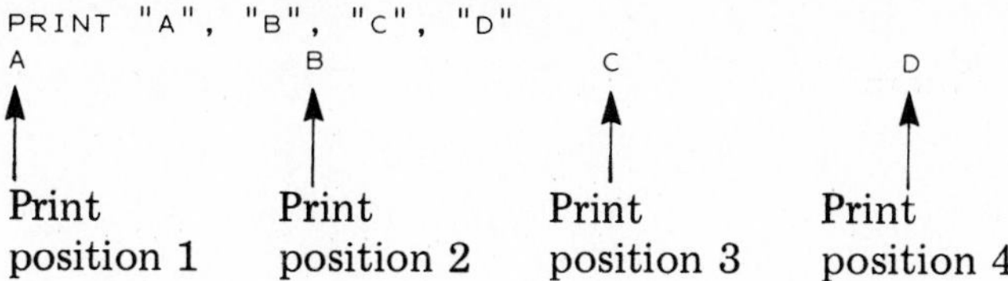

Your turn. Complete the output for this direct statement the way the computer would do it.

```
PRINT "A", "B", "C", "D", "E", "F", "G"
```

— — — — — — — — — —

```
A              B              C              D
   E              F              G
```

With strings, as with numbers, the comma causes the computer to move to the next standard print position.

35. Comma spacing is useful for printing *headings.* For example, here is a rewrite of our inches to centimeters program in frame 6 to include headings and a flag to signal the end of data.

```
10 REM**INCHES VERSUS CENTIMETERS TABLE
20 PRINT "INCHES","CENTIMETERS"
30 READ I
40 PRINT I,2.54*I
50 GOTO 30
90 DATA 1,8,12

RUN
INCHES        CENTIMETERS
1             2.54
8             20.32
12            30.48
ERROR-   6 IN 30
```

Note the use of comma spacing in lines 20 and 40. The numerical values printed by line 40 line up nicely under the headings printed by line 20.

Your turn. Rewrite the ounces to grams program (frame 7), so that a RUN looks like the one on the following page.

```
RUN
OUNCES         GRAMS
1              28.35
13             368.55
16             453,6
```

— — — — — — — — — — —

```
1Ø REM***OUNCES TO GRAMS TABLE
2Ø PRINT "OUNCES","GRAMS"
3Ø READ Z
4Ø PRINT Z,28.35*Z
5Ø GOTO 3Ø
9Ø DATA 1,13,16
```

38. Now, let's look at semicolon spacing with strings.

```
PRINT "A"; "B"; "C"; "D"; "E"
ABCDE
```

Semicolon spacing causes the computer to catenate strings, that is, to print them one after the other with no spaces.

Show what happens when the computer executes the following PRINT statement.

```
PRINT "THIS"; "IS"; "COMPUTER"; "PROGRAMMING?"
```

____

— — — — — — — — — — —

```
THISISCOMPUTERPROGRAMMING?
```

39. The output in frame 38 is rather crowded and hard to read. If you want spaces between strings, you must put them where you want them. For example:

```
PRINT "THIS ";"IS ";"COMPUTER ";"PROGRAMMING?"
```

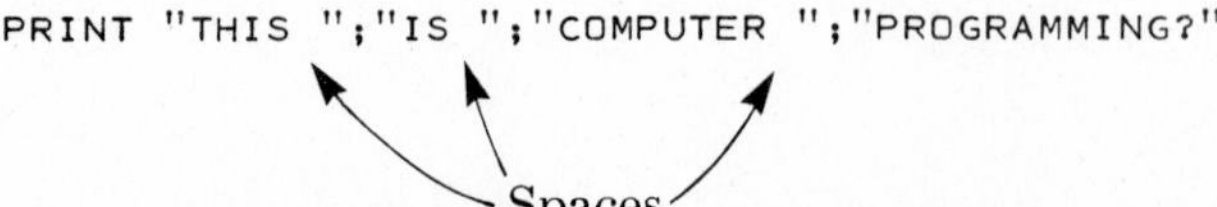

____

Show what the computer will print this time.

— — — — — — — — — —

```
THIS IS COMPUTER PROGRAMMING?
```

40. Let's try a program that causes strings stored by string variables to print information.

```
 5 DIM A$(2Ø),B$(2Ø),C$(2Ø)
1Ø LET A$="COMPUTERS "
2Ø LET B$="ARE"
3Ø LET C$=" INTERESTING."
4Ø PRINT A$;B$;C$
5Ø PRINT A$,B$,C$
```

First, we make room for the strings.

Note the spaces inside the quotation marks in lines 10 and 30.

Show what the computer will print when the program is RUN.

RUN

— — — — — — — — — —

```
RUN
COMPUTERS ARE INTERESTING.
COMPUTERS ARE          INTERESTING.
          ↑            ↑
     Position 2    Position 3
```

41. You may have guessed by now that a READ statement may also be used to assign strings to string variables. Show how you think the RUN for the following program to print the names of computer club members will look.

```
 5 DIM M$(2Ø)
1Ø READ M$
2Ø PRINT M$
3Ø GOTO 1Ø
4Ø DATA JERRY,BOBBY,MARY,DANNY
5Ø DATA MIMI,KARL,DOUG,SCOTT
```

Remember, this means "up to 20."

— — — — — — — — — —

```
RUN
JERRY
BOBBY
MARY
DANNY
MIMI
KARL
DOUG
SCOTT
ERROR-    6 AT LINE 10
```

Well, we could go on like this for a long time. But, there are other things for you to know. So, EXPERIMENT! What happens if??? Try it and find out. Try short strings, long strings (what if a string is more than 10 characters). Mix up strings and numbers. Try strings with leading spaces; trailing space. Aha! You and your friendly ATARI computer can do it all.

And now, it's your turn again to write a program. You have probably used dice before, either on "board" games or other games. We want you to apply your accumulated knowledge of BASIC to write a program that simulates (imitates) the roll of a die. (A "die" is one "dice.") Below is a RUN of our program. Examine it and use it as a guide to writing a program that will produce a RUN similar to this one. Use standard print positions. Take your time, and try *your* solution on a computer before looking at ours, if possible.

```
RUN

HOW MANY ROLLS? 7

ONE         THREE       THREE        SIX
  FOUR        FIVE        TWO

HOW MANY ROLLS? 2

ONE         SIX

HOW MANY ROLLS?
```

And so on.

— — — — — — — — — —

Don't look at the answer until *you* have written *your* program.

```
100 REM***DIE ROLLER
110 PRINT : PRINT "HOW MANY ROLLS"; : INPUT R
120 K=1 : PRINT
200 REM***'ROLL THE DIE' R TIMES
210 S=INT(6*RND(1))+1
220 ON S GOTO 230,240,250,260,270,280
230 PRINT "ONE", : GOTO 290
240 PRINT "TWO", : GOTO 290
250 PRINT "THREE", : GOTO 290
260 PRINT "FOUR", : GOTO 290
270 PRINT "FIVE", : GOTO 290
280 PRINT "SIX",
290 IF K<R THEN LET K=K+1 : GOTO 210
300 PRINT : PRINT : GOTO 110
```

Why two PRINTs in line 300? Try it with just one.

SELF-TEST

Try this Self-Test, so you can evaluate how much you have learned so far.

1. Pretend that *you* are the computer and complete each RUN.

(a)
```
10 READ A
20 PRINT A
30 DATA 27
RUN
```

(b)
```
10 READ A
20 READ B
30 PRINT A-B
40 DATA 27,15
RUN
```

(c)
```
10 READ A,B
20 PRINT A-B
30 DATA 27,15
RUN
```

(d)
```
10 READ A,B
20 PRINT A-B
30 DATA 27
40 DATA 15
RUN
```

2. Show the RUNs for the following programs.

(a)
```
10 READ X
20 PRINT X,  <-- Comma at end of PRINT statement
30 GOTO 10
40 DATA 3,7,0,-2,5,-1,7,8,0,-3
RUN
```

(b)
```
10 READ X
20 PRINT X;"   ";  <-- Semicolon at end of PRINT statement
30 GOTO 10
40 DATA 3,7,0,-2,5,-1,7,8,0,-3
RUN
```

3. Complete each RUN as if *you* were the computer.

(a)
```
10 READ X
20 IF X >= 0 THEN PRINT "X = " ; X,  <-- Comma
30 GOTO 10
40 DATA 3,7,0,-2,5,-1,7,8,0,-3
RUN
```

(b)
```
10 READ X
20 IF X >= 0 THEN PRINT "X = " ; X;  <-- Semicolon
30 GOTO 10
40 DATA 3,7,0,-2,5,-1,7,8,0,-3
RUN
```

4. Show the results if we RUN the following short program.

```
420 PRINT "ANSWER","NO. OF","PERCENT OF"
430 PRINT "(Y OR N)","ANSWERS","TOTAL"
```

5. Modify the questionnaire analysis program beginning in frame 19 so that the results are printed as follows.

```
ANSWER     NO. OF     PERCENT
(Y OR N)   ANSWERS    OF TOTAL

YES        23         46
NO         27         54
TOTAL      50         100
```

Hint: Rewrite beginning with line 420. The required information is printed in three columns, occupying the first three standard print positions.

6. Write a program, using READ and DATA statements, to compute the distance traveled in one turn of the rear wheel for bicycles with various wheel diameters. Use the following DATA statement with the line number of your choice.

`DATA 16,20,24,26,27` ← Wheel diameters

On the following page is a run of *our* program.

```
RUN

WHEEL DIAMETER: 16
DISTANCE IN ONE TURN: 50.24

WHEEL DIAMETER: 20
DISTANCE IN ONE TURN: 62.8

WHEEL DIAMETER: 24
DISTANCE IN ONE TURN: 75.36

WHEEL DIAMETER: 26
DISTANCE IN ONE TURN: 81.64

WHEEL DIAMETER: 27
DISTANCE IN ONE TURN: 84.78

ERROR-    6 AT ____________
```

Remember, distance in one turn is circumference of the wheel. C = 3.14*D where D = diameter of the wheel.

←Line number of *your* READ statement

7. Write a program to simulate coin flipping. The program should direct the computer to do the following steps. Type H for HEADS and T for TAILS *across* the page as shown in the RUN below. Also ask *how many* flips the user wants and do exactly that many, then stop. In other words, count the flips, and, when the count has reached the number requested, stop. Here are two RUNs of our program.

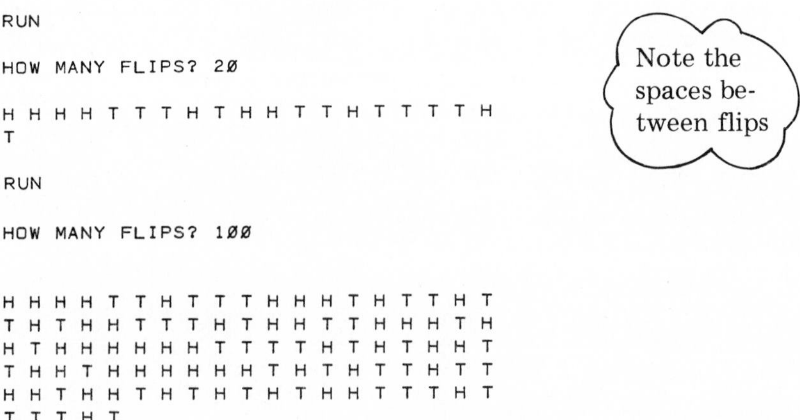

```
RUN

HOW MANY FLIPS? 20

H H H H T T T H T H H T T H T T T T H
T

RUN

HOW MANY FLIPS? 100

H H H H T T H T T T H H H T H T T H T
T H T H H T T T H T H H T T H H H T H
H T H H H H H H T T T T H T H T H H T
T H H T H H H H H H T H T H T T H T T
H H T H H T H T H T H T H H T T T H T
T T T H T
```


The first RUN of our program on our computer produced 9 heads (H) and 11 tails (T). The second RUN produced 53 heads (H) and 47 tails (T). Your computer may give quite different results.

8. Why not let the computer count the number of heads and the number of tails? Modify your program for question 7 so that the computer counts the number of heads and tails. Use the variable H to keep track of the number of heads and the variable T to keep track of the number of tails. Two RUNs of the modified program are shown below.

```
RUN

HOW MANY FLIPS? 20

T H H T T H H H T H H H T H H T T T H
T

11 HEADS AND 9 TAILS

RUN

HOW MANY FLIPS? 37
H T H H H T T T H T T H T T T H H H H
T H H H H T H T T T T T T T T H T T

16 HEADS AND 21 TAILS
```

9. Write a program to *count* the numbers in all the DATA statements in a program. Do *not* count the *flag*! For example, if the following DATA statements are in the program, the computer should dutifully tell us that there are 25 numbers.

```
15Ø DATA 2,3,5,7,11,13,17,19,23,29,31,37,41
16Ø DATA 43,47,53,59,61,67,71,73,79,83,89,97,1E97
```

↑ The flag

Our program RUNs like this.

```
RUN
THERE ARE 25 ITEMS OF DATA.
```

10. Now write a program that will print a pattern of asterisks according to a plan entered as DATA statement values. This might be a way of laying a pattern of floor tiles, or loom weaving patterns, or just "computer art." Use a flag to avoid an out-of-data error message. Shown on the following page are our DATA statement values and the pattern produced by our program. Our program prints five different lines of asterisks and spaces.

```
3,4,4,5,1,5,1,5,1,5,2,2,2,5,1,5,1,5,1,5,4,4,3
```
← DATA values

```
RUN

*********************
* * * * * * * * * * *
* * * * * * * * * * *
***   ***   ***   ***
*******  ***  *******
***   ***   ***   ***
*******  ***  *******
***   ***   ***   ***
*******  ***  *******
***   ***   ***   ***
*** *****   ***** ***
*** *****   ***** ***
*** *****   ***** ***
***   ***   ***   ***
*******  ***  *******
***   ***   ***   ***
*******  ***  *******
***   ***   ***   ***
*******  ***  *******
***   ***   ***   ***
* * * * * * * * * * *
* * * * * * * * * * *
*********************
```

Hint: The pattern consists of five different types of lines. The first and last lines are "type 3" lines. The first and last numbers in the DATA statement are 3. Got the idea?

Answers to Self-Test

The frame numbers in parentheses refer to the frames in the chapter where the topic is discussed. You may wish to refer to these for quick review.

1. (a)
```
RUN
27
```
(b)
```
RUN
12
```
(c)
```
RUN
12
```
(d)
```
RUN
12
```
(frames 1–6)

2. (a)
```
RUN
3       7       Ø      -2
5      -1       7       8
Ø      -3
ERROR-    6 AT LINE 1Ø
```
(b)
```
RUN
3 7 Ø -2 5 -1 7 8 Ø -3
ERROR-    6 AT LINE 1Ø
```
(frames 1–5)

3. (a)
```
RUN
X = 3      X = 7      X = Ø      X = 5
X = 7      X = 8      X = Ø
ERROR-    6 AT LINE 1Ø
```

(b)
```
RUN
X = 3X = 7X = 5X = 7X = 8X = Ø
ERROR-    6 AT LINE 1Ø
```

How would you rewrite line 20 in order to provide more space between items? For example: X = 3 X = 7 etc.

(frames 32–33)

4.
```
RUN
ANSWER      NO. OF      PERCENT OF
(Y OR N)    ANSWERS     TOTAL
```

(frame 35)

5.
```
42Ø PRINT "ANSWER","NO. OF","PERCENT OF"
43Ø PRINT "(Y OR N)","ANSWERS","TOTAL"
44Ø PRINT
45Ø LET T=Y+N
46Ø PRINT "YES", Y,1ØØ*Y/T
47Ø PRINT "NO",N,1ØØ*N/T
48Ø PRINT "TOTAL",T,1ØØ
```

In the above program segment, we have used T to compute the *Total* number of votes (T = Y + N). Then, in lines 460 and 470, the expressions 100*Y/T and 100*N/T are the percent Yes votes and No votes.

(frame 18–20, 35)

6.
```
1ØØ REM***DISTANCE IN ONE TURN OF A WHEEL
11Ø READ D
12Ø PRINT
13Ø PRINT "WHEEL DIAMETER: " ;D
14Ø PRINT "DISTANCE IN ONE TURN: " ;3.14*D
15Ø GOTO 11Ø
16Ø DATA 16,2Ø,24,26,27
```

(frame 1)

7.
```
1ØØ REM***COIN FLIPPER
11Ø PRINT : PRINT "HOW MANY FLIPS" ; : INPUT N
12Ø IF N<1 THEN END
13Ø REM***FLIP COIN N TIMES
14Ø K=Ø : PRINT
15Ø C=INT(2*RND(1))
16Ø IF C=Ø THEN PRINT "T ";
17Ø IF C=1 THEN PRINT "H ";
18Ø K=K+1
19Ø IF K<N THEN 15Ø
2ØØ GOTO 11Ø
21Ø END
```

There is more than one way to write this program. In ours, we use the variable K to count the number of times the coin has been flipped. In line 140, we set K to zero. Then, each time through the loop, we increase K by 1 (line 180) and compare K with N (line 190). If K is still less than N, we increase K by 1 and go around again. If N is less than one, no flips are done—this is checked by line 120. Your program may be entirely different. If it works, you have solved the problem! (frames 37, 42)

8. We modified our program of question 7. The complete program is shown below. The variable T is used to count the number of tails and the variable H to count the number of heads. Look for T and H in lines 140, 160, 170, and 210.

```
100 REM***COIN FLIPPER
110 PRINT : PRINT "HOW MANY FLIPS";:INPUT N
120 IF N<1 THEN END
130 REM***FLIP COIN N TIMES
140 K=0 : T=0 : H=0 : PRINT
150 C=INT(2*RND(1))
160 IF C=0 THEN PRINT "T "; : T=T+1
170 IF C=1 THEN PRINT "H "; : H=H+1
180 K=K+1
190 IF K<N THEN 150
200 PRINT : PRINT
210 PRINT H:" HEADS AND ";T;" TAILS"
220 END
```

(frames 33, 37, 42)

9.

```
100 REM***COUNT ITEMS IN DATA STATEMENTS, EXCEPT FLAG
110 K=0
120 READ N
130 IF N<>1E97 THEN LET K=K+1 : GOTO 120
140 IF N=1E97 THEN PRINT "THERE ARE" ;K;"ITEMS OF DATA."
150 DATA 2,3,5,7,11,13,17,19,23,29,31,37,41
160 DATA 43,47,53,59,61,67,71,73,79,83,89,97,1E97
999 END
```

Do you recognize the numbers in the DATA statements? They are all the prime numbers (those numbers with themselves and 1 as their only factors) less than 100. (frames 10, 11, 19)

10.
```
100 REM***PATTERN PRINTING PROGRAM
110 READ X : IF X=-1 THEN END
120 ON X GOTO 210,220,230,240,250
200 REM***PATTERN LINES
210 PRINT "*******  ***  *******" : GOTO 110
220 PRINT "*** *****   ***** ***" : GOTO 110
230 PRINT "*********************" : GOTO 110
240 PRINT "* * * * * * * * * * *" : GOTO 110
250 PRINT "***   ***   ***   ***" : GOTO 110
300 REM*** DATA TO MAKE A RUG DESIGN
310 DATA 3,4,4,5,1,5,1,5,1,5,2,2,2,5,1,5,1,5,1,5,4,4,3,-1
RUN
*********************
* * * * * * * * * * *
* * * * * * * * * * *
***   ***   ***   ***
*******  ***  *******
***   ***   ***   ***
*******  ***  *******
***   ***   ***   ***
*******  ***  *******
***   ***   ***   ***
*** *****   ***** ***
*** *****   ***** ***
*** *****   ***** ***
***   ***   ***   ***
*******  ***  *******
***   ***   ***   ***
*******  ***  *******
***   ***   ***   ***
*******  ***  *******
***   ***   ***   ***
* * * * * * * * * * *
* * * * * * * * * * *
*********************
```

Here is another way to do it.

```
10 REMARK PATTERN PRINTING PROGRAM
20 READ X
30 IF X=-1 THEN END
40 IF X=1 THEN 100
50 IF X=2 THEN 120
60 IF X=3 THEN 140
70 IF X=4 THEN 160
80 IF X=5 THEN 180
90 GOTO 20
100 PRINT "*******  ***  *******"
110 GOTO 20
120 PRINT "*** *****   ***** ***"
130 GOTO 20
140 PRINT "*********************"
150 GOTO 20
160 PRINT "* * * * * * * * * * *"
170 GOTO 20
180 PRINT "***   ***   ***   ***"
190 GOTO 20
900 DATA 3,4,4,5,1,5,1,5,1,5,2,2
910 DATA 2,5,1,5,1,5,1,5,4,4,3,-1
```

(frames 18, 19)

CHAPTER SIX

FOR-NEXT Loops

In this chapter we introduce another important computer programming concept: the FOR-NEXT loop. The IF-THEN statement and the FOR-NEXT loop greatly extend the usefulness of the computer as a tool. Close attention to the explanation and problems in this chapter will help you understand the functions of these statements in BASIC and will open a new dimension in your computer programming capability. When you complete this chapter you will be able to:

- use the FOR and NEXT statements;
- use the STEP clause in FOR statements.

1. The Loop Demonstration Program on the following page is a counting program that prints the value for F as we increase F from 1 through 6. Line 10 merely initializes F at 1. To initialize, remember, means to assign the first value to a variable. Line 20 prints the current value for F. Line 30 increases F by 1 each time through the program.

Line 40 is an IF statement that tests the value of F. As long as F is less than or equal to 6, line 40 sends the computer back to line 20 to print the value of F. Once F exceeds 6, the program will stop since there are no more statements in the program. Just for practice, rewrite the program on the following page using multiple statements in one line. But think carefully: Can you do the *entire* program in just one line?

```
5 REM***LOOP DEMONSTRATION
1Ø LET F=1
2Ø PRINT "F = "; F
3Ø LET F=F+1
4Ø IF F <= 6 THEN 2Ø


RUN
F = 1
F = 2
F = 3
F = 4
F = 5
F = 6
```

— — — — — — — — — —

```
1Ø LET F = 1
2Ø PRINT "F = "; F : LET F=F+1 : IF F <= 6 THEN 2Ø
RUN                                             ▲
F = 1
F = 2
F = 3
F = 4
F = 5
F = 6
```

This means go back and start executing line 20 again (only if the comparison is true, of course). Notice that line 10 would also fit on this line, but the value for F would get "initialized" back to 1 every time the statement was executed. So we could *not* put the entire program in just one line.

2. The space-saving, time-saving FOR-NEXT loop accomplishes a given number of *iterations* or repetitions more easily. Look at the FOR-NEXT loop below. Instead of IF-THEN, this time we use the FOR and NEXT statements to tell the computer how many times to go through the loop.

```
5 REM***FOR-NEXT LOOP DEMONSTRATION
1Ø FOR F=1 TO 6
2Ø PRINT "F = "; F
3Ø NEXT F
RUN
F = 1
F = 2
F = 3
F = 4
F = 5
F = 6
```

In every FOR-NEXT loop, the FOR statement is the beginning point of the loop and the NEXT statement is always the last statement in the loop. The statement or statements between FOR and NEXT are executed, in order, over and over again, with the FOR statement indicating to the computer how many times the loop is to be executed.

(a) You can see from the RUN of the FOR-NEXT loop that each time through the loop the value of F is automatically increased by ________________.

(b) How many times did the computer go through the loop? ________

(c) Why did the computer stop after going through the loop the above number of times? ______________________________

____

(d) What other statement must you have? ______________________________

— — — — — — — — — — —

(a) 1
(b) 6
(c) because the FOR statement told it to go from 1 to 6.
(d) a NEXT statement

3. As you can see in the program below, the computer will continue with the rest of the program when it has completed the loop as specified by the FOR statement.

```
5 REM***ANOTHER FOR-NEXT LOOP
10 FOR D=5 TO 10  <——— Note that the loop doesn't have to
20 PRINT "D = "; D          start with 1.
30 NEXT D
40 PRINT
50 PRINT "AHA! OUT OF THE LOOP BECAUSE"
60 PRINT "D = "; D: " WHICH EXCEEDS 10."

RUN
D = 5
D = 6
D = 7
D = 8
D = 9
D = 10

AHA! OUT OF THE LOOP BECAUSE
D = 11 WHICH EXCEEDS 10
```

In the program, the FOR-NEXT loop occupies which lines? ______________

— — — — — — — — — — —

lines 10, 20, and 30

4. How does the FOR-NEXT loop work? Follow the arrows.

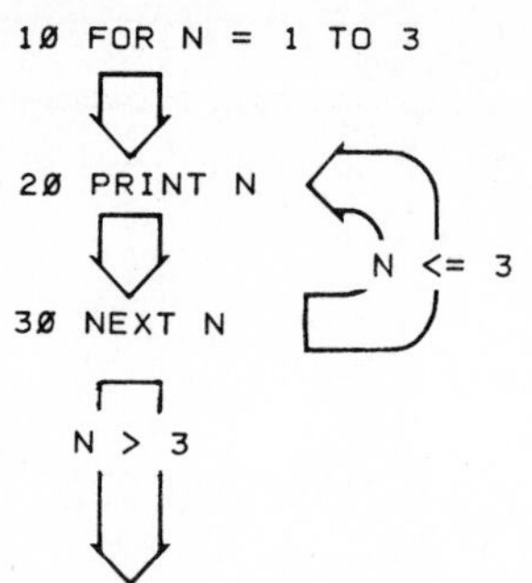

In line 10, N is set equal to 1.

In line 30, N is increased by one, and the computer compares the increased value of N to the upper limit for N indicated in the FOR statement.

Let's look at the FOR statement.

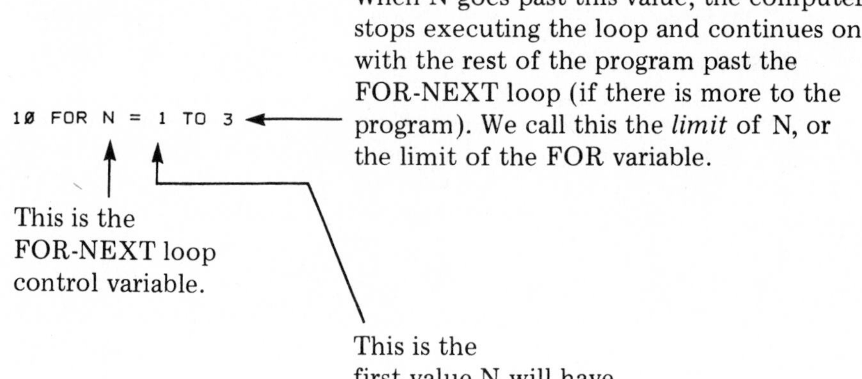

Here is a RUN of the program above.

```
10 FOR N=1 TO 3
20 PRINT N
30 NEXT N
RUN
1
2
3
```

Each time the computer comes to a NEXT N statement, it increases the value of N by one, and checks the new value against the limit for N. In this case, the limit is 3, because the FOR statement reads: FOR N = 1 TO 3. When the value of N is greater than 3, the computer continues to the next statement after the NEXT statement, if there is one. If not, the computer has finished executing the program and stops. Got that? Let's see.

Statement 10 means that for the first time through the loop, N = 1. The second time through, N = N + 1 = 1 + 1 = 2. The third time through, N = __________ = __________ = __________.

— — — — — — — — — — —

N = N + 1 = 2 + 1 = 3

5. Write a program with three statements that will print the word LOOP six times. Use a FOR-NEXT loop, and use C as the FOR-NEXT loop control variable. Show what your program will print when it is RUN.

— — — — — — — — — — —

```
10 FOR C = 1 TO 6
20 PRINT "LOOP"
30 NEXT C
RUN
LOOP
LOOP
LOOP
LOOP
LOOP
LOOP
```

6. FOR-NEXT statements can be used in a multiple statement line. Here is a FOR-NEXT program, all on one line. Follow the arrows.

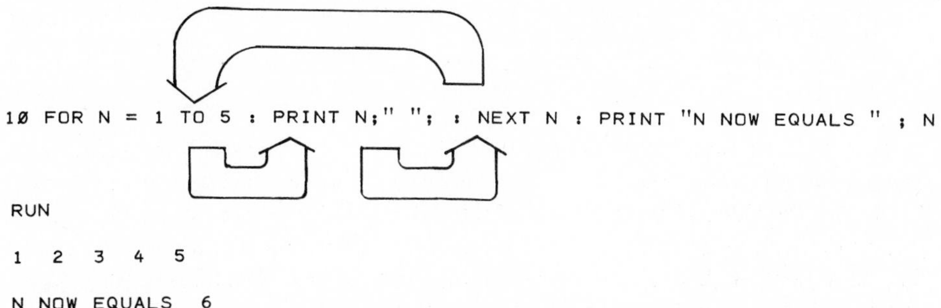

When the computer had finished the FOR-NEXT loop and had made its exit from the loop, what was the value for N? _______

— — — — — — — — — — —

6

Notice that the value for N after loop exit is one more than the upper limit for N as given in the FOR statement. That is how the computer recognized that it had performed the proper number of loops and was ready to go on to the next statement in the program beyond the FOR-NEXT loop.

7. Let's say you enter the following multiple-statement line.

```
10 PRINT "TESTING "; : FOR X = 1 TO 4 : PRINT X; " "; : NEXT X
```

What will your computer print when you type RUN? ______________________

____

— — — — — — — — — — — —

```
TESTING 1 2 3 4
```

8. Finish writing this program so that the computer will produce the RUN shown. Use a FOR-NEXT loop with Y as the control variable.

```
10 PRINT "THIS YEAR CATHY IS 10 YEARS OLD"
20 ______________________________________
30 ______________________________________
40 ______________________________________

RUN
THIS YEAR CATHY IS 10 YEARS OLD
AND THE NEXT YEAR SHE WILL BE 11
AND THE NEXT YEAR SHE WILL BE 12
AND THE NEXT YEAR SHE WILL BE 13
AND THE NEXT YEAR SHE WILL BE 14
```

— — — — — — — — — — — —

```
20 FOR Y = 11 TO 14
30 PRINT "AND THE NEXT YEAR SHE WILL BE "; Y
40 NEXT Y
```

9. Another thing to notice about FOR-NEXT loops is that variables may be used instead of numbers, providing, of course, that the variables have been assigned values earlier in the program. In the example below, values are assigned by LET statements. Values could also have been assigned by INPUT or READ statements.

```
10 A=3 : B=8
20 FOR C=A TO B
30 PRINT " "; C ;
40 NEXT C
RUN
 3 4 5 6 7 8
```

This prints a space before each number.

Rewrite the FOR statement (line 20), substituting numerical values for variables A and B. Use the values that were assigned by the program above.

20 ______________________

— — — — — — — — — —

```
20 FOR C = 3 TO 8
```

10. Play computer and show the RUN for this FOR-NEXT demonstration program.

```
10 X=0 : Y=4
20 FOR Z=X TO Y
40 PRINT " "; Z
50 NEXT Z
RUN
```

____

— — — — — — — — — —

```
RUN
 0 1 2 3 4
```

11. Now you write a program where variables are used to set the initial and upper limits of the FOR-NEXT loop control variable. Have your program READ the values to be used for the initial and upper limits from a DATA statement.

Use Z for the control variable, and use X and Y for the variables that set the initial and upper limits. Select your DATA statement values so that your program will produce the following RUN.

```
RUN
 100 101 102 103 104 105
```

— — — — — — — — — — —

```
10 READ X
20 READ Y
30 FOR Z=X TO Y
40 PRINT " "; Z
50 NEXT Z
60 DATA 100,105
```

Statements 10 and 20 could be combined in one statement: 10 READ X, Y.

12. In this next program, an INPUT value (line 40) is used to establish the upper limit of the FOR statement (line 100), which tells the computer how many times to repeat "X = ?" When the program is RUN, the PRINT statements in lines 10-80 tell the user how to use the program.

```
5 REM***FRIENDLY MEAN FROM INPUT VALUES
10 PRINT "FOR MY NEXT ENCORE I WILL COMPUTE"
20 PRINT "THE MEAN OF A LIST OF NUMBERS."
30 PRINT
40 PRINT "HOW MANY NUMBERS IN THE LIST"; : INPUT N
50 PRINT
60 PRINT "EACH TIME I TYPE 'X =?' YOU TYPE IN"
70 PRINT "ONE NUMBER AND THEN PRESS RETURN."
80 PRINT
90 T=0
100 FOR K=1 TO N
110 PRINT "X = "; : INPUT X
120 T=T+X
130 NEXT K
140 M=T/N
150 PRINT
160 PRINT "TOTAL = "; T
170 PRINT "MEAN = "; M
```

(a) In the program above, the FOR-NEXT loop occupies lines ____________ __________________.

(b) What is the FOR-NEXT loop control variable? _______

(c) The upper limit for the control variable is determined by the value assigned to which other variable? _______

— — — — — — — — — — —

(a) 100, 110, 120, 130
(b) K
(c) N

13. In the program of frame 12, which line in the FOR-NEXT loop will keep a running tally of the values entered for line 110? ______________

— — — — — — — — — — —

```
120 T = T + X
```

14. This is a RUN of the program in frame 12.

```
RUN
FOR MY NEXT ENCORE, I WILL COMPUTE
THE MEAN OF A LIST OF NUMBERS.

HOW MANY NUMBERS IN THE LIST? 5

EACH TIME I TYPE 'X =?' YOU TYPE IN
ONE NUMBER AND THEN PRESS RETURN.

X =? 16
X =? 46
X =? 38
X =? 112
X =? 23

TOTAL = 235
MEAN = 47
```

Values entered by user. (16, 46, 38, 112, 23)

Show the numerical values in the FOR statement for the above RUN.

```
100 FOR K = ______ TO ______
```

— — — — — — — — — — —

1 TO 5 (The value entered for INPUT N was 5.)

15. Here is the beginning of another RUN of the same program.

```
RUN
FOR MY NEXT ENCORE, I WILL COMPUTE
THE MEAN OF A LIST OF NUMBERS.

HOW MANY NUMBERS IN THE LIST: 4
```

← Value entered by user. (4)

How many times will "X = ?" be printed? ______ How many times will the statements between the FOR-NEXT statements be executed? ______

— — — — — — — — — — —

4; 4

Just to prove it to you, this is the rest of the same RUN.

```
EACH TIME I TYPE 'X =?' YOU TYPE IN
ONE NUMBER AND THEN PRESS RETURN.

X =? 2
X =? 4
X =? 6
X =? 8

TOTAL = 2Ø
MEAN = 5
```

16. Complete the following program to compute the product (P) of N numbers. Think carefully about the effect of your statements when the program is RUN.

```
5 REM***PRODUCT CALCULATED FROM A LIST OF NUMBERS
1Ø PRINT "YOU WANT ANOTHER ENCORE? I'LL COMPUTE"
2Ø PRINT "THE PRODUCT OF A LIST OF NUMBERS."
3Ø PRINT
4Ø PRINT "HOW MANY NUMBERS IN THE LIST"; : INPUT N
5Ø PRINT
6Ø PRINT "EACH TIME I TYPE 'X =?' YOU TYPE IN"
7Ø PRINT "ONE NUMBER AND THEN PRESS RETURN."
8Ø PRINT

1ØØ ____________________________ <---- Initialize

11Ø ______________________________________
12Ø PRINT "X = "; : INPUT X
13Ø P=P*X

14Ø ______________________________________
15Ø PRINT : PRINT "PRODUCT = "; P

RUN
YOU WANT ANOTHER ENCORE? I'LL COMPUTE
THE PRODUCT OF A LIST OF NUMBERS.

HOW MANY NUMBERS IN THE LIST? 5

EACH TIME I TYPE 'X =?' YOU TYPE IN
ONE NUMBER AND THEN PRESS RETURN.

X =? 7
X =? 12
X =? 4
X =? 3
X =? 19

PRODUCT = 19152
```

— — — — — — — — — —

```
1ØØ LET P=1
11Ø FOR K=1 TO N
14Ø NEXT K
```

17. Any BASIC expression may be used to set both the initial and the maximum value of a FOR-NEXT loop control variable. The computer evaluates these expressions (that is, does the arithmetic) *before* the loop is executed the first time, and does *not* recompute these values each time through the loop.

Look at the FOR statement in this next program, and then decide whether the computer executed the loop the proper number of times.

```
10 Q=4
20 FOR P=Q TO 2*Q-1
30 PRINT " "; P;
40 NEXT P


RUN
 4 5 6 7
```

The computer was right!

In the following program, fill in the blanks in line 20 with expressions using the variable Q, so that when the program is RUN, it will produce the printout shown below.

```
10 Q=4

20 FOR P=________ TO ________

30 PRINT " "; P;
40 NEXT P

RUN
 2 3 4 5 6 7 8 9 10 11 12
```

— — — — — — — — — —

```
20 FOR P=Q/2 TO Q*3 OR 20 FOR P=Q-2 TO Q+8
```

Note: If your answer is different and you think it is correct, try it on your computer and see if you get the same RUN that we did.

18. In the FOR-NEXT loops you have seen so far, the FOR-NEXT loop control variable takes the first value given in the FOR statement, and keeps that value until the computer comes to the NEXT statement. Then the FOR variable increases its value by one each time through the loop until it reaches the maximum value allowed by the FOR statement.

```
FOR X = 5 TO 10
```

First value of X (points to 5) — Maximum value for X (points to 10)

X = 5, then 6, then 7, then 8, then 9, and then 10

However, you can write a FOR statement that causes the value of the FOR-NEXT loop control variable to increase by multiples of other than one, or by frational increments. You can also have the value of the FOR-NEXT variable *decrease* each time through the loop.

```
10 FOR X=1 TO 10 STEP 2
```

Tells the computer to increase the value of X by 2 every time through the FOR-NEXT loop, until X is greater than 10.

```
10 FOR Y-3 TO 6 STEP 1.5
```

Tells the computer to increase the value of Y by 1.5 every time through the FOR-NEXT loop, until Y is greater than 6.

```
10 FOR Z=10 TO 5 STEP -1
```

Note that Z will start at Z = 10 and go to Z = 5

Tells the computer to decrease the value of Z by 1 each time through the FOR-NEXT loop, until Z is less than 5.

Some demonstration programs will show the effects of STEP in action.

```
10 FOR B=1 TO 10 STEP 2
20 PRINT " "; B;
30 NEXT B
40 PRINT
50 PRINT
60 PRINT "LOOP TERMINATES BECAUSE"
70 PRINT "B = "; B; ", WHICH IS GREATER THAN 10."

RUN
 1 3 5 7 9

LOOP TERMINATES BECAUSE
B = 11, WHICH IS GREATER THAN 10.
```

The PRINT statement in line 40 "bumps" the computer off the line where it is held by the semicolon at the end of line 20. The PRINT statement in line 50 causes the space before line 60 is printed.

Note that the loop starts with the first value in the FOR statement (1) and increases by increments of 2, until the value of B = 11 which exceeds the maximum value allowed (10). At that point, the computer terminates the loop and continues running the rest of the program.

Play computer again, and fill in the RUN for this program.

```
10 D=3 : FOR F=D TO 4*D STEP D : PRINT " "; F; : NEXT F
RUN
```

____

— — — — — — — — — — —

```
3 6 9 12
```

19. In this example, the STEP in the FOR statement is followed by a negative number. STEP may be used to decrease the value of the FOR variable in any size step, going from a large value to a smaller one.

```
10 FOR J=100 TO 10 STEP -10
20 PRINT " "; J;
30 NEXT J
RUN
 100 90 80 70 60 50 40 30 20 10
```

Now you write one where the FOR-NEXT loop control variable E decreases in steps of 3 from 27 to 18. Show the program and the RUN.

— — — — — — — — — —

```
10 FOR E = 27 TO 18 STEP -3
20 PRINT " "; E;
30 NEXT E

RUN
  27 24 21 18
```

20. As we mentioned, the steps in a FOR-NEXT loop can be fractional values, as in the following example.

```
10 FOR X = 5 TO 7.5 STEP .25
20 PRINT " "; X;
30 NEXT X
RUN
 5 5.25 5.5 5.75 6 6.25 6.5 6.75 7 7.25 7.5
```

Show the RUN for this program if we changed line 10 to the following.

```
10 FOR X = 5 TO 7.5 STEP .5
RUN
```

— — — — — — — — — —

```
RUN
 5 5.5 6 6.5 7 7.5
```

21. The FOR-NEXT loop is useful for such things as repeated calculations, counting or keeping tallies, and dealing with cyclical or recurring events.

One such recurring event is the monthly compounding of interest on a savings account. In the following program, monthly interest (I) is calculated in line 180 by multiplying the initial amount of money (P for Principal) by the Rate of interest (R).

The rate of interest is converted to a decimal fraction: R = 5 percent = 5/100 = .05

Since 5 percent is the yearly rate of interest, only 1/12 of the calculated amount of interest is added to the principal each month.

```
100 REM***MONTHLY INTEREST COMPOUNDING
110 PRINT "PRINCIPAL" ; : INPUT P
120 PRINT "YEARLY INTEREST RATE (IN %)" ; : INPUT R
130 PRINT "HOW MANY MONTHS"; : INPUT M
140 PRINT
150 PRINT "MONTH", "AMOUNT"
160 FOR K=1 TO M
170 PRINT K, P
180 I=(P*(R/100))/12
190 P=P+I
200 NEXT K

RUN
PRINCIPAL? 200
YEARLY INTEREST RATE (IN %)? 5
HOW MANY MONTHS? 6

MONTH     AMOUNT
1         200
2         200.833333
3         201.670138
4         202.51043
5         203.354223
6         204.201532
```

This table shows the amount of money in the account at the beginning of each month.

(a) Which lines are included in the FOR-NEXT loop? ____________________

(b) Which variable keeps track of and is used to print the number corresponding to the month for each line in the table? ____________________

(c) Line 150 prints the column headings for the table. The words used in the headings are separated by commas. In line 170, the values to be printed under the headings are also separated by commas, so that the spacing of headings and the numbers that go under headings match up. What would happen if the statement that prints the heading were included in the FOR-NEXT loop? ____________________

____

(d) Which line keeps a running tally of Principal plus Interest? ____________

— — — — — — — — — —

(a) 160, 170, 180, 190, 200
(b) the FOR variable K
(c) The heading would be printed every time through the loop, between each line of the table.
(d) 190

Note: If you want to brush up on your business math, a useful book would be Locke, *Business Mathematics* (a Self-Teaching Guide), John Wiley & Sons, New York, 1972.

22. Yes, we admit, it is rather strange to see a "dollars and cents" answer printed as 200.833333 or 201.670138. Fortunately, BASIC has a nifty way for rounding off numbers to a desired number of decimal places.

Recall how the INT function works (Chapter 4, Frame 20). The INT function chops off a number at the decimal point, keeps the integer part and discards the decimal fraction part. For example,

```
INT (200.833333) = 200
```

However, when dealing with dollars and cents, we don't want to lose the cents! So, we do it like this.

(1) Multiply by 100.	100*200.833333 = 20083.333
(2) Add .5.	20083.333 + .5 = 20083.8333
(3) Keep the integer part.	INT(20083.8333) = 20083.
(4) Divide by 100.	20083/100 = 200.83

Your turn. Use the above procedure to round $123.45678 to the nearest penny.

(1) Multiply by 100.	100*123.45678 = ________________
(2) Add .5.	________________
(3) Keep the integer part.	________________
(4) Divide by 100.	________________

— — — — — — — — — —

(1) 100*123.456789 = 12345.678
(2) 12345.678 + .5 = 12346.178
(3) INT(12346.178) = 12346.
(4) 12346/100 = 123.46

23. The following program is a step by step demonstration of the rounding method shown in the previous frame.

```
100 REM**STEP BY STEP DEMONSTRATION OF ROUNDING

110 PRINT "NUMBER TO BE ROUNDED"; : INPUT A
120 PRINT "START WITH YOUR NUMBER,    A = ";A

130 A = 100*A
140 PRINT "(1) MULTIPLY BY 100,       A = ";A

150 A = A + .5
160 PRINT "(2) ADD .5,                A = ";A

170 A = INT(A)
180 PRINT "(3) KEEP INTEGER PART,     A = ";A

190 A = A/100
200 PRINT "(4) DIVIDE BY 100,         A = ";A

210 PRINT "A IS NOW ROUNDED TO 2 DECIMAL PLACES"
220 PRINT
230 GOTO 110

RUN

NUMBER TO BE ROUNDED? 123.45678
START WITH YOUR NUMBER,    A = 123.45678
(1) MULTIPLY BY 100,       A = 12345.678
(2) ADD .5,                A = 12346.178
(3) KEEP INTEGER PART,     A = 12346.
(4) DIVIDE BY 100,         A = 123.46
A IS NOW ROUNDED TO 2 DECIMAL PLACES
```

One more example. You fill in the values of A. (Try using our program on your Atari!)

```
NUMBER TO BE ROUNDED. 203.7249

START WITH YOUR NUMBER,    A = ____________

(1) MULTIPLY BY 100,       A = ____________

(2) ADD .5,                A = ____________

(3) KEEP INTEGER PART,     A = ____________

(4) DIVIDE BY 100,         A = ____________

A IS NOW ROUNDED TO 2 DECIMAL PLACES
```

```
    203.7249
(1) 20372.49
(2) 20372.99
(3) 23072
(4) 203.72
```

24. In our rounding program, the actual work of rounding is done by lines 130, 150, 170 and 190. We can combine these four lines into a single statement to round a number, as follows.

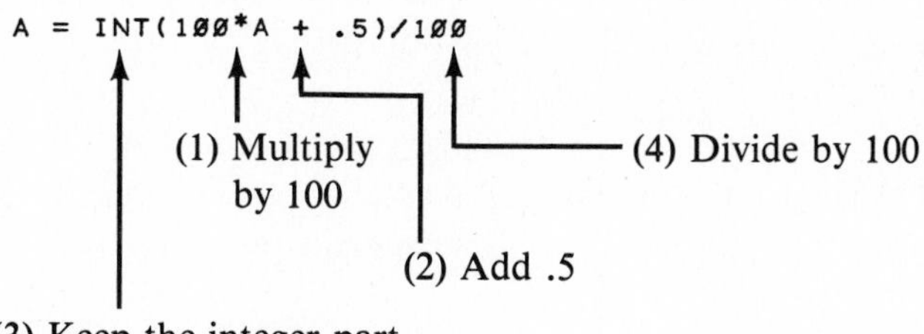

Remember, the above statement rounds the value of A to *two* decimal places.

(1) Write a statement to round the value of P to *two* decimal places.

____

(2) Write a statement to round the value of X to *one* decimal place.

____

(3) Write a statement to round the value of B to *three* decimal places.

____

— — — — — — — — — —

(1) `P = INT(1ØØ*P + .5)/1ØØ`
(2) `X = INT(1Ø*X + .5)/1Ø`
(3) `B = INT(1ØØØ*B + .5)/1ØØØ`

Try this. Add the statement 195 P = INT(100*P + .5)/100 to the MONTHLY INTEREST COMPOUNDING program in frame 21. This should cause the numbers under AMOUNT to be rounded to the nearest penny. A RUN will look like this.

```
RUN
PRINCIPAL?2ØØ
YEARLY INTEREST RATE (IN %)?5
HOW MANY MONTHS?6

MONTH    AMOUNT
1        2ØØ
2        2ØØ.83
3        2Ø1.67
4        2Ø2.51
5        2Ø3.35
6        2Ø4.2  <——— Read this as 204.20
```

25. Can you have a FOR-NEXT *inside* another FOR-NEXT loop? Absolutely. It is called *nested* FOR-NEXT loops and is perfectly "legal" provided you follow the rule illustrated below.

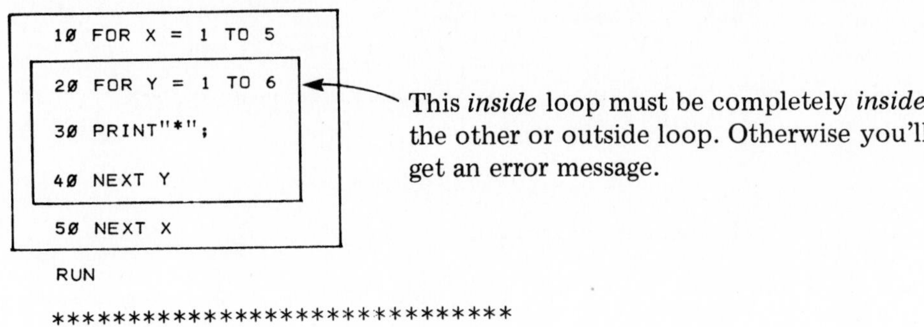


```
RUN
******************************
```

Count the stars. How many are there? Do you see any relationship between the number of stars printed and the numbers 5 and 6 which appear in the two FOR statements?

A loop within a loop is called a ______________ FOR-NEXT loop. The inside loop must be ______________ the outside loop.

— — — — — — — — — — —

nested; inside

26. Here are two programs using nested FOR-NEXT loops.

```
5 REM*** PROGRAM A
1Ø FOR N=1 TO 4
2Ø FOR L=1 TO 3
3Ø PRINT "NESTED"
4Ø NEXT L
5Ø PRINT "        LOOP "
6Ø NEXT N
```

```
5 REM***PROGRAM B
1Ø FOR N=1 TO 4
2Ø FOR L=1 TO 3
3Ø PRINT "NESTED"
4Ø NEXT N
5Ø PRINT "        LOOP"
6Ø NEXT L
```

Which program (A or B) has correctly nested FOR-NEXT loops? ________

— — — — — — — — — — —

program A

27. Program A in frame 26 produces a repeated pattern of printout. Look at the program closely and then show what the computer will print when the program is RUN.

```
RUN
NESTED
NESTED
NESTED
        LOOP
NESTED
NESTED
NESTED
        LOOP
NESTED
NESTED
NESTED
        LOOP
NESTED
NESTED
NESTED
        LOOP
```

28. The following program uses nested loops to print a rectangular pattern of "stars."

```
10 FOR R = 1 TO 3

20 FOR C = 1 TO 7
30 PRINT "*";
40 NEXT C

50 PRINT
60 NEXT R
```

This *inner loop* causes the computer to print one row of seven stars.

```
RUN
*******
*******
*******
```

(1) What is the purpose of the empty PRINT statement in line 50?

____

____

(2) Why does the computer print 3 rows of stars? ______________________

____

____

---

(1) It moves the cursor to the beginning of the next line *after* a row of stars has been printed by the inside loop.

(2) The outer loop, controlled by lines 10 and 60, causes the inner loop to be executed for R = 1, 2, and 3. Each time, a row of stars is printed.

29. Show what will be printed if we run the following program.

```
10 FOR A=1 TO 4
20 FOR B=1 TO 3
30 PRINT "?";
40 NEXT B
50 PRINT
60 NEXT A

RUN
```

```
???
???
???
???
```

The computer will print four (4) rows, each with three (3) question marks.

30. Write a program to print 7 rows with 12 dollars signs ($) in each row. A RUN should look like the following.

```
RUN
$$$$$$$$$$$$
$$$$$$$$$$$$
$$$$$$$$$$$$
$$$$$$$$$$$$
$$$$$$$$$$$$
$$$$$$$$$$$$
$$$$$$$$$$$$
```

```
10 FOR A=1 TO 7
20 FOR Z=1 TO 12
30 PRINT "$";
40 NEXT Z
50 PRINT
60 NEXT A
```

You may have used different variables.

SELF-TEST

Now that you have completed Chapter 6, you have acquired enough understanding of computer programming to be able to learn a lot more by experimenting at a computer terminal. As you look at our demonstration programs, you may see some possibilities that we do not specifically deal with. Build on your knowledge by trying out your own ideas.

But right now, find out if you really know how to use FOR-NEXT loops by doing the following programs.

1. Show what will be printed if we RUN the following program.

```
10 S=0
20 FOR K=1 TO 4
30 S=S+K
40 NEXT K
50 PRINT S
RUN
```

2. Show what will be printed if we RUN the following program.

```
10 P=1 : FOR K=1 TO 4 : P=P*K : NEXT K : PRINT P
RUN
```

3. Examine this program. Which of the three RUNs was produced by the program? ________

```
10 N=1
20 FOR K=1 TO N
30 PRINT "*";
40 NEXT K
50 PRINT
60 N=N+1
70 IF N>10 THEN END
80 GOTO 20
```

RUN 1

```
       *
      ***
     *****
    *******
   *********
  ***********
 *************
***************
```

RUN 2

```
********
 ********
  ********
   ********
    ********
     ********
      ********
       ********
```

RUN 3

```
*
**
***
****
*****
******
*******
********
*********
**********
```

4. Write a program to print a table of N, N^2, and N^3. Use INPUT statements to indicate what list of numbers you wish included in the table. A RUN should look like this.

```
RUN
FIRST NUMBER? 4Ø
LAST NUMBER? 45

N               N-SQUARED        N-CUBED
4Ø              16ØØ             64ØØØ
41              1681             68921
42              1764             74Ø88
43              1849             795Ø7
44              1936             85184
45              2Ø25             91125
```

5. Show what will be printed if we RUN the following program.

```
1Ø S=Ø
2Ø FOR K=1 TO 7 STEP 2
3Ø S=S+K
4Ø NEXT K
5Ø PRINT S
RUN
```

6. On the following page, complete this program to print a table projecting growth rate of a population at specified intervals over a given time period (years). The formula for population growth is:

$$Q = P(1 + R/100)^N$$

where N is the number of years.

We want the population *rounded* to the nearest whole number.

```
100 REM***REQUEST DATA AND PRINT HEADING
110 PRINT "INITIAL POPULATION"; : INPUT P
120 PRINT "GROWTH RATE"; : INPUT R
130 PRINT "INITIAL VALUE OF N"; : INPUT A
140 PRINT "FINAL VALUE OF N"; : INPUT B
150 PRINT "STEP SIZE"; : INPUT H
160 PRINT : PRINT "N", "POPULATION" : PRINT
200 REM***COMPUTE AND PRINT TABLE

210 ______________________________

220 ______________________________

230 ______________________________

240 ______________________________

RUN
INITIAL POPULATION? 230
GROWTH RATE? 1
INITIAL VALUE OF N? 0
FINAL VALUE OF N? 100
STEP SIZE? 25

N           POPULATION
0           230
25          295
50          378
75          485
100         622

RUN
INITIAL POPULATION? 205
GROWTH RATE? 1
INITIAL VALUE OF N? 0
FINAL VALUE OF N? 100
STEP SIZE? 10

N           POPULATION
0           205
10          226
20          250
30          276
40          305
50          337
60          372
70          411
80          454
90          502
100         554
```

For U.S.A., 1970 (in millions of people).

Results are expressed in millions, rounded to the nearest million.

7. Write a program to compute and print the sum of whole numbers from 1 to N where the value of N is supplied in response to an INPUT statement. A RUN might look like the one on the following page.

```
RUN
GIVE ME A NUMBER (N) AND I WILL COMPUTE
THE SUM OF THE NUMBERS FROM 1 TO N.

WHAT IS N? 3
THE SUM IS 6                 Because 1+2+3 = 6

WHAT IS N? 5
THE SUM IS 15                Because 1+2+3+4+5 = 15

WHAT IS N?                   And so on.
```

8. Look back at the simple number guessing game in Chapter 1, frame 9. Use a FOR-NEXT loop to modify the program so that the user has only eight chances to guess the number. If he fails in eight guesses print an appropriate message before starting over again.

9. What will soon appear on the screen if we store and run the following program?

```
100 FOR R=1 TO 23
110 FOR C=1 TO 37
120 S=INT(6*RND(1))+1
130 IF S=1 THEN PRINT "*";
140 IF S>1 THEN PRINT " ";
150 NEXT C

160 PRINT
170 NEXT R

180 GOTO 180
```

Answers to Self-Test

The frame numbers in parentheses refer to the frames in the chapter where the topic is discussed. You may wish to refer back to these for a quick review.

1.
```
RUN
 1Ø
```

The answer is the *sum* of the values of K defined by the FOR statement (K = 1, 2, 3, and 4). (frames 1–7)

2.
```
RUN
 24
```

The answer is the *product* of the values of K defined by the FOR statement (K = 1, 2, 3, and 4). (frames 1–6, 16)

3. RUN 3. The FOR-NEXT loop (lines 20, 30, 40) causes the computer to print a *row* of N stars. The loop is done for N = 1, 2, 3, . . . 10. (frames 1–6, 28)

4.
```
10 INPUT "FIRST NUMBER"; A
20 INPUT "LAST NUMBER"; B
30 PRINT
40 PRINT "N","N-SQUARED", "N-CUBED"
50 FOR N=A TO B
60 PRINT N, N^2, N^3
70 NEXT N
```

(frames 9, 21)

5.
```
RUN
 16
```

Similar to question 1, but this time the values of K defined by the FOR statement are K = 1, 3, 5, and 7. (frame 18)

6.
```
200 REM***COMPUTE AND PRINT TABLE
210 FOR N=A TO B STEP H
220 LET Q=P*(1+R/100)^N
230 PRINT N, INT(Q+.5)
240 NEXT N
```

(frames 18–24)

Line 230 prints Q, rounded to nearest whole number.

7.
```
1Ø PRINT "GIVE ME A NUMBER (N) AND I WILL COMPUTE"
2Ø PRINT "THE SUM OF THE NUMBERS FROM 1 TO N."
3Ø PRINT
4Ø PRINT "WHAT IS N";
5Ø INPUT N
55 LET S=Ø
6Ø FOR W=1 TO N
7Ø LET S=S+W
8Ø NEXT W
9Ø PRINT "THE SUM IS";S
1ØØ GOTO 3Ø
```

If you wish, you can put these on one line.

(frame 2)

8.
```
100 REMARK***THIS IS A SIMPLE COMPUTER GAME
110 LET X=INT (100*RND(1))+1
120 PRINT
130 PRINT "I'M THINKING OF A NUMBER FROM 1 TO 100"
140 PRINT "GUESS MY NUMBER!!!"
150 FOR A=1 TO 8 : PRINT "YOUR GUESS"; : INPUT G
160 IF G<X THEN PRINT "TRY A BIGGER NUMBER" : GO TO 190
170 IF G>X THEN PRINT "TRY A SMALLER NUMBER" : GO TO 190
180 IF G=X THEN PRINT "THAT'S IT!!! YOU GUESSED MY NUMBER." : GO TO 110
190 NEXT A : PRINT "TOO MANY GUESSES. THE NUMBER WAS" ;X : GO TO 110
```
(frames 2, 4)

9. The "stars" will come out. About 1/6 of the screen will show stars; the other 5/6 will be "blanks." The stars and blanks are selected at random by lines 120, 130, and 140. Happy stargazing!

CHAPTER SEVEN

Subscripted Variables

In Chapters 7 and 8 we will present another useful tool, the *subscripted variable.* First we will discuss BASIC variables with a *single* subscript.

You will learn, for example, how to count votes from a survey and how to accumulate or count dollars and assign them to different groupings. And you will get lots more practice using FOR-NEXT loops.

Many new programming ideas are introduced in this chapter. Read the chapter slowly and carefully. Experiment on your computer; you will find that these new techniques give you much more range and flexibility. When you complete this chapter, you will be able to:

- recognize and use subscripted variables with a single (one) subscript;
- assign values to subscripted variables;
- use subscripted variables with variables for subscripts;
- use one-dimensional arrays to store the values of subscripted variables;
- use the DIM statement to tell the computer the maximum size of the array(s) used by a program.

1. The concept we discuss here will require your close attention. Take it slowly, and read carefully as we enter the mysterious realm of *subscripted variables.*

Until now, we have used only *simple* BASIC variables. A simple variable consists of a letter (any letter A to Z) or a letter *followed* by a single digit (any digit 0 to 9). For example, the following are simple variables.

P R K P1 P2

Now we want to introduce a new type of variable, called a subscripted variable.

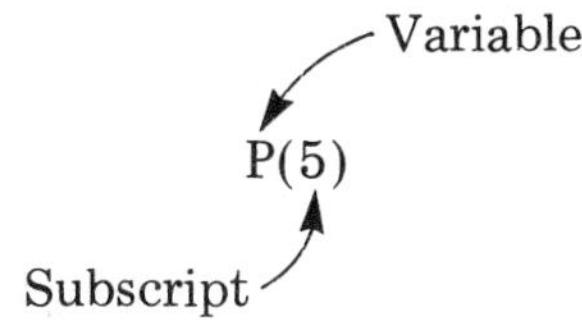

Say it: "P sub 5"

A subscripted variable consists of a letter (any letter A to Z) followed by a subscript enclosed in *parentheses.* P(3) is a subscripted variable; P3 is *not* a subscripted variable.

Which of the following are subscripted variables? Circle the answer(s).

X(1) X X1 C(23) D

— — — — — — — — — —

X(1); C(23)

Note: X, X1, and X(1) are three distinct variables. All three can appear in the same program. They may confuse *you,* but the computer will recognize them as three different variables.

2. A subscripted variable (like the simple variables we have been using) names a memory location inside the computer. You can think of it as a box, a place to store a number.

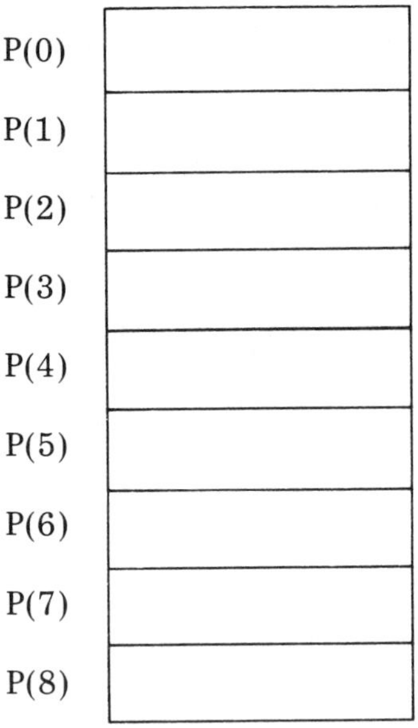

P(0)	
P(1)	
P(2)	
P(3)	
P(4)	
P(5)	
P(6)	
P(7)	
P(8)	

A set of subscripted variables is also called an *array*. This set of subscripted variables is a *one-dimensional array,* also known as a vector. In Chapter 8, we will discuss two-dimensional arrays.

Pretend you are the computer, and LET P(2) = 36. In other words use your pencil or pen and write the number 36 in the box labeled P(2) in the drawing above. Then LET P(3) = 12. (Do it.) Now LET P(7) = P(2)+P(3). Check yourself by looking at our answer following the dashed line.

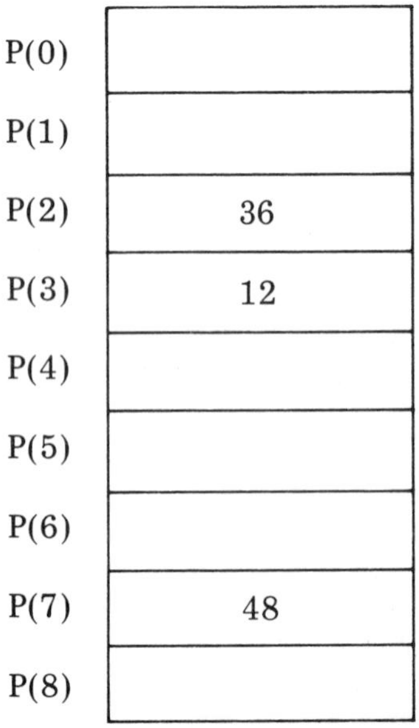

P(0)	
P(1)	
P(2)	36
P(3)	12
P(4)	
P(5)	
P(6)	
P(7)	48
P(8)	

3. Subscripted variables can have variables for subscripts. The subscripted variable, Y(J), has the variable J for a subscript.

If J = 1 then Y(J) is Y(1)

If J = 2 then Y(J) is Y(2)

If J = 7 then Y(J) is Y(7)

Let us assume that the values (in the boxes below) have been assigned to the corresponding variables. Note that both simple and subscripted variables are shown here.

Y(1)	4	Z(1)	4.7	A	1
Y(2)	−3	Z(2)	9.2	B	2
Y(3)	5	X(1)	2	C	3
Y(4)	6	X(2)	3	D	4

Write the value of each variable below.

Y(1) = ______ A = ______ Y(A) = ______

Y(2) = ______ B = ______ Y(B) = ______

Y(C) = ______ X(A) = ______ X(B) = ______

Z(A) = ______ Z(B) = ______ Y(D) = ______

— — — — — — — — — —

4	1	4
−3	2	−3
5	2	3
4.7	9.2	6

4. So far we have only used single variables as subscripts. However, the subscript can be more complex. Below are two examples, still using the variables and values in the boxes in frame 3.

Y(A + 1) = Y(1 + 1) = Y(2) = −3

Y(2*B) = Y(2*2) = Y(4) = 6

Notice that the expressions inside the subscript parentheses are computed using the same rules for BASIC arithmetic as an expression in a PRINT statement, or inside a function parentheses.

Now you complete some examples as we did above, showing both the value calculated for the subscript and the value assigned to the subscripted variable with that subscript. (Refer to the boxes in frame 3.)

Y(A+2) = ______________________________

Y(2*A–1) = ______________________________

Y(A+B) = ______________________________

Y(B*C–D) = ______________________________

Y(A+3) = ______________________________

Y(D–3) = ______________________________

Y(D–C+A) = ______________________________

Y((C+D)–(A+B)) = ______________________________

— — — — — — — — — — —

Y(A + 2) = Y(1 + 2) = Y(3) = 5
Y(2*A – 1) = Y(2*1 – 1) = Y(2 – 1) = Y(1) = 4
Y(A + B) = Y(1 + 2) = Y(3) = 5
Y(B*C – D) = Y(2*3 – 4) = Y(6 – 4) = Y(2) = –3
Y(A + 3) = Y(1 + 3) = Y(4) = 6
Y(D – 3) = Y(4 – 3) = Y(1) = 4
Y(D – C + A) = Y(4 – 3 + 1) = Y(1 + 1) = Y(2) = –3
Y((C + D) – (A + B)) = Y((3 + 4) – (1 + 2)) = Y(7 – 3) = Y(4) = 6

5. You will recall that previously you had to tell the computer how much space to reserve in its memory for the strings to be assigned to string variables in your program. In a similar fashion, you must also DIMension subscripted variables for the maximum number of values to be assigned to a particular subscripted variable. That is, you must tell the computer the *largest* subscript it is to permit for a subscripted variable by using a DIM statement. "DIM" is the abbreviation for the "dimension" of an array of subscripted variables. The DIM statement(s) in your program must be placed so that they are executed before the subscripted variable(s) are actually used in the program, or an error message will result and the execution of the program will stop. The format for dimensioning an array is shown below. Note that it is similar to dimensioning a string variable.

```
105 DIM X(100)
```

Variable for which space is being reserved ↗ (X) ↖ Maximum subscript to be permitted (100)

The above DIM statement specifies a subscripted variable which can have a maximum subscript of ______________.

— — — — — — — — — — —

```
100
```

6. Suppose we wanted to specify that the maximum subscript is 50. Write the DIM statement.

```
105 ______________________________
```

— — — — — — — — — — —

```
105 DIM X(50)
```

7. So how can subscripted variables contribute to the ease and versatility of programming in BASIC? One common use of subscripted variables is to store a list of numbers entered via INPUT or READ statements. This can be done with a FOR-NEXT loop. The control variable can also be used as the variable for the subscript in a subscripted variable, causing the subscript to increase by one each time through the loop. To illustrate, again we will turn to The World's Most Expensive Adding Machine.

```
100 REM***WORLD'S MOST EXPENSIVE
105 REM***ADDING MACHINE (AGAIN)
110 DIM X(10)
120 PRINT "HOW MANY NUMBERS";
130 INPUT N
140 PRINT
150 FOR K=1 TO N
160 PRINT "X=";
170 INPUT X
180 X(K)=X
190 NEXT K
200 T=0
210 FOR K=1 TO N
220 LET T=T+X(K)
230 NEXT K
240 PRINT "THE TOTAL IS "; T

RUN
HOW MANY NUMBERS?5

X=?37
X=?23
X=?46
X=?78
X=?59
THE TOTAL IS 243
```

For the RUN shown, N is 5. Therefore, 5 numbers will be entered by the operator and stored in X(1) through ______________________.

— — — — — — — — — — —

```
X(5)
```

8. Notice especially lines 170 and 180 in the previous frame. First, the input value is assigned to the simple numeric variable X. Then the subscripted variable X(K) is assigned the *same* value by letting X(K) = X.

Now suppose the computer is running the program in frame 7. It has just completed the FOR-NEXT loop in lines 150 to 190. The numbers entered by the user are now stored as follows.

N	5
X(1)	37
X(2)	23
X(3)	46
X(4)	78
X(5)	59

The computer is ready to proceed with line 200. This statement initializes the variable T, that is, gives T its first value. Show the value of T after line 200 has been executed.

T	

— — — — — — — — — — — —

T	0

9. Next, the computer will execute the FOR-NEXT loop in lines 210 to 230. How many times will the FOR-NEXT loop be executed? ____________________

— — — — — — — — — — — —

5 times, because line 210 says FOR K = 1 TO N and N is equal to 5

10. The FOR-NEXT loop in lines 210 to 230 will be done 5 times, first for K = 1, then for K = 2, K = 3, K = 4, and finally for K = 5. Let's look at line 220, where K is used as a subscript.

```
220 LET T=T+X(K)
```

This statement tells the computer to add the value of X(K) to the *old* value of T and then assign the results as the *new* value of T.

What is the value of T after line 220 has been executed for K = 1? ________

For K = 2? ________ For K = 3? ________ For K = 4? ________

For K = 5? ________

— — — — — — — — — — —

37; 60; 106; 184; 243

11. Let's use the World's Most Expensive Adding Machine to compute the sum of whole numbers, 1 through 12.

```
RUN

HOW MANY NUMBERS? 12

X =? 1
X =? 2
X =? 3
X =? 4
X =? 5
X =? 6
X =? 7
X =? 8
X =? 9
X =? 10
X =? 11
ERROR-    AT LINE 180
```

This time we got an error message telling us that we had a bad subscript. What was the largest subscript for X(K) that the computer would accept *before* it gave us an error message? ____________________

— — — — — — — — — — —

10

12. Change line 110 to allow us to input more numbers by substituting the following statement:

```
110 DIM X(100)
```

Now RUN the program again using the 12 numbers that gave us trouble before.

```
RUN

HOW MANY NUMBERS: 12

X =? 1
X =? 2
X =? 3
X =? 4
X =? 5
X =? 6
X =? 7
X =? 8
X =? 9
X =? 10
X =? 11
X =? 12
THE TOTAL IS 78
```

Now the program can be used to compute the sum of *at most* how many numbers? ________

— — — — — — — — — — —

100. If 100 numbers are entered they will be stored in X(1) through X(100), the limit specified by the DIM statement in line 110. We can, of course, also use the program to compute the sum of fewer than 100 numbers.

13. A DIM statement may have its dimensions assigned by a variable. Look at the examples below.

```
DIM X(N)            DIM A(B)            DIM D(Y+2)
```

You may only dimension an array *once* during the RUN of a program. The computer will give you an error message and stop executing the program if it comes to a DIM statement for the same array a second time and tries to redimension the array during the same RUN.

Look at the program segment below, and the beginning of the RUN. We have deleted line 110 and placed the DIM statement at the beginning of line 150.

```
.
.
.
120 PRINT "HOW MANY NUMBERS";
130 INPUT N
140 PRINT
150 DIM X(N) : FOR K=1 TO N

:

:
RUN
HOW MANY NUMBERS:8
```

What will be the dimensioned size of the array during this RUN of the program?

____

— — — — — — — — — — —

8 (the value assigned to N by the INPUT statement)

14. Where else in the program segment shown in frame 13 could DIM X(N) be placed?

____

____

— — — — — — — — — —

In line 130 *after* INPUT N, or in line 140 either before or after PRINT. But notice that the DIM statement must be placed after the input value has been entered, but *before* the FOR-NEXT loop so that the array X(K) is dimensioned *only once* during the same RUN. The DIM X(N) statement could also be on a single line by itself, using a line number between 130 and 140 or between 140 and 150.

15. Look at the first FOR-NEXT loop (lines 150–190) in the program in frame 7. The first value assigned to K is 1, so the first subscripted variable X(K) is X(1). Since the array *could* start with X(0), an array dimensioned as DIM X(100) can actually hold how many values? ____________

Show how we could modify the FOR statement so that we could take advantage of every element (subscripted variable value) in the array for storing values, provided that N = 100. ______________________________

— — — — — — — — — —

```
101
FOR K=0 TO N
```

16. Instead of using an INPUT statement to get values for X(1), X(2), and so on, we can use READ and DATA statements. We'll put the value of N and the values of X(1) through X(N) in a DATA statement, as follows.

```
DATA 5, 37, 23, 46, 78, 59
     ▲  ▲   ▲   ▲   ▲   ▲
```

Value of N Values of X(1) through X(5)

```
100 REM ** WORLD'S MOST EXPENSIVE
105 REM ** ADDING MACHINE YET AGAIN
110 DIM X(100)
200 REM ** READ N & X(1) THRU X(N)
210 READ N
220 FOR J=1 TO N
230 READ X : X(J)=X
240 NEXT J
300 REM ** PRINT VALUE OF N & X ARRAY
310 PRINT "N="; N
320 PRINT "X(1) THRU X(";N;") ARE:"
330 FOR K=1 TO N
340 PRINT " "; X(K);
350 NEXT K
360 PRINT
400 REM ** TOTAL OF X ARRAY VALUES
410 T=0
420 FOR L=1 TO N
430 T=T+X(L)
440 NEXT L
500 REM ** PRINT TOTAL; START AGAIN
510 PRINT "THE TOTAL IS "; T
520 PRINT
530 GOTO 210
900 REM ** HERE ARE TWO SETS OF DATA
910 DATA 5,37,23,46,78,59
920 DATA 12,1,2,3,4,5,6,7,8,9,10,11,12
```

In the first FOR-NEXT loop (lines 220–240), we used J as the subscript. This choice was entirely arbitrary. What subscript did we use in lines 330 to 350?

________ Lines 420 to 440? ________

— — — — — — — — — — —

K; L

17. If we had wanted to, could we have used J as the subscript in all three places? ________________

— — — — — — — — — — —

Yes. These are three separate and distinct FOR-NEXT loops. We could have used *any* variable as the subscript except N, T, or X.

18. The following questions refer back to the program in frame 16.

(a) For the second set of data, which statement assigns the first item in the DATA statement to a variable? ________________

(b) Which statements assign the rest of the data to a subscripted variable?

____

(c) Which statement prints values stored in an array instead of from the DATA statement? ______________________

(d) Which statement tallies or adds up all the values stored in the array?

____

(a) `21Ø READ N`
(b) `23Ø READ X : X(J)=X`
(c) `34Ø PRINT X(K);`
(d) `43Ø T=T+X(L)`

Note: Refer back to frame 8 for an explanation and suggestion regarding line 230.

19. Suppose we RUN the program in frame 16. Show what the RUN will look like. (Hint: Check all the PRINT statements.)

```
RUN
N=5
X(1) THRU X(5) ARE:
 37 23 46 78 59
THE TOTAL IS 243

N=12
X(1) THRU X(12) ARE:
 1 2 3 4 5 6 7 8 9 1Ø 11 12
THE TOTAL IS 78

ERROR-   6 AT LINE 21Ø
```

20. So that you can better understand and use subscripted variables in your programming, here's a little more practice at doing what a computer does when dealing with subscripted variables.

For this segment of a computer program, fill in the boxes showing the values of D(G) at the affected locations after this FOR-NEXT loop has been run.

```
10 DIM D(3)
20 FOR G=1 TO 3
30 D(G)=2*G-1
40 NEXT G
```

D(1) [ ] D(2) [ ] D(3) [ ]

D(1)	1	For G = 1, 2*G − 1 = 2*1 − 1 = 2 − 1 = 1
D(2)	3	For G = 2, 2*G − 1 = 2*2 − 1 = 4 − 1 = 3
D(3)	5	For G = 3, 2*G − 1 = 2*3 − 1 = 6 − 1 = 5

21. For the following FOR-NEXT loop, fill in the boxes showing the values in R(1) through R(4) after the loop has been carried out.

```
10 DIM R(10)
20 FOR R=1 TO 4
30 R(R)=R+2
40 NEXT R
```

(Remember R and (R) are different variables.)

R(1) [ ] R(2) [ ] R(3) [ ] R(4) [ ]

R(1)	3	For R = 1, R+2 = 1+2 = 3
R(2)	4	For R = 2, R+2 = 2+2 = 4
R(3)	5	For R = 3, R+2 = 3+2 = 5
R(4)	6	For R = 4, R+2 = 4+2 = 6

22. Let's do one more of these. Show what values will be in the boxes after this FOR-NEXT loop has been executed.

```
10 DIM P(10)
20 FOR N=1 TO 6
30 P(N)=2*N
40 NEXT P
```

P(1)		P(2)		P(3)	
P(4)		P(5)		P(6)	

P(1)	2	P(2)	4	P(3)	6
P(4)	8	P(5)	10	P(6)	12

23. Next, assume that numbers are stored in C(1) through C(5), as follows:

C(1)	18	C(2)	34	C(3)	12
C(4)	20	C(5)	17		

What will be printed if the following FOR-NEXT loop is carried out?

```
100 DIM C(10)
110 FOR A=1 TO 5
120 PRINT " "; C(A);
130 NEXT A
RUN
```

```
RUN
 18 34 12 20 17
```

24. Suppose numbers are stored in C(1) through C(5) as shown in frame 23. What will be printed if the following FOR-NEXT loop is carried out?

```
100 DIM C(10)
110 FOR A=5 TO 1 STEP -1
120 PRINT " "; C(A);
130 NEXT A
RUN
```

— — — — — — — — — — —

```
RUN
 17 20 12 34 18
```

The values are printed in reverse order. If you missed this, review Chapter 6, frames 18 and 19.

25. Assume that an election is approaching and you have conducted a poll among your friends, using the following questionnaire.

> Who will you vote for in the coming election? Circle the number to the left of your choice.
> 1. Sam Smoothe
> 2. Gabby Gruff

Let's write a program to count the votes each candidate received in the poll. You have 35 responses to your questionnaire, each response being either a "1" or a "2". First, record the votes in DATA statements.

```
910 DATA 1,1,2,2,2,1,1,2,2,2,1,1,1,2
920 DATA 1,2,1,1,2,2,1,1,1,2,1,2,2,2,
930 DATA 1,1,2,1,-1
```

End-of-data flag (not a vote)

How many votes did Sam Smoothe receive? _______

— — — — — — — — — — —

17

26. How many votes did Gabby Gruff receive? ________ (Do your answers total 32?)

— — — — — — — — — — —

15

27. To answer those last two questions, you probably counted the 1's in the DATA statements to find out how many votes Sam Smoothe received. Then you counted the 2's to find out how many votes Gabby Gruff received.

Your computer can count votes by using subscripted variables to keep a running total of the 1's and 2's read from the DATA statements. When it comes to the end-of-data flag (–1) it stops counting and prints the results. Here is a program to count the votes.

```
100 REM***VOTE COUNTING PROGRAM
110 REM***INITIALIZE
120 DIM C(2) : C(1)=0 : C(2)=0
200 REM***READ AND COUNT VOTES
210 READ V
220 IF V=-1 THEN 310
230 C(V)=C(V)+1 ←———————— Crucial vote-counting statement.
240 GOTO 210
300 REM***PRINT RESULTS
310 PRINT "SAM SMOOTHE:"; C(1)
320 PRINT "GABBY GRUFF:"; C(2)

910 DATA 1,1,2,2,2,1,1,2,2,2,1,1,1,2
920 DATA 1,2,1,1,2,2,1,1,1,2,1,2,2,2
930 DATA 1,1,2,1,-1

RUN
SAM SMOOTHE:17
GABBY GRUFF:15
```

Is the DIM statement really necessary? Why or why not? ____________________

____

— — — — — — — — — — —

Yes, arrays must always be DIMensioned.

28. After the computer executes line 120, what are the values of C(1) and C(2)?

C(1) [ ]

C(2) [ ]

— — — — — — — — — — —

Both have a value of 0. These are the initial values prior to counting votes. We call the process *initializing* as shown in the REMark statement in line 110.

29. When your programs get so long that they start exceeding the computer's memory capacity, delete the REMarks to save memory space, as well as to save you time in typing in the programs you don't intend to store for later use.

To save memory space, which statements could be deleted from the program and still have it RUN as shown in frame 27? ____________________

— — — — — — — — — — —

```
100,110,200, AND 300
```

30. Look again at the crucial vote-counting statement from frame 27.

```
230 LET C(V)=C(V)+1
```

It is the subscripted variable equivalent of a similar statement which has been used in earlier programs to keep count, such as this one:

```
LET N=N+1
```

Note how the variable *subscript* of C is used to determine whether either the value of C(1) is increased by one, or the value of C(2) is increased by one. Since V can have only two values, either 1 or 2, line 230 is actually a double-purpose line. Depending on the value of V, line 230 is actually equivalent to:

`LET C(1)=C(1)+1,` or `LET C(2)=C(2)+1`

When the preceding program is RUN, what values will the computer have stored for C(1) and C(2) after the *first* vote has been read and processed? (That is, lines 210 through 230 have been done for the first vote in the first DATA statement.)

C(1) [ ] C(2) [ ]

What values will be stored for C(1) and C(2) after the *second* vote has been read and processed?

C(1) [ ] C(2) [ ]

What values will be stored in C(1) and C(2) after the third vote has been read and processed?

C(1) [ ] C(2) [ ]

— — — — — — — — — — —

C(1)	1	C(2)	0
C(1)	2	C(2)	0
C(1)	2	C(2)	1

31. In the program we have been discussing (frame 27), line 220 checks for the end-of-data flag with the following statement.

```
IF V=-1 THEN 31Ø
```

If we switch lines 220 and 230, this section of the program would look like this:

```
21Ø READ V
22Ø LET C(V)=C(V)+1
23Ø IF V=-1 THEN 31Ø
24Ø GOTO 21Ø
```

(a) What would be the last value assigned to V from the DATA statement?

____

(b) If the computer used this value for V in line 220, what would the subscripted variable look like? ________________

(c) Since negative subscripts are not allowed, what error message would our computer print? ________________________

— — — — — — — — — —

(a) -1
(b) C(-1)
(c) ERROR—a bad subscript. Moral: Beware of *where* you place the test for the end-of-data flag. The best place is usually right after the READ or INPUT statement where the flag might appear.

32. Suppose the following poll is conducted.

> Which candidate will you vote for in the coming election? Circle the number to the left of your choice.
> 1. Sam Smoothe
> 2. Gabby Gruff
> 3. No opinion

The results of this poll are shown below.

```
2,2,2,1,2,1,1,2,1,1,3,2,1,3
2,1,1,3,1,3,2,2,1,1,3,2,1,3
1,1,2,1,2,1,1
```

Modify the vote-counting program from frame 27 to process this data. You will have to add a line to set C(3) to zero and a PRINT statement to print the NO OPINION total. You will also have to change the DATA statements for the new data, as well as the DIM statement. Here is how it should RUN.

```
RUN
SAM SMOOTHE:17
GABBY GRUFF:12
NO OPINION:6
```

Write your program below.

— — — — — — — — — — —

```
100 REM ** VOTE COUNTING PROGRAM
110 REM ** INITIALIZE
120 DIM C(3)
130 C(1)=0 : C(2)=0 : C(3)=0
200 REM ** READ AND COUNT VOTES
210 READ V
220 IF V=-1 THEN 310
230 C(V)=C(V)+1
240 GOTO 210
300 REM ** PRINT RESULTS
310 PRINT "SAM SMOOTHE:"; C(1)
320 PRINT "GABBY GRUFF:"; C(2)
330 PRINT "NO OPINION:"; C(3)
910 DATA 2,2,2,1,2,1,1,2,1,1,3,2,1,3
920 DATA 2,1,1,3,1,3,2,2,1,1,3,2,1,3
930 DATA 1,1,2,1,2,1,1,-1
```

Did you remember the flag?

33. Suppose we have a questionnaire with 4 possible answers, or 5 or 6. Instead of writing a separate program for each, let's write one program to count votes for a questionnaire with N possible answers. The value of N will appear in a DATA statement prior to the actual answers, or votes. For example, the data for the questionnaire in frame 25 would look like this.

```
900 REM ** THE DATA
901 REM ** FIRST DATA IS NUMBER OF
902 REM ** POSSIBLE CHOICES
910 DATA 2
920 DATA 1,1,2,2,2,1,1,2,2,2,1,1,1,2
930 DATA 1,2,1,1,2,2,1,1,1,2,1,2,2,2
940 DATA 1,1,2,1,-1
```

Line 910 is the value of N. In this case, N is 2 and possible votes are 1 or 2. How would the data for the questionnaire in frame 32 be placed in DATA statements?

```
900 REM ** THE DATA
901 REM ** FIRST DATA IS NUMBER OF
902 REM ** POSSIBLE CHOICES

910 DATA ______________________________

919 REM ** THE VOTES & THE FLAG (-1)

920 ______________________________

930 ______________________________

940 ______________________________
```

— — — — — — — — — — —

```
910 DATA 3
920 DATA 2,2,2,1,2,1,1,2,1,1,3,2,1,3
930 DATA 2,1,1,3,1,3,2,2,1,1,3,2,1,3
940 DATA 1,1,2,1,2,1,1,-1
```

This time N = 3 (line 910) and possible votes or 1, 2, or 3.

34. Your turn. Write a program to read and count votes for a questionnaire with N different possible answers (votes), where N is less than or equal to 20. You will have to do the following things.

(1) DIMension for the *maximum* subscript for C. Remember, we said N is less than or equal to 20.
(2) Read the value of N.
(3) Set C(1) through C(N) to zero. (Use a FOR-NEXT loop.)
(4) Read and count votes until a flag is read.
(5) Print the results, as shown in the sample runs below.

Example: N = 2

```
RUN
ANSWER # 1 : 17
ANSWER # 2 : 15
```

Example: N = 5

```
RUN
ANSWER # 1 : 12
ANSWER # 2 : 7
ANSWER # 3 : 9
ANSWER # 4 : 9
ANSWER # 5 : 10
```

Here's a good opportunity to practice writing multiple statements per line. Our sample runs above were produced using these two sets of data.

```
910 DATA 2
920 DATA 1,1,2,2,2,1,1,2,2,2,1,1,1,2
930 DATA 1,2,1,1,2,2,1,1,1,2,1,2,2,2
940 DATA 1,1,2,1,-1

910 DATA 5
920 DATA 4,3,4,2,4,1,1,5,5,3,5,4,5,1
930 DATA 3,2,5,5,4,4,5,1,2,3,3,3,5,2
940 DATA 2,3,1,5,4,1,1,1,2,3,1,4,1,5
950 DATA 1,2,3,4,1,-1
```

Write your program below. (You need not show the DATA statements.)

— — — — — — — — — —

```
100 REM***VOTE COUNTING PROGRAM
110 REM***INITIALIZE
120 DIM C(20) : READ N : FOR K=1 TO N : C(K)=0 : NEXT K
200 REM***READ AND COUNT VOTES
210 READ V : IF V <> -1 THEN LET C(V)=C(V)+1 : GOTO 210
300 REM***PRINT RESULTS
310 FOR K=1 TO N : PRINT "ANSWER #"; K; ":"; C(K) : NEXT K
```

35. The problems in frames 25–34 dealt with counting votes. Each time through the loop that reads data (a data loop) you added one (1) to an array element (LET C(V) = C(V)+1). Almost any vote counting application you might want to try is going to be similar to the solutions in frame 34. Now you can volunteer to be the official ballot counter for all the elections in your community—PTA, computer club, school class offices, church groups, ad infinitum.

On to more serious business. A similar, but not identical application of simple one-dimension arrays deals with counting things or money, instead of votes.

Let's set the stage. You are the sponsor for the neighborhood computer club for eight local kids. The kids want to buy a new superduper color graphics terminal for the neighborhood computer system. It's only $1200 in kit form. Raising funds is the problem. The kids agree to sell milk chocolate candy bars for $1.00 each to raise money. (The club makes 55¢ profit per sale, not bad!). But you must do the recordkeeping. You assign each kid a number. Whenever a kid comes by for candy bars, you identify the kid, by number, and note how many bars were taken. The money will be turned in later.

Here are the ID numbers assigned to each club member.

1. Jerry	5. Karl
2. Bobby	6. Mimi
3. Mary	7. Doug
4. Danny	8. Scott

When Danny first takes 6 bars you note it as 4,6. The 4 is Danny's ID number for the computer, and 6 is the number of candy bars he took. When Doug takes 12 bars, your note is ________, ________. When Mary takes 6, the note is ________, ________.

— — — — — — — — — — —

7,12; 3,6

36. After a few weeks of this, you've accumulated quite a pile of notes. It's time to tally and see how much money you've raised thus far. The information from your notes will be placed into DATA statements. (You could enter the information using INPUT, but it could take much too long!) Start at line 910 (a good place to put DATA assuming the rest of the program won't have line numbers past 900.)

```
900 REM ** DATA IN PAIRS: KID ID NO.
901 REM ** FOLLOWED BY QUANTITY
910 DATA 4,6,7,12,3,6,1,8,4,5,5,3,8,20
```

This shows that Danny took *another* five candy bars.

```
920 2,4,3,8,6,6,5,10,7,12,8,4,1,3
```

Mary took *another* 8.

```
930 DATA -1,-1
```

(a) Each item of data has (how many?) ________ numbers.

(b) DATA 6,6 means ________________________.

(c) The end-of-data flag has (how many?) ________ numbers. Why?________

____

(a) two
(b) Mimi took 6 bars
(c) Two. Each data element has two numbers. Two values will be read with one READ statement. An ERROR would result if there were only one (flag) value for the two variables in the READ statement.

37. Just as you complete entering the DATA, Bobby shows up to take another six bars. Show how you could add this data without changing any of the existing DATA statements. Use the highest line number permissible and still have the end-of-data flags as the last values read by the program.

____

```
929 DATA2,6
```

The line number cannot be larger than 929, or the flags in line 930 will not be the *last* data item read by the program. Moral: Be careful *where* you add DATA into an existing program.

38. We need an array with eight elements. That means we need a subscripted variable with subscripts from 1 to 8, to represent the eight members of the club. The *value* added to each element (or subscripted variable) in the array will be the number of candy bars each kid took. But first, initialize the array by writing one multiple-statement line that will dimension the array and assign a zero to each element. We will call this the A array and use A(X) for the subscripted variable.

```
100 REM***CANDY BAR COUNTER
110 REM***INITIALIZE

120 DIM ________________________
```

```
120 DIM A(8) : FOR X=1 TO 8 : LET A(X)=0 : NEXT X
```

You could omit the LET.

39. Now let's read the *data in pairs* (two items at a time). Use K for kid and Q for quantity of candy bars, and test for end of DATA, all on one line. If we run out of data, have the program branch to line 310.

```
200 REM***READ DATA AND TALLY
210 ______________________________
```

— — — — — — — — — — — —

```
210 READ K,Q : IF K=-1 THEN 310
```

40. Now the hard one! We must accumulate the number of bars in the correct array element corresponding to the kid who took them. Think of the subscript K in the subscripted variable A(K) as the kid's ID code.

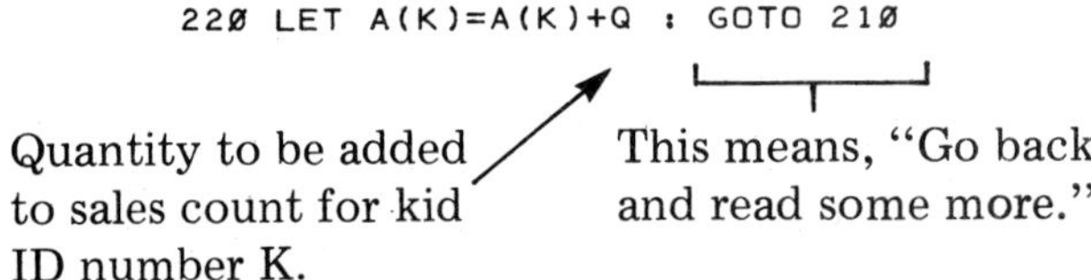

If K (for kid) is 2 and Q (quantity) is 4, then line 220 will cause array element A(______) to increase by ________.

— — — — — — — — — — — —

A(2); 4

41. If the array elements look like those on the left *before,* how will they look *after* reading and adding the additional DATA given here?

```
920 DATA 4,6,3,8,6,6,7,2,4,3
```

Before		After	
A(1) =	8	A(1) =	
(2) =	4	(2) =	
(3) =	6	(3) =	
(4) =	4	(4) =	
(5) =	3	(5) =	
(6) =	2	(6) =	
(7) =	12	(7) =	
(8) =	7	(8) =	

— — — — — — — — — — — —

A(1) =	8
(2) =	4
(3) =	14
(4) =	13
(5) =	3
(6) =	8
(7) =	14
(8) =	7

42. Here's our program so far.

```
100 REM ** CANDY BAR COUNTER
110 REM ** INITIALIZE
120 DIM A(8)
130 FOR X=1 TO 8 : A(X)=0 : NEXT X
200 REM ** READ DATA AND TALLY
210 READ K,Q : IF K=-1 THEN 310
220 LET A(K)=A(K)+Q : GOTO 210
900 REM ** DATA IN PAIRS: KID ID NO.
901 REM ** FOLLOWED BY QUANTITY
910 DATA 4,6,7,12,3,6,1,8,4,5,5,3,8,20
920 DATA 2,4,3,8,6,6,5,10,7,12,8,4,1,3
929 DATA 1,6
930 DATA -1,-1
```

It starts and it accumulates. Before it stops, we must have it print our report. Let's start the report with a heading.

```
300 REM ** PRINT THE REPORT
310 PRINT "KID ID #", "QUANTITY"
```

Now we print the results using a FOR-NEXT loop.

```
320 FOR X=1 TO 8
330 PRINT X, A(X)
340 NEXT X
```

or

```
320 FOR X=1 TO 8:PRINT X, A(X):NEXT X
```

Using the data in the DATA statement, show below how the report will look after running our program.

```
RUN
KID ID #  QUANTITY
1         17
2         4
3         14
4         11
5         13
6         6
7         24
8         24

READY
```

43. So far our report shows us who has what but doesn't give us names or totals or profits. With some help, the computer can do all those things.

Let's start with the total. In BASIC each array has an element we haven't used yet. It's the zero (0) element. Remember, when you DIMension an array of eight elements with a DIM statement, DIM A(8), you really get 9: 0, 1, 2, 3, 4, 5, 6, 7, and 8.

Since we haven't assigned any kid the ID number 0 (zero), the "A array" element with the subscript 0 has not been used or assigned a value. So the A(0) element can be used for accumulating totals, although we could use some other variable. Look at statement 410, which accumulates the total number of bars sold in A(0).

```
400 REM ** TALLY TOTAL SALES & PROFIT
410 FOR X=1 TO 8:A(0)=A(0)+A(X):NEXT X
```

If the A array starts at zero, we must remember to change the FOR statement in the initializing routine to start assigning zeros at A(0). Replace (rewrite) the initializing line for this program so that all the array elements are given the initial value of zero.

130 ____________________

```
130 FOR K=0 TO 8 : A(X)=0 : NEXT X
```

44. The statement that tallies up all the candy sold by the club uses the A(0) element in the A array to accumulate the value stored in A(1) through A(8).

If the array looks as it did in frame 41 (after reading data), then what value will be stored in A(0) after one time through the loop in line 410? __________

After three times through the loop in 410? __________

8, 26

45. Write lines 420 and 430 to print the total and the profit (55¢ on each bar). Here is what we want line 420 to print:

```
TOTAL IS 113
PROFIT IS 62.15
```

42Ø ______________________________

43Ø ______________________________

```
42Ø PRINT "TOTAL IS ";A(Ø)
43Ø PRINT "PROFIT IS ";A(Ø)*Ø.55
```

46. Here is a complete list and run so far.

```
1ØØ REM ** CANDY BAR COUNTER
11Ø REM ** INITIALIZE
12Ø DIM A(8)
13Ø FOR X=Ø TO 8:A(X)=Ø:NEXT X
2ØØ REM ** READ DATA & TALLY
21Ø READ K,Q:IF K=-1 THEN 31Ø
215 IF K=-1 THEN 31Ø
22Ø A(K)=A(K)+Q:GOTO 21Ø
3ØØ REM ** PRINT THE REPORT
31Ø PRINT "KID ID #","QUANTITY"
32Ø FOR X=1 TO 8:PRINT X,A(X):NEXT X
4ØØ REM ** TALLY TOTAL SALES & PROFIT
41Ø FOR X=1 TO 8:A(Ø)=A(Ø)+A(X):NEXT X
42Ø PRINT "TOTAL IS ";A(Ø)
43Ø PRINT "PROFIT IS ";A(Ø)*Ø.55
9ØØ REM ** DATA IN PAIRS: KID ID NO.
9Ø1 REM ** FOLLOWED BY QUANTITY
91Ø DATA 4,6,7,12,3,6,1,8,4,5,5,3,8,2Ø
92Ø DATA 2,4,3,8,6,6,5,1Ø,7,12,8,4,1,3
929 DATA 1,6
93Ø DATA -1,-1

RUN
KID ID #    QUANTITY
1           17
2           4
3           14
4           11
5           13
6           6
7           24
8           24
TOTAL IS 113
PROFIT IS 62.15
```

That's a nice report . . . but wait! In this day of impersonalization, wouldn't it be nice to print each kid's name instead of a number? How can we do it? Easily. We can have the computer READ the names from DATA statements.

String variables must be DIMensioned, just as an array must be DIMensioned. Just don't forget the properly placed $ that identifies a string variable. You may prefer to DIMension each array in the same multiple-statement line where the array is first used or initialized.

Write a DIM statement to initialize N$(X) for a string long enough to use for the longest name of any member of the computer club.

140 ________________________________

— — — — — — — — — — —

140 DIM N$(8) (Number in parentheses must be at least 5.)

47. Let's say that we have placed the club members' names in a DATA statement, in the same order as their ID numbers.

```
DATA JERRY, BOBBY, MARY, DANNY, KARL, MIMI, DOUG, SCOTT
```

(Note that on your video screen this line will "wrap around" to the next line. The computer doesn't care and will consider names or numbers that are "split" between the end of one display line and the beginning of the next as unbroken.)

Since our BASIC does not allow arrays of strings, only numeric arrays, we must tell the computer to READ and PRINT each name at the time that it is printing the report. Therefore, the statement that reads the names from the data statement must be *inside* the FOR-NEXT loop that prints the report (lines 320 and 340).

```
300 REM***PRINT THE REPORT
310 PRINT
320 PRINT "NAME", "QUANTITY":PRINT
330 FOR X=1 TO 8: READ N$
340 PRINT N$,A(X):NEXT X
```

Notice that no "end of data" flag is needed since the FOR-NEXT loop only goes around 8 times, and there are 8 names in the DATA statement.

There is now the touchy problem of *where* to place the DATA statement that contains the club members' names. Keep in mind that we want to avoid an error message just because a READ statement with a numeric variable came upon a DATA statement containing strings!

Where should the DATA statement with club members names be placed in the program? ________________________________

____

— — — — — — — — — — —

At the end, since all numeric data is read earlier in the program.

48. Now here is the real test of your understanding. Ready to play computer? Show what a RUN of this program would look like.

```
100 REM ** CANDY BAR COUNTER
110 REM ** INITIALIZE
120 DIM A(8)
130 FOR Z=0 TO 8:A(X)=0:NEXT X
140 DIM N$(8)
200 REM ** READ DATA & TALLY
210 READ K,Q:IF K=-1 THEN 310
215 IF K=-1 THEN 310
220 A(K)=A(K)+Q:GOTO 210
300 REM ** PRINT THE REPORT
310 PRINT
320 PRINT "NAME","QUANTITY"
330 FOR X=1 TO 8:READ N$
340 PRINT N$,A(X):NEXT X
400 REM ** TALLY TOTAL SALES & PROFIT
410 FOR X=1 TO 8:A(0)=A(0)+A(X):NEXT X
420 PRINT "TOTAL IS ";A(0)
430 PRINT "PROFIT IS ";A(0)*0.55
900 REM ** DATA IN PAIRS: KID ID NO.
901 REM ** FOLLOWED BY QUANTITY
910 DATA 4,6,7,12,3,6,1,8,4,5,5,3,8,20
920 DATA 2,4,3,8,6,6,5,10,7,12,8,4,1,3
929 DATA 1,6
930 DATA -1,-1
940 DATA JERRY,BOBBY,MARY,DANNY,KARL,MIM
I,DOUG,SCOTT
```

```
RUN
NAME          QUANTITY
JERRY         17
BOBBY         4
MARY          14
DANNY         11
KARL          13
MIMI          6
DOUG          24
SCOTT         24
TOTAL IS 113
PROFIT IS 62.15
```

49. Let's look at one other application of singly-subscripted variables. This one neither counts votes nor accumulates anything.

No doubt you've read about computer dating. Ever wonder how it works? You answer a series of questions that are then stored in the computer; other people who wish to be matched do likewise. Then the responses are compared to test for "compatibility." Let's do a simplified version of a computer dating program which you can alter for your own uses.

We'll use a multiple-choice questionnaire with only five questions. (Ask anything you'd like!) Responses will be stored in DATA statements, with the name first, and the five responses following. My responses appear in line 910 on the next page.

```
900 REM ** QUESTIONAIRE RESPONSES
901 REM ** NAME FOLLOWED BY ANSWERS
902 REM ** 'HIS' IN LINE 910
910 DATA LEROY,3,3,4,2,1
```

Now, you create DATA statements in lines 920–970 for these respondents, plus an end-of-data flag.

	Q1	Q2	Q3	Q4	Q5
JOAN	1	4	2	2	1
TONI	2	2	2	3	3
LAURA	2	3	3	1	2
MARY	3	3	4	2	1
IRENE	3	1	4	2	1

```
920 ____________________________________

930 ____________________________________

940 ____________________________________

950 ____________________________________

960 ____________________________________

970 DATA END
```

— — — — — — — — — — —

```
920 DATA JOAN,1,4,2,2,1
930 DATA TONI,2,2,2,3,3
940 DATA LAURA,2,3,3,1,2
950 DATA MARY,3,3,4,2,1
960 DATA IRENE,3,1,4,2,1
970 DATA END
```

50. Now, you write the rest of the program with some gentle supervision. First, you will need a DIM statement that will allow the program to compare "his" responses (stored in array C), with "her" responses (stored in array A). Also initialize string variable N$ for "his" and H$ for "her."

```
100 REM***COMPUTER DATING SIMULATION
105 REM***INITIALIZE

110 ____________________________________
```

— — — — — — — — — — —

```
110 DIM C(5),A(5),N$(10),H$(10)
```

Note: You can DIMension more than one array in one DIM statement.

51. Next, READ the first data statement which contains "his" name, and READ "his" five responses. The responses should be read into array C using the method shown in frames 8 and 18.

Then print "his" name and responses all on one line, so that later you can compare them with "hers."

```
200 REM**'HIS' NAME & RESPONSES
```

```
210 READ N$
220 FOR X=1 TO 5:READ C:C(X)=C:NEXT X
230 PRINT N$,
240 FOR X=1 TO 5:PRINT C(X);" "; :NEXT X:
PRINT
```

Did you remember this PRINT statement? It returns the cursor to the beginning of the next line.

Note: You may have used more or less line numbers, but the statements must perform as indicated, probably the same order.

52. Next, READ *one* set of "her" names and responses into array A, and print "her" responses so you can visually compare the "his" responses with "her" responses. After you read "her" name in line 310, check to see if it is the end-of-data flag (the word END). Use the string comparison IF H$ = "END" THEN END. The output we want so far should look like this.

```
RUN
LEROY     3 3 4 2 1
JOAN      1 4 2 2 1
```

Complete the program segment to produce this output or printout.

```
300 REM ** 'HER' NAMES & RESPONSES
310 ____________________
320 ____________________
330 ____________________
340 ____________________
```

```
310 READ H$:IF H$="END" THEN END
320 FOR X=1 TO 5:READ A:A(X)=A:NEXT X
330 PRINT H$,
340 FOR X=1 TO 5:PRINT A(X);" "; :NEXT X:
PRINT
```

53. Now comes the crucial part. This is where you compare the contents of array C with the contents of array A and add the number of matches into variable M. Think about that and complete the program below, so that a RUN of the complete program looks like the one here.

```
RUN
LEROY         3 3 4 2 1
JOAN          1 4 2 2 1
 2 MATCHES

TONI          2 2 2 3 3
 Ø MATCHES

LAURA         2 3 3 1 2
 1 MATCHES

MARY          3 3 4 2 1
 5 MATCHES

IRENE         3 1 4 2 1
 4 MATCHES
```

```
4ØØ REM ** COMPARE & COUNT 'MATCHES'
41Ø M=Ø
42Ø FOR X=1 TO 5
43Ø IF __________ THEN 45Ø  <------ Compare
44Ø LET M= ______  <------ Add matches
45Ø __________  <------ Close the loop to compare another
46Ø PRINT ______"MATCHES"
47Ø PRINT
48Ø GOTO ______  <------ Read another set of responses
```

— — — — — — — — — —

```
41Ø M=Ø
42Ø FOR X=1 TO 5
43Ø IF C(X)<>A(X) THEN 45Ø
44Ø M=M+1
45Ø NEXT X
46Ø PRINT M;" MATCHES"
47Ø PRINT
48Ø GOTO 31Ø
```

Following is a complete listing and RUN of our computer dating program.

```
100 REM ** COMPUTER DATING SIMULATION
105 REM ** INITIALIZE
110 DIM C(5),A(5),N$(10),H$(10)
200 REM ** 'HIS' NAME & RESPONSES
210 READ N$
220 FOR X=1 TO 5:READ C:C(X)=C:NEXT X
230 PRINT N$,
240 FOR X=1 TO 5:PRINT C(X);" ";:NEXT X:
PRINT
300 REM ** 'HER' NAMES & RESPONSES
310 READ H$:IF H$="END" THEN END
320 FOR X=1 TO 5:READ A:A(X)=A:NEXT X
330 PRINT H$,
340 FOR X=1 TO 5:PRINT A(X);" ";:NEXT X:
PRINT
400 REM ** COMPARE & COUNT 'MATCHES'
410 M=0
420 FOR X=1 TO 5
430 IF C(X)<>A(X) THEN 450
440 M=M+1
450 NEXT X
460 PRINT M;" MATCHES"
470 PRINT
480 GOTO 310
900 REM ** QUESTIONAIRE RESPONSES
901 REM ** NAME FOLLOWED BY ANSWERS
902 REM ** 'HIS' IN LINE 910
910 DATA LEROY,3,3,4,2,1
920 DATA JOAN,1,4,2,2,1
930 DATA TONI,2,2,2,3,3
940 DATA LAURA,2,3,3,1,2
950 DATA MARY,3,3,4,2,1
960 DATA IRENE,3,1,4,2,1
970 DATA END

RUN
LEROY        3  3  4  2  1
JOAN         1  4  2  2  1
2 MATCHES

TONI         2  2  2  3  3
0 MATCHES

LAURA        2  3  3  1  2
1 MATCHES

MARY         3  3  4  2  1
5 MATCHES

IRENE        3  1  4  2  1
4 MATCHES
```

SELF-TEST

If you can complete the Self-Test on subscripted variables, you will be ready for the next chapter, which will expand your programming ability to include the use of more complex subscripted variables. Therefore, it is important that you have the information in this chapter well in hand.

1. Indicate which of the following are legal BASIC subscripted variables.

____ (a) X	____ (b) X2	____ (c) X(2)
____ (d) 2(X)	____ (e) XX(2)	____ (f) X(K)
____ (g) X_2	____ (h) X(I–J)	

2. Assume that values have been assigned to variables as shown below. Note that both simple and subscripted variables are shown.

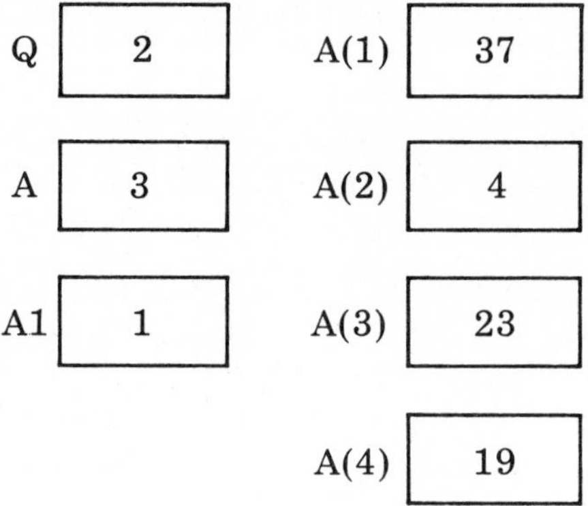

Remember, A, A1, and A(1) are distinct variables. Write the value of each variable below.

(a) A(Q) ________________________

(b) A(A) ________________________

(c) A(A1) ________________________

(d) A(A(2)) ________________________

(e) A(A(Q)) ________________________

(f) A(A–Q) ________________________

(g) A(A+A1) ________________________

(h) A(2*Q) ________________________

3. What will be printed if we RUN the following program?

```
100 REM ** MYSTERY PROGRAM
110 DIM X(10)
120 READ N
130 FOR K=1 TO N
140 READ X:X(K)=X
150 NEXT K
160 FOR K=1 TO N
170 IF X(K)<0 THEN 190
180 PRINT X(K);" ";
190 NEXT K
900 REM ** VALUES OF N AND X ARRAY
910 DATA 7
920 DATA 23,-44,37,0,-12,-58,87
```

4. In the preceding program of question 3, what is the largest value of N for which the program can be used? ___________ What would happen if we tried to RUN the program using the following DATA?

```
910 DATA 12
920 DATA 3,6,-2,0,9,0,7,3,-5,4,-1,7
```

____

5. Modify the vote-counting program of frame 27 so that the total votes (for both candidates) are also printed. The printout might look like this.

```
RUN
SAM SMOOTHE: 19
GABBY GRUFF: 16

TOTAL VOTES: 35
```

6. Modify the vote-counting program of frame 27 so that the printout is % of total votes, rounded to the nearest *whole number* %.

```
RUN

SAM SMOOTHE: 54%
GABBY GRUFF: 46%
```

7. You are selected chairman of the United Collection in your neighborhood. You have 5 people who collect money door-to-door and turn in the money to you at the end of each day. You record their names and dollar amounts collected on a form. This data is then entered into your computer for further processing. Write a BASIC program that will accumulate the current amount each person has collected and the total amount collected by all 5 people. Your report should show the names of each collector with the amounts collected.

```
RUN

NAME        AMOUNT COLLECTED
FRED          125
JOANN         2Ø5
MARYJO        1ØØ
JERRY         1ØØ
BOB           2ØØ
TOTAL 73Ø
```

8. Your computer club kids decide they want to find out who is the best programmer in their group. As club sponsor, you decide to give them a multiple choice test on the programming concepts and correct the test using the computer. The multiple choice answers will be the numbers 1, 2, 3, 4, or 5. There are 10 questions on the test. You enter the 10 *correct* answers in the first DATA statements in the program. These are read into array K. In subsequent DATA statements, you first enter the name of the club member, followed by the 10 answers that person gave for the test. (Enter in array R.) Your task is to write a BASIC program that will correct the tests and print a report that looks similar to the one below.

```
RUN
NAME        SCORE
DANNY         5
KARL          5
MIRIAM        4
SCOTT         7
```

9. Are you curious about your chances of winning at any game using dice? If you developed a program to simulate the rolling of one die and counted how many times each side appeared, you would get a better idea of your chances of winning.

   Write a BASIC program to simulate the roll of one die, 1000 times (or make that an input variable). After each simulated roll, accumulate or add to the correct array element one appearance or "vote." After 1000 rolls, print the contents of your array in report form showing how many times each die side appeared during the computer simulation. Your report should look like the one below. There is room to write your program on the next page.

```
RUN
HOW MANY SIMULATED ROLLS? 1ØØØ
DICE ROLL          NO. OF OCCURENCES
  1                  159
  2                  152
  3                  173
  4                  142
  5                  189
  6                  185
```

Answers to Self-Test

The frame numbers in parentheses refer to the frames in the chapter where the topic is discussed. You may wish to refer back to these for quick review.

1. (c), (f), and (h) are legal subscripted variables. Longer variable names such as item (e) may be legal on *your* computer. Check the reference manual for your computer. (frame 1)

2. (a) 4
   (b) 23
   (c) 37
   (d) 19 A(A(2)) = A(4) = 19
   (e) 19 A(A(Q)) = A(A(2)) = A(4) = 19
   (f) 37 A(3–2) = A(1) = 37
   (g) 19 A(3 + 1) = A(4) = 19
   (h) 19 A(2 + 2) = A(4) = 19
   (frame 4)

3.
```
RUN

 23 37 Ø 87
```

(frames 7–8)

4. 10
The computer would print an error message.

(frames 11–12)

5. Add the following statements.

```
33Ø PRINT
34Ø PRINT "TOTAL VOTES:";C(1)+C(2)
```

(frames 43–46)

6. Beginning at line 310, make these changes.

```
31Ø LET T=C(1)+C(2)
32Ø LET S=INT(1ØØ*C(1)/T + .5)
33Ø LET G=INT(1ØØ*C(2)/T + .5)
34Ø PRINT "SAM SMOOTHE:";S;"%"
35Ø PRINT "GABBY GRUFF:";G;"%"
```

(frame 27 and Chapter 4)

7.
```
1Ø REM
15 REM
2Ø DIM N$(1Ø),T(5):G=Ø:FOR X=1 TO 5:T(
X)=Ø:NEXT X
25 REM
3Ø READ P,D:IF P=-1 THEN 6Ø
4Ø T(P)=T(P)+D:G=G+D:GOTO 3Ø
5Ø REM
6Ø PRINT "NAME","AMOUNT COLLECTED"
7Ø FOR P=1 TO 5:READ N$:PRINT N$,T(P):
NEXT P
8Ø PRINT "TOTAL:",G
9ØØ REM
91Ø DATA 2,45,1,75,3,25,4,1ØØ,3,25
92Ø DATA 5,125,3,5Ø,1,5Ø,2,12Ø,2,4Ø
93Ø DATA 5,75,-1,-1
94Ø DATA FRED,JOANN,MARYJO,JERRY,BOB

RUN
NAME            AMOUNT COLLECTED
FRED            125
JOANN           2Ø5
MARYJO          1ØØ
JERRY           1ØØ
BOB             2ØØ
TOTAL           73Ø

READY
```

(frame 35–53)

8.

```
10 REM
20 REM
30 DIM K(10),R(10),N$(10)
40 REM
50 PRINT "NAME","SCORE" : PRINT
60 REM
70 FOR X=1 TO 10
80 READ K : K(X)=K
90 NEXT K
100 REM
110 READ N$ : IF N$="END" THEN END
120 FOR X=1 TO 10
130 READ R : R(X)=R : NEXT X
140 S=0
150 REM
160 FOR X=1 TO 10
170 IF K(X)<>R(X) THEN 190
180 S=S+1
190 NEXT
200 PRINT N$,S : GOTO 110
900 REM
910 DATA 3,4,3,3,5,1,2,3,2,1
920 REM
930 DATA DANNY,1,2,3,4,5,1,2,3,4,5
940 DATA KARL,1,3,2,4,1,2,3,2,1
950 DATA MIRIAM,3,2,2,1,4,1,2,3,1,2
960 DATA SCOTT,1,2,3,3,5,1,2,3,2,2
970 DATA END

RUN
NAME                SCORE
DANNY               5
KARL                5
MIRIAM              4
SCOTT               7
```

(frame 49–53)

9.

```
10 REM
20 DIM D(6)
30 FOR X=1 TO 6 : D(X)=0 : NEXT X
40 PRINT "HOW MANY SIMULATED ROLLS";
50 INPUT R
60 FOR X=1 TO R
70 N=INT(6*RND(1))+1 : D(N)=D(N)+1
80 NEXT X
90 PRINT "SPOTS","# OF OCCURENCES"
100 REM
110 FOR X=1 TO 6
120 PRINT X,D(X)
130 NEXT X

RUN
HOW MANY SIMULATED ROLLS?1000
SPOTS      # OF OCCURENCES
1          168
2          144
3          172
4          182
5          159
6          175
```

(frames 25–31)

CHAPTER EIGHT

Double Subscripts

In Chapter 7 you were introduced to singly-subscripted variables and their many applications. There are no new statements in this chapter, just some new uses and variations of what you already know.

In this chapter we'll extend your use of ATARI BASIC to variables with *two* subscripts, which we call doubly-subscripted variables. Doubly-subscripted variables are used with arrays of numbers which might require several columns and rows, such as in complex voter analysis problems, detailed dollar analysis problems, and a whole host of board game applications. When you complete this chapter, you will be able to:

- use variables with two subscripts;
- assign values to doubly-subscripted variables in a two-dimensional array (also called a table or matrix);
- use the DIM statement to tell the computer the dimensions of two-dimensional arrays.

1. In Chapter 7, we described subscripted variables such as X(7) and T(K). These are *singly-subscripted* variables. That is, each variable has exactly *one* subscript.

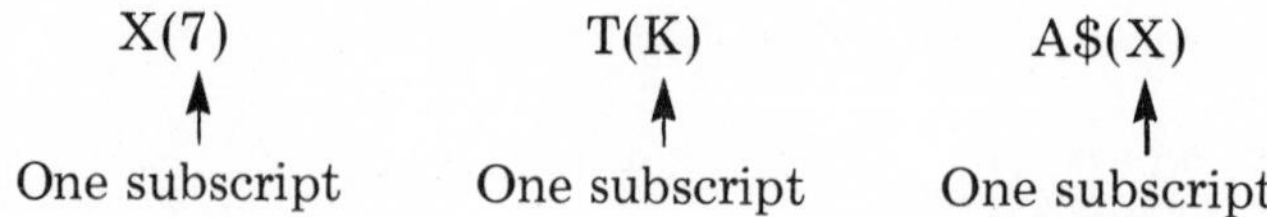

In this chapter, we will use *doubly-subscripted* variables, variables that have *two* subscripts.

T(2,3)

↑↑

Two subscripts,
separated by a comma

T(3) is a subscripted variable with how many subscripts? __________

T(7,5) is a subscripted variable with how many subscripts? __________

— — — — — — — — — — —

1; 2

2. It is convenient to think of doubly-subscripted variables arranged in an *array* of *rows* and *columns,* as shown below.

	Column 1	Column 2	Column 3	Column 4
Row 1	A(1,1) ☐	A(1,2) ☐	A(1,3) ☐	A(1,4) ☐
Row 2	A(2,1) ☐	A(2,2) ☐	A(2,3) ☐	A(2,4) ☐
Row 3	A(3,1) ☐	A(3,2) ☐	A(3,3) ☐	A(3,4) ☐

The above array has _______ rows and _______ columns.

— — — — — — — — — — —

3; 4

3. With the arrangement shown in frame 2, we can relate subscripts to particular places (locations, or "boxes" for values) in rows and columns. These are called the *elements* in the array. For example:

A(2,3)

↑↑

Row

Column

A(1,1) is in row 1, column 1. A(1,2) is in row 1, column 2. What subscripted variable is in row 3, column 2? __________

— — — — — — — — — — —

A(3,2)

4. The rectangular arrangement of doubly-subscripted variables shown in frame 2 is called a *table, matrix,* or *two-dimensional array.*

In Chapter 7 we described arrays of singly-subscripted variables which are also called *lists, vectors,* or *one-dimensional arrays.*

This is a *list*:	X(1)	X(2)	X(3)
This is a *table*:	C(1,1)	C(1,2)	C(1,3)
	C(2,1)	C(2,2)	C(2,3)
	C(3,1)	C(3,2)	C(3,3)

(a) A list is also called a ____________ or a ____________

(b) A table is also called a ____________ or a ____________.

— — — — — — — — — —

(a) vector, one-dimensional array (one subscript)
(b) matrix, two-dimensional array (two subscripts)

5. A doubly subscripted variable is simply the name of a location in the computer. As with any other variable, you can think of it as the name for a box, a place to store a number. Here is a table of doubly-subscripted variables.

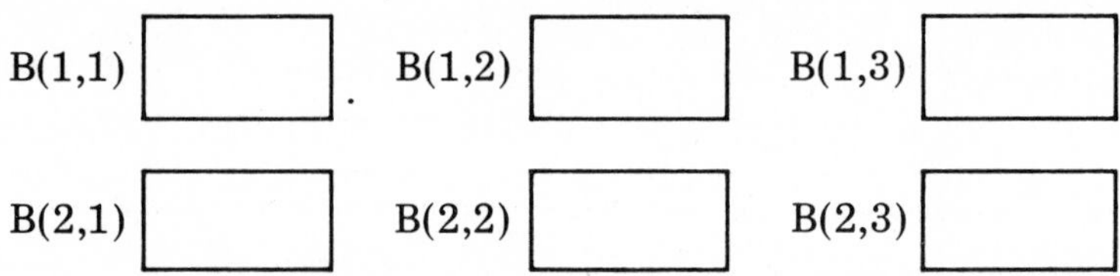

Pretend you are the computer and assign the value of 73 to variable B(2,1). In other words, take pencil in hand and write the number 73 in the box labeled B(2,1). Then do the same for the following.

```
LET B(1,3)=Ø
LET B(1,1)=49
LET B(2,3)=B(2,1) - B(1,1)
LET B(1,2)=2*B(2,1)
LET B(2,2)=INT(B(2,1)/B(2,3))
```

— — — — — — — — — —

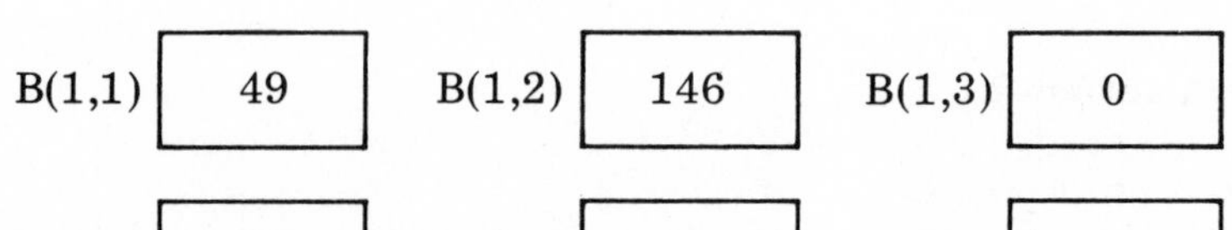

6. As we learned in Chapter 7, subscripts can be variables. The subscripted variable P(R,C) has variable subscripts.

If R = 1 and C = 2, then P(R,C) is P(1,2).

If R = 4 and C = 3, then P(R,C) is P(4,3).

If R = 7 and C = 5, then P(R,C) is ___________.

— — — — — — — — — — —

P(7,5)

7. Let's assume that the following values (in the boxes) have been assigned to the corresponding variables. Note that there are both simple and subscripted variables.

Variable	Value	Variable	Value	Variable	Value	Variable	Value
R	2	T(1,1)	7	T(1,2)	0	T(1,3)	−12
C	3	T(2,1)	9	T(2,2)	5	T(2,3)	8
A	1	T(3,1)	16	T(3,2)	13	T(3,3)	10
B	2						

Write the value of each variable below, and the value of subscripts.

T(2,3) = ______________________ T(1,1) = ______________________

R = ______________________ A = ______________________

C = ______________________ T(A,A) = ______________________

T(R,C) = ______________________ T(B,R) = ______________________

T(A,B) = ______________________ T(R,A) = ______________________

T(R+1,C−2) = ______________________

— — — — — — — — — — —

8 7
2 1
3 7
8 5
0 9
16 T(R+1,C−2) = T(2+1,3−2) = T(3,1)

8. Election time again. (Before starting on this, you may wish to review the vote-counting application in Chapter 7.) The questionnaire below requires two answers.

> Q1. Who will you vote for in the coming election? Circle the number to the left of your choice.
> 1. Sam Smoothe
> 2. Gabby Gruff
> 3. No opinion
>
> Q2. What age group are you in? Circle the number to the left of your age group.
> 1. Under 30
> 2. 30 or over

Since there are two questions, each reply consists of two numbers: the answer to question 1 and the answer to question 2. We will use V (for Vote) to represent the answer to question 1 and A (for Age) to represent the answer to question 2.

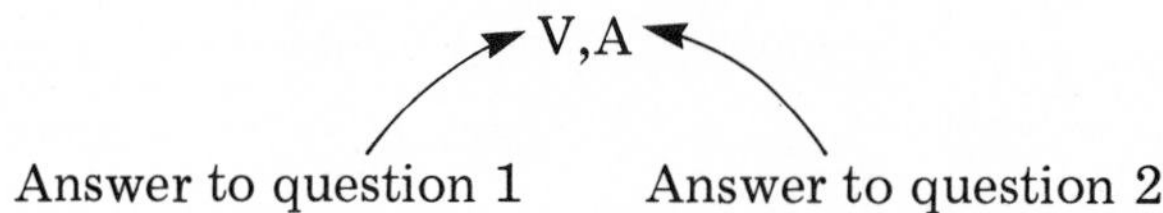

The possible values of V are 1, 2, or 3. What are the possible values of A?

____

— — — — — — — — — — —

1 or 2

9. We sent out some questionnaires. Some typical replies are shown below.

Reply	Meaning
1,1	one vote for Sam Smoothe, voter is under 30
1,2	one vote for Sam Smoothe, voter 30 or over
3,1	no opinion, voter is under 30

What does the reply 2,2 mean? ____________________________________

— — — — — — — — — — —

one vote for Gabby Gruff, voter is 30 or over

10. We want to write a program to summarize data for a two-question questionnaire. We will use subscripted variables to count votes as shown on the following page.

		Under 30		30 or over
Sam Smoothe	C(1,1)		C(1,2)	
Gabby Gruff	C(2,1)		C(2,2)	
No opinion	C(3,1)		C(3,2)	

In other words, C(1,1) will hold the count for Sam Smoothe by people under 30. C(1,2) will hold the total for Sam Smoothe by people 30 or over.

C(2,1) will hold the total for ______________________ by people

______________________.

What subscripted variable will hold the No opinion count for people 30 or over? ______________

— — — — — — — — — — — —

Gabby Gruff; under 30; C(3,2)

11. Here are 29 replies to our questionnaire. Remember, each reply is a *pair* of numbers and represents *one* vote. The first number of each pair is the answer to question 1. The second number of each pair is the answer to question 2.

3,1	2,2	3,2	1,2	1,2	2,1
2,2	1,1	1,2	3,1	3,2	2,2
3,1	2,1	2,2	1,1	1,1	1,2
1,1	2,1	2,1	1,2	2,1	3,1
2,1	3,1	2,1	3,1	2,2	

Write the appropriate count in each box below.

		Under 30		30 or over
Sam Smoothe	C(1,1)		C(1,2)	
Gabby Gruff	C(2,1)		C(2,2)	
No opinion	C(3,1)		C(3,2)	

— — — — — — — — — — —

C(1,1)	4	C(1,2)	5
C(2,1)	7	C(2,2)	5
C(3,1)	6	C(3,2)	2

12. Naturally, we want the computer to do the counting. Below is the beginning of our program.

```
100 REM***VOTE COUNTING, TWO QUESTIONS
110 DIM C(3,2)
```

The DIM statement (line 110) defines an array with at most 3 rows and 2 columns. That is, the DIM statement defines an array of doubly-subscripted variables in which the maximum value of the first subscript is 3 and the maximum value of the second subscript is 2. You must always DIM doubly-subscripted arrays or you'll get an error message.

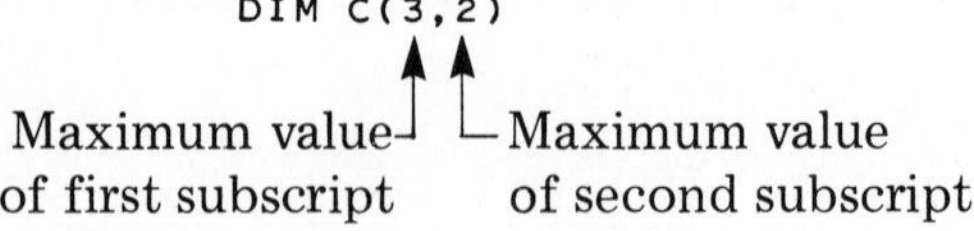

Next, we want to set all counts to zero. That is, we want to assign zero to C(1,1), C(1,2), and so on up to C(3,2). Even though other versions of BASIC might do this automatically, it is good programming practice to initialize every program. *You* complete this part of the program.

```
200 REM***INITIALIZE: SET ALL COUNTS TO ZERO
```

— — — — — — — — — — —

Here are four ways to do it!

Method 1

```
210 LET C(1,1)=0
220 LET C(1,2)=0
230 LET C(2,1)=0
240 LET C(2,2)=0
250 LET C(3,1)=0
260 LET C(3,2)=0
```

Method 2

```
210 FOR K=1 TO 3
220 LET C(K,1)=0
230 LET C(K,2)=0
240 NEXT K
```

Method 3

```
210 FOR K=1 TO 3
220 FOR L=1 TO 2
230 LET C(K,L)=0
240 NEXT L
250 NEXT K
```

Method 4

```
210 FOR K=1 TO 3 : FOR L=1 TO 2 : LET C(K,L)=0 : NEXT L : NEXT K
```

We will usually use Methods 3 and 4 because they are easily generalized to arrays of different sizes. Using Method 3, we can add more rows by changing line 210, more columns by changing line 220. (Of course, we would also have to change the DIM statement.)

13. The array is now set up. Let's READ and count the votes.

```
300 REM***READ AND COUNT VOTES
310 READ V,A : IF V=-1 THEN 410
320 LET C(V,A)=C(V,A)+1 : GOTO 310
```

Line 320 is the crucial vote-counting statement. It adds 1 (vote) to the array element specified by V and A. Suppose this is the array before executing lines 310 and 320.

C(1,1)	0	C(1,2)	4
C(2,1)	2	C(2,2)	7
C(3,1)	5	C(3,2)	0

Show how the array would look after this additional data was processed.

```
91Ø DATA 3,1,2,2,3,2,1,2
```

C(1,1)		C(1,2)	
C(2,1)		C(2,2)	
C(3,1)		C(3,2)	

— — — — — — — — — — —

C(1,1)	0	C(1,2)	5
C(2,1)	2	C(2,2)	8
C(3,1)	6	C(3,2)	1

14. Since line 310 is a READ statement, some DATA statements must be given somewhere. Here they are, featuring the data from frame 11.

```
9ØØ REM ** DATA IN PAIRS:
9Ø1 REM ** VOTE FOLLOWED BY AGE GROUP
91Ø DATA 3,1, 2,2, 3,2, 1,2, 1,2, 2,1
92Ø DATA 2,2, 1,1, 1,2, 3,1, 3,2, 2,2
93Ø DATA 3,1, 2,1, 2,2, 1,1, 1,1, 1,2
94Ø DATA 1,1, 2,1, 2,1, 1,2, 2,1, 3,1
95Ø DATA 2,1, 3,1, 2,1, 3,1, 2,2, -1,-1
```

Remember, each reply is a *pair* of numbers representing *one* vote. To emphasize this, we have typed a space after each reply (pair of values) in the DATA statements above. Why is the flag –1,–1 instead of just –1? ____________________

____

____

— — — — — — — — — — —

If the computer could not find a value for READ variable A as well as variable V in line 310, it would print a data error message and stop.

15. Only one task remains—print the results! For the data shown in frame 14, the results should look like the one on the following page when the program is RUN.

```
RUN
CAND.        UNDER 3Ø   3Ø +

SMOOTHE      4          5
GRUFF        7          5
NO OPIN      6          2
```

You do it. Complete the program segment to print the results—C(1,1), C(1,2), and so on—as shown above.

```
4ØØ REM***PRINT THE RESULTS
```

— — — — — — — — — —

We did it like this.

```
4ØØ REM ** PRINT THE RESULTS
41Ø PRINT "CAND.","UNDER 3Ø","3Ø +"
42Ø PRINT
43Ø PRINT "SMOOTHE",C(1,1),C(1,2)
44Ø PRINT "GRUFF",C(2,1),C(2,2)
45Ø PRINT "NO OPIN",C(3,1),C(3,2)
```

16. Here's a listing of the complete vote-counting program.

```
1ØØ REM ** VOTE COUNTING, 2 QUESTIONS
11Ø DIM C(3,2)
2ØØ REM ** INITIALIZE
21Ø FOR K=1 TO 3:FOR L=1 TO 2
22Ø C(K,L)=Ø
23Ø NEXT L:NEXT K
3ØØ REM ** READ AND COUNT DATA
31Ø READ V,A:IF V=-1 THEN 41Ø
32Ø C(V,A)=C(V,A)+1:GOTO 31Ø
4ØØ REM ** PRINT THE RESULTS
41Ø PRINT "CAND.","UNDER 3Ø","3Ø +"
42Ø PRINT
43Ø PRINT "SMOOTHE",C(1,1),C(1,2)
44Ø PRINT "GRUFF",C(2,1),C(2,2)
45Ø PRINT "NO OPIN",C(3,1),C(3,2)
9ØØ REM ** DATA IN PAIRS:
9Ø1 REM ** VOTE FOLLOWED BY AGE GROUP
91Ø DATA 3,1,2,2,3,2,1,2,1,2,2,1
92Ø DATA 2,2,1,1,1,2,3,1,3,2,2,2
93Ø DATA 3,1,2,1,2,2,1,1,1,1,1,2
94Ø DATA 1,1,2,1,2,1,1,2,2,1,3,1
95Ø DATA 2,1,3,1,2,1,3,1,2,2,-1,-1
```

Suppose the questionnaire had been the following.

> Q1. Who will you vote for in the coming election? Circle the number to the left of your choice.
> 1. Sam Smoothe
> 2. Gabby Gruff
> 3. No opinion
>
> Q2. What is your political affiliation? Circle the number to the left of your answer.
> 1. Democrat
> 2. Republican
> 3. Other

Modify the vote-counting program so that answers are counted as follows.

	Democrat	Republican	Other
Sam Smoothe	C(1,1)	C(1,2)	C(1,3)
Gabby Gruff	C(2,1)	C(2,2)	C(2,3)
No opinion	C(3,1)	C(3,2)	C(3,3)

You will have to change lines 110, 210, 410, 430, 440, and 450.

110 ______________________________

210 ______________________________

410 ______________________________

430 ______________________________

440 ______________________________

450 ______________________________

— — — — — — — — — — —

```
110 DIM C(3,3)
210 FOR K=1 TO 3:FOR L=1 TO 3
410 PRINT "CAND.","DEM.","REPUB.","OTHER"
420 PRINT
430 PRINT "SMOOTHE",C(1,1),C(1,2),C(1,3)
440 PRINT "GRUFF",C(2,1),C(2,2),C(2,3)
450 PRINT "NO OPIN.",C(3,1),C(3,2),C(3,3)
```

Note: Even though we changed the questionnaire, we didn't have to change the crucial vote-counting statement in line 320.

17. Here is a LISTing of the modified program and new DATA statements for the questionnaire in frame 16. You be the computer and print the output for the program when it is RUN.

```
100 REM ** VOTE COUNTING, 2 QUESTIONS
110 DIM C(3,2)
200 REM ** INITIALIZE
210 FOR K=1 TO 3:FOR L=1 TO 2
220 C(K,L)=0
230 NEXT L:NEXT K
300 REM ** READ AND COUNT DATA
310 READ V,A:IF V=-1 THEN 410
320 C(V,A)=C(V,A)+1:GOTO 310
400 REM ** PRINT THE RESULTS
410 PRINT "CAND.","DEM.","REPUB.","OTHER"
420 PRINT
430 PRINT "SMOOTHE",C(1,1),C(1,2),C(1,3)
440 PRINT "GRUFF",C(2,1),C(2,2),C(2,3)
450 PRINT "NO OPIN.",C(3,1),C(3,2),C(3,3)
900 REM ** DATA IN PAIRS:
901 REM ** VOTE FOLLOWED BY POLITICAL AFFILIATION
910 DATA 3,1,1,1,1,2,2,3,1,3,3,1,2,1
920 DATA 2,2,3,2,3,3,1,1,2,3,1,2,2,1
930 DATA 3,3,3,2,3,2,2,2,1,1,1,1,3,2
940 DATA 3,2,2,1,3,1,1,2,1,3,2,2,2,1
950 DATA 3,1,1,3,1,3,2,3,3,3,1,2,1,3
960 DATA 2,3,2,1,3,1,1,2,3,3,2,3,2,1
970 DATA 3,1,3,3,-1,-1

RUN
```

```
CAND.        DEM.     REPUB.     OTHER

SMOOTHE      4        5          5
GRUFF        6        3          5
NO OPIN.     6        5          5
```

18. Look at this section of the program.

```
43Ø PRINT "SMOOTHE",C(1,1),C(1,2),C(1,3)
44Ø PRINT "GRUFF",C(2,1),C(2,2),C(2,3)
45Ø PRINT "NO OPIN.",C(3,1),C(3,2),C(3,3)
```

We have used the subscripted variables with the actual numerical values for the subscripts. Instead, we could have used a FOR-NEXT loop to print the results for each candidate and no opinion, and could do this using just three multiple-statement lines. Think about it carefully, then rewrite lines 430, 440, and 450 so that FOR-NEXT loops are used to print the values stored in the C array. The RUN should look exactly as it did before.

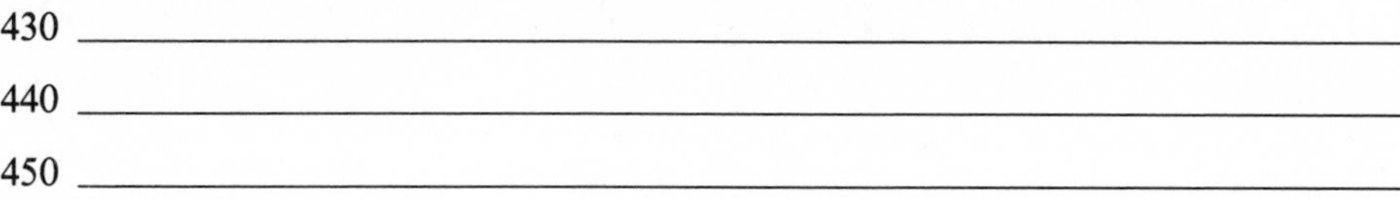

430 ______

440 ______

450 ______

```
43Ø PRINT "SMOOTHE", : FOR X=1 TO 3 : PRINT C(1,X), : NEXT : PRINT
44Ø PRINT "GRUFF", : FOR X=1 TO 3 : PRINT C(2,X), : NEXT : PRINT
45Ø PRINT "NO OPIN", : FOR X=1 TO 3 : PRINT C(3,X), : NEXT
```

Note that a PRINT statement must end lines 430 and 440. You must use PRINT to tell the computer to start a new line at character position 0. Also, the above program lines will each occupy more than one line on your display.

19. Do you remember the problem on counting candy bars? You might want to review it in Chapter 7 before we go on.

Before, we were selling one chocolate candy bar for $1.00, on which the profit was $.55. Now let's add another product—a bag of jelly beans which sells for $.50, on which we profit $.30. Our job is to re-program our computer to tabulate individual sales and overall profits. Here's the report we'd like to produce.

```
RUN
KID ID #    TOTAL $     CHOC        J.BEANS
1           Ø           Ø           Ø
2           3           3           Ø
3           Ø           Ø           Ø
4           6           3           6
5           1Ø          6           8
6           Ø           Ø           Ø
7           Ø           Ø           Ø
8           12          6           12
TOTALS:     31          18          26
PROFITS:    17.7        9.9         7.8
```

(a) From the report above, who had the greatest overall dollar sales? ______

(b) Who sold the most chocolate bars? ______

(c) The most jelly beans? ______

(d) Can you tell who made us the most profit? ______

(a) 8 (c) 8
(b) 5 and 8 (d) not directly from the report. (It's number 8.)

20. For recordkeeping purposes we will prepare some preprinted forms to keep track of who takes what. Now, when one of the kids asks for candy we fill in a form like the one on the following page.

Name	Danny
ID No.	4
1. Milk Chocolate	3
2. Jelly Beans	6

This shows that Danny (number 4) took 3 chocolate bars and 6 bags of jelly beans. When we convert that into computer data we use this format.

kid number, candy number (1 or 2), quantity

Thus, to show the data on this one slip requires 6 data items.

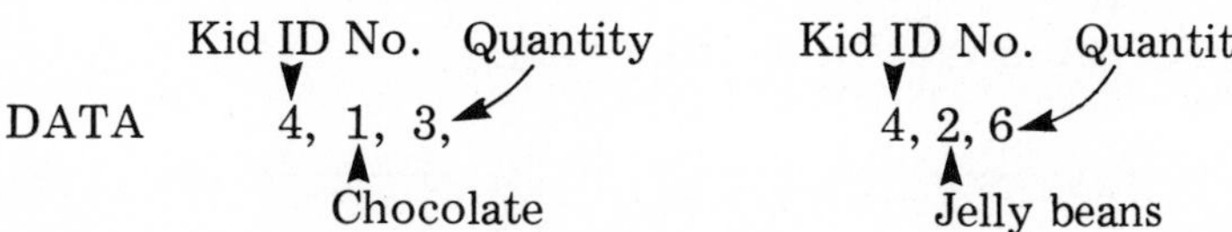

(Notice how we designed the form to conform to our system of data entry!)

From the three forms below, complete the DATA statements. Include end-of-data flags.

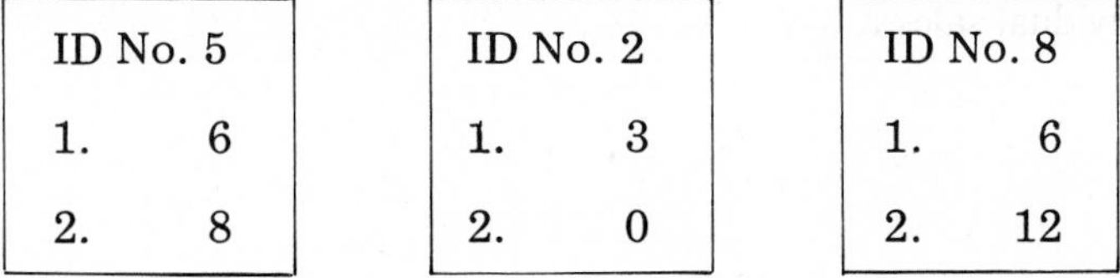

ID No. 5	
1.	6
2.	8

ID No. 2	
1.	3
2.	0

ID No. 8	
1.	6
2.	12

```
900 REM***KID ID NUMBER, CANDY ID NUMBER, QUANTITY
910 DATA 4,1,3, 4,2,6
920 ____________________________________________
930 ____________________________________________
```

This data is not even necessary, since this kid didn't take any jelly beans to sell.

```
920 DATA 5,1,6, 5,2,8, 2,1,3, 2,2,0
930 DATA 8,1,6, 8,2,12, -1,-1,-1
```

← End-of-data flag

21. Our array will look like this.

Array A.	1 = chocolate	2 = jelly beans
1 = Jerry		
2 = Bobby		
3 = Mary		
4 = Danny		
5 = Karl		
6 = Mimi		
7 = Doug		
8 = Scott		

Here is another way to visualize the same A-array.

A		A	
(1,1)		(1,2)	
(2,1)		(2,2)	
(3,1)		(3,2)	
(4,1)		(4,2)	
(5,1)		(5,2)	
(6,1)		(6,2)	
(7,1)		(7,2)	
(8,1)		(8,2)	

Your first task is to write the statement(s) to initialize the array and zero it out, that is, set the dimensions and set the values for all the variables to zero. Don't forget the zero element. We'll be using it, too!

```
1ØØ REM***CANDY BAR & JELLY BEAN COUNTER
11Ø REM***INITIALIZE

12Ø ______________________________________

13Ø ______________________________________

14Ø ______________________________________

15Ø ______________________________________
```

— — — — — — — — — —

```
12Ø DIM A(8,2)
13Ø FOR X=Ø TO 8:FOR Y=Ø TO 2
14Ø A(X,Y)=Ø
15Ø NEXT Y:NEXT X
```

22. Now READ a set of data (K,C,Q) and test for the end-of-data condition. When you encounter the end-of-data flag, jump to line 310.

```
2ØØ REM***READ DATA AND TEST FOR FLAG

21Ø ______________________________________
```

— — — — — — — — — —

```
21Ø READ K,C,Q : IF K=-1 THEN 31Ø
```

23. The heart of this program is found in line 220, where the "accumulation" takes place.

```
22Ø A(K,C)=A(K,C)+Q : GOTO 21Ø
```

(GOTO 21Ø ← Go back and read some more.)

K is the kid ID number, C is the candy number (1 = chocolate, 2 = jelly beans), and Q is the quantity. Assume we have the following DATA.

```
91Ø DATA 4,1,3
```

(a) The value of what array element (subscripted variable) will be increased?

____

(b) By how much will it be increased? _______

— — — — — — — — — —

(a) A(4,1)
(b) 3

24. If the array looked like this before:

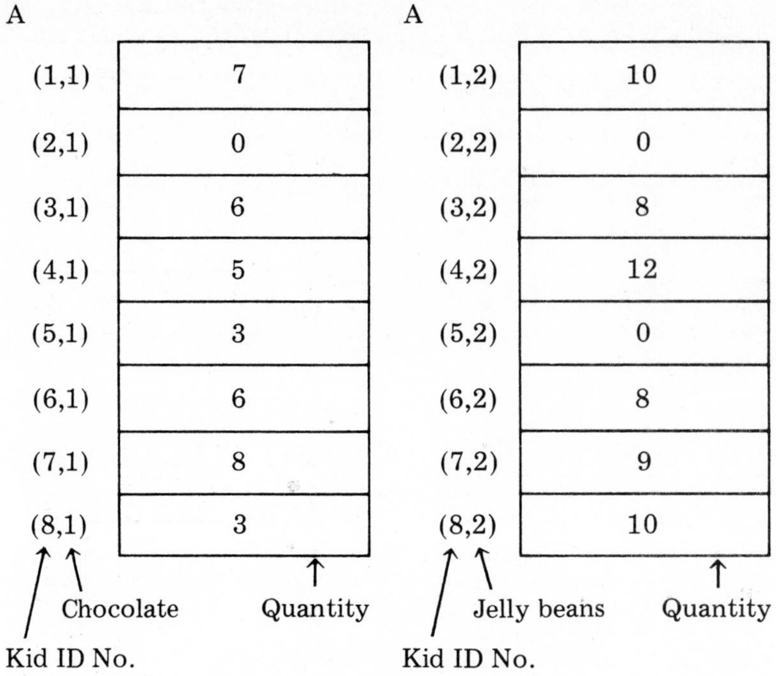

A	Chocolate Quantity	A	Jelly beans Quantity
(1,1)	7	(1,2)	10
(2,1)	0	(2,2)	0
(3,1)	6	(3,2)	8
(4,1)	5	(4,2)	12
(5,1)	3	(5,2)	0
(6,1)	6	(6,2)	8
(7,1)	8	(7,2)	9
(8,1)	3	(8,2)	10

(Kid ID No., Chocolate, Quantity; Kid ID No., Jelly beans, Quantity)

How will it look *after* accumulating the data in these DATA statements?

```
910 DATA 4,1,3, 4,2,6
920 DATA 5,1,6, 5,2,8, 2,1,3, 2,2,0
930 DATA 8,1,6, 8,2,12
```

A		A	
(1,1)		(1,2)	
(2,1)		(2,2)	
(3,1)		(3,2)	
(4,1)		(4,2)	
(5,1)		(5,2)	
(6,1)		(6,2)	
(7,1)		(7,2)	
(8,1)		(8,2)	

— — — — — — — — — — — —

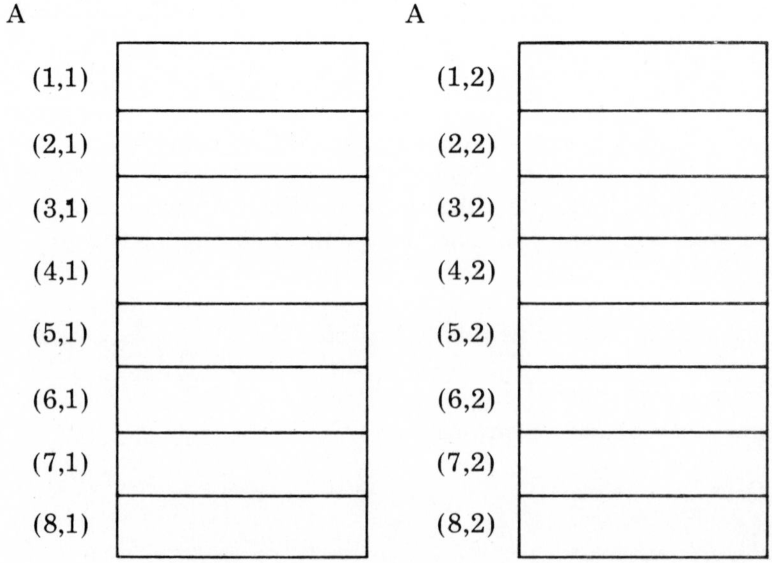

A		A	
(1,1)	7	(1,2)	10
(2,1)	3	(2,2)	0
(3,1)	6	(3,2)	8
(4,1)	8	(4,2)	18
(5,1)	9	(5,2)	8
(6,1)	6	(6,2)	8
(7,1)	8	(7,2)	9
(8,1)	9	(8,2)	22

25. Here is our program, so far.

```
100 REM ** CANDY COUNTER
110 REM ** INITIALIZE
120 DIM A(8,2)
130 FOR X=0 TO 8:FOR Y=0 TO 2
140 A(X,Y)=0
150 NEXT Y:NEXT X
200 REM ** READ DATA & TEST FOR FLAG
210 READ K,C,Q:IF K=-1 THEN 310
220 A(K,C)=A(K,C)+Q:GOTO 210

910 DATA 4,1,3, 4,2,6
920 DATA 5,1,6, 5,2,8, 2,1,3, 2,2,0
930 DATA 8,1,6, 8,2,12, -1,-1,-1
```

Now let's print a preliminary report like the one in frame 19, but without any totals. You fill in the blanks in the program on the following page. This is how the report should look when the program is RUN.

```
RUN
KID ID #    CHOC        J.BEANS
1           0           0

2           3           0

3           0           0

4           3           6

5           6           8

6           0           0

7           0           0

8           6           12
```

```
400 REM***REPORT #1

410 PRINT "KID ID #"________________________________

420 FOR K=1 TO 8

430 PRINT K,  <----------------- The comma is important.

440 FOR C=1 TO__________

450 PRINT________________,  <---------- The comma is important.

460 NEXT C

470 PRINT

480 NEXT__________
```

— — — — — — — — — —

```
410 PRINT "KID ID #", "CHOC", "J.BEANS"
440 FOR C=1 TO 2
450 PRINT A(K,C),
480 NEXT K
```

26. In frame 25, why are the commas placed at the end of lines 430 and 450?

____

— — — — — — — — — —

to suppress the normal carriage return after the PRINT (that is, to keep the computer output on the same line)

27. Why did we include line 470 PRINT where we did? ______________

____

____

— — — — — — — — — —

to force a carriage return (start a new line of display), so the next KID ID No. will be printed in the correct place or position when line 420 is executed again.

28. Running our program now gives these results.

```
RUN
KID ID #    CHOC        J.BEANS
1           Ø           Ø

2           3           Ø

3           Ø           Ø

4           3           6

5           6           8

6           Ø           Ø

7           Ø           Ø

8           6           12
```

Now, let's complete the program so it will print everything shown in frame 19.

When we DIMensioned our array DIM (8,2) it included the 0,0 elements shown below. We are going to use these zero elements to accumulate totals.

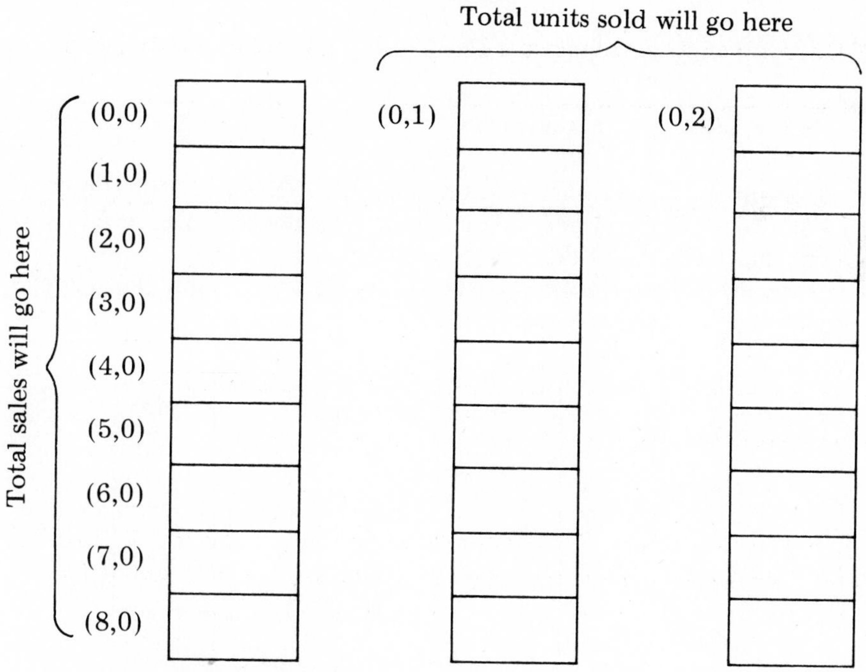

Total units sold will go here

(0,0) (0,1) (0,2)

(1,0)

(2,0)

(3,0)

(4,0)

(5,0)

(6,0)

(7,0)

(8,0)

Total sales will go here

You fill in the blank lines in the program on the following page. Line 120 is fixed to set all array elements (boxes) to zero, starting at the 0,0 element. Line 320 adds the total sales per kid (remember, jelly beans sell for $.50 per bag). And line 350 adds units sold.

```
100 REM ** CANDY COUNTER
110 REM ** INITIALIZE
120 DIM A(8,2)
130 FOR X=Ø TO 8:FOR Y=Ø TO 2
140 A(X,Y)=Ø
150 NEXT Y:NEXT X
200 REM ** READ DATA & TEST FOR FLAG
210 READ K,C,Q:IF K=-1 THEN 310
220 A(K,C)=A(K,C)+Q:GOTO 210
300 REM ** TOTAL OF UNITS SOLD AND
301 REM ** TOTAL OF SALES IN DOLLARS

310 FOR K=1 TO ______________
320 A(K,Ø)=A(K,1)*1.ØØ+A(K,2)*.5Ø
330 A(Ø,Ø)=A(Ø,Ø)+A(K,Ø)

340 FOR C= ______________________

350 A(Ø,C)=A(Ø,C)+A(K,________)

360 NEXT C : _____________
370 REM ** CALCULATE PROFITS

380 P1=A(Ø,1)*.55 : P2=______________
390 P=P1+P2
```

— — — — — — — — — — —

```
310 FOR K=1 TO 8
340 FOR C=1 TO 2
350 A(Ø,C)=A(Ø,C)+A(K,C)
360 NEXT C : NEXT K
380 P1=A(Ø,1)*.55 : P2=A(Ø,2)*.3Ø
```

29. Did you understand what went on in lines 320, 330, and 350? If not, go back and review the problem a little more. These statements are *crucial* for your complete understanding of this type of problem.

Write the *line numbers* in the labeled boxes below to show which lines generate values for those boxes.

		(0,1)		(0,2)	
(0,0)					
(1,0)					
(2,0)					
(3,0)					
(4,0)					
(5,0)					
(6,0)					
(7,0)					
(8,0)					

— — — — — — — — — — —

(0,0)	330	(0,1)	350	(0,2)	350
(1,0)	320				
(2,0)	320				
(3,0)	320				
(4,0)	320				
(5,0)	320				
(6,0)	320				
(7,0)	320				
(8,0)	320				

30. In frame 28, what does line 330 do?

```
33Ø A(Ø,Ø)=A(Ø,Ø)+A(K,Ø)
```

____

— — — — — — — — — — —

accumulate grand total sales in A(0,0)

31. In line 390, how would you describe what the statement P = P1 + P2 accomplishes?

```
39Ø P = P1 + P2
```

____

____

— — — — — — — — — — —

computes total profits and assigns them to variable P

32. Time to redo our report printing section to update *everything* shown in the RUN on the following page (the same RUN as in frame 19). Fill in the blanks.

```
RUN
KID ID #   TOTAL $    CHOC       J.BEANS
1          Ø          Ø          Ø

2          3          3          Ø

3          Ø          Ø          Ø

4          6          3          6

5          1Ø         6          8

6          Ø          Ø          Ø

7          Ø          Ø          Ø

8          12         6          12

TOTALS:    31         18         26

PROFITS:   17.7       9.9        7.8
```

```
4ØØ REM ** PRINT REPORT
41Ø PRINT "KID ID #"______________________
42Ø FOR K=1 TO 8

43Ø PRINT______________

44Ø FOR C=______________

45Ø PRINT A______________

46Ø NEXT C :______________

47Ø NEXT K
48Ø PRINT "TOTALS:",A(Ø,Ø ),A(Ø,1),A(Ø,2)

49Ø PRINT "PROFITS:"______________________
```

— — — — — — — — — —

```
4ØØ REM ** PRINT REPORT
41Ø PRINT "KID ID #","TOTAL $","CHOC","J
.BEANS"
42Ø FOR K=1 TO 8
43Ø PRINT K,
44Ø FOR C=Ø TO 2
45Ø PRINT A(K,C),
46Ø NEXT C:PRINT
47Ø NEXT K
48Ø PRINT "TOTALS:",A(Ø,Ø),A(Ø,1),A(Ø,2)

49Ø PRINT :PRINT "PROFITS:",P,P1,P2
```

Now the program is done and the RUN should look just like the one above. On the following page is a complete listing of the program.

```
100 REM ** CANDY COUNTER
110 REM ** INITIALIZE
120 DIM A(8,2)
130 FOR X=0 TO 8:FOR Y=0 TO 2
140 A(X,Y)=0
150 NEXT Y:NEXT X
200 REM ** READ DATA & TEST FOR FLAG
210 READ K,C,Q:IF K=-1 THEN 310
220 A(K,C)=A(K,C)+Q:GOTO 210
300 REM ** TOTAL OF UNITS SOLD AND
301 REM ** TOTAL OF SALES IN DOLLARS
310 FOR K=1 TO 8
320 A(K,0)=A(K,1)*1+A(K,2)*0.5
330 A(0,0)=A(0,0)+A(K,0)
340 FOR C=1 TO 2
350 A(0,C)=A(0,C)+A(K,C)
360 NEXT C:NEXT K
370 REM ** CALCULATE PROFITS
380 P1=A(0,1)*0.55:P2=A(0,2)*0.3
390 P=P1+P2
400 REM ** PRINT REPORT
410 PRINT "KID ID #","TOTAL $","CHOC","J
.BEANS"
420 FOR K=1 TO 8
430 PRINT K,
440 FOR C=0 TO 2
450 PRINT A(K,C),
460 NEXT C:PRINT
470 NEXT K
480 PRINT "TOTALS:",A(0,0),A(0,1),A(0,2)

490 PRINT :PRINT "PROFITS:",P,P1,P2
910 DATA 4,1,3, 4,2,6
920 DATA 5,1,6, 5,2,8, 2,1,3, 2,2,0
930 DATA 8,1,6, 8,2,12, -1,-1,-1
```

32. Here is one final double array application. In a small class of 8 students, each student has taken 4 quizzes. The scores are shown below.

	Quiz 1	Quiz 2	Quiz 3	Quiz 4
Student 1	65	57	71	75
Student 2	80	90	91	88
Student 3	78	82	77	86
Student 4	45	38	44	46
Student 5	83	82	79	85
Student 6	70	68	83	59
Student 7	98	92	100	97
Student 8	85	73	80	77

Let S(B,J) be the score obtained by student B on quiz J. S(5,2) is the score obtained by student ____ on quiz ____. What is the value of S(5,2)? ____

— — — — — — — — — — —

5; 2; 82

33. Another class might have 30 students and 5 quizzes per student. Still another class might have 23 students and 7 quizzes per student, and so on. Let's begin a program to read scores for N students and Q quizzes per student.

```
100 REM ** QUIZ-SCORE PROGRAM
110 DIM S(30,10)
```

The DIM statement permits up to _______ students and up to _________ quizzes.

— — — — — — — — — — — —

30; 10

34. Next, we want to read the values of N and Q for a particular set of scores—in this case, the scores shown in frame 32. For this set of scores the value of N (number of students) is _______ and the value of Q (number of quizzes) is _______.

— — — — — — — — — — — —

8; 4

35. We will put the values of N and Q and the scores in DATA statements. Now the program looks like this.

```
100 REM ** QUIZ-SCORE PROGRAM
110 DIM S(30,10)

900 REM ** LINE 910:VALUES OF N AND Q
910 DATA 8,4  <---------------------- Values of N,Q
919 REM ** SCORES
920 DATA 65,57,71,75     }
930 DATA 80,90,91,88     }
940 DATA 78,82,77,86     }
950 DATA 45,38,44,46     }--- N by Q array of quiz scores from frame 32
960 DATA 83,82,79,85     }
970 DATA 70,68,83,59     }
980 DATA 98,92,100,97    }
990 DATA 85,73,80,77     }
```

Your turn. Complete line 120, below, to READ the values of N and Q.

120 ____________________

— — — — — — — — — — — —

`120 READ N,Q` (That's all there is to it!)

36. The values of N and Q read by line 120 (in frame 35) will be read from which DATA statement? Line ________.

— — — — — — — — — —

910

37. Now let's read the N by Q array of scores using FOR-NEXT loops. Fill in the blanks.

```
13Ø FOR X=1 TO N: FOR Y=______;READ______NEXT Y:NEXT X
```

— — — — — — — — — —

```
13Ø FOR X=1 TO N:FOR Y=1 TO Q:READ S(X,Y):NEXT Y:NEXT X
```

38. The numerical values read by line 130 are stored in the DATA statements, lines ________ through ________.

— — — — — — — — — —

920; 990

39. Now that we have the array in the computer, what shall we do with it? One thing someone might want is the average score for each student. Let's do it, beginning at line 200.

```
2ØØ REM ** COMPUTE & PRINT AVERAGES
21Ø PRINT "STUD. #","AVERAGE"
22Ø FOR B=1 TO N   ┐
23Ø LET T=Ø        │
24Ø FOR J=1 TO Q   ├── Compute total of quiz scores for student B
25Ø LET T=T+S(B,J) │
26Ø NEXT J         ┘
27Ø LET A=T/Q  <───── Compute average for student B
28Ø PRINT B,A  <───── Print student number and average
29Ø NEXT B     <───── Go back and compute scores for next student
```

Lines 230 through 280 are done for each student. That is, for B=1, then B=2, and so on up to B=N. For B=1, what is the value of T computed by lines 230 through 260? T=________.

— — — — — — — — — —

268. This is the sum of the 4 scores for student 1. Remember, Q=4. Therefore, line 250 will be done for J=1, J=2, J=3, and J=4.

40. For B = 1, what is the value of A computed by line 270?

A = T/Q = ________________________.

— — — — — — — — — — —

67. A = T/Q = 268/4 = 67.

41. Here is the complete program and a RUN.

```
100 REM ** QUIZ-SCORE PROGRAM
110 DIM S(30,10)
120 READ N,Q
130 FOR X=1 TO N:FOR Y=1 TO Q
140 READ S:S(X,Y)=S
150 NEXT Y:NEXT X
200 REM ** COMPUTE & PRINT AVERAGES
210 PRINT "STUD. #","AVERAGE"
220 FOR B=1 TO N
230 T=0
240 FOR J=1 TO Q
250 T=T+S(B,J)
260 NEXT J
270 A=T/Q
280 PRINT B,A
290 NEXT B
900 REM ** LINE 910:VALUES OF N AND Q
910 DATA 8,4
919 REM ** SCORES
920 DATA 65,57,71,75
930 DATA 80,90,91,88
940 DATA 78,82,77,86
950 DATA 45,38,44,46
960 DATA 83,82,79,85
970 DATA 70,68,83,59
980 DATA 98,92,100,97
990 DATA 85,73,80,77
```

```
RUN
STUD. #         AVERAGE
1               67
2               87.25
3               80.75
4               43.25
5               82.25
6               70
7               96.75
8               78.75
```

Your turn. Beginning with line 300, write a program segment to compute and print the average score for each quiz. For the data used in the program, the results might look like this.

```
RUN
QUIZ #          AVERAGE
1               75.5
2               72.75
3               78.125
4               76.625
```

— — — — — — — — — —

```
300 REMARK COMPUTE AND PRINT AVERAGE OF EACH QUIZ
310 PRINT "QUIZ #","AVERAGE"
320 FOR J=1 TO Q
330 LET T=0
340 FOR B=1 TO N
350 LET T=T+S(B,J)
360 NEXT B
370 LET A=T/N
380 PRINT J,A
390 NEXT J
```

42. Suppose some students take a multiple-choice quiz, 10 questions with four possible answers per question. We want to know how many students gave answer number 1 to question number 1, how many gave answer number 2 to question number 1, and so on.

Here are the answers given by 7 students. Each set of answers is in a DATA statement. The last DATA statement is a "fictitious student" and really means "end of data."

```
900 REM ** STUDENT ANSWERS TO QUIZ
910 DATA 2,3,1,1,1,2,4,3,4,1
920 DATA 2,3,2,4,1,2,4,2,1,1
930 DATA 2,3,2,4,1,2,4,2,1,1
940 DATA 3,2,4,1,1,2,3,3,4,1
950 DATA 2,3,4,1,1,3,4,3,4,1
960 DATA 2,1,2,3,1,2,4,3,4,2
970 DATA 3,4,1,1,1,4,3,1,4,2
980 DATA -1,0,0,0,0,0,0,0,0,0
```

In each line of data, the first number is the answer to question 1, the second number is the answer to question 2, and so on.

"Fictitious student"

Student 1 (line 910) gave answer 1 to question 3. Student 5 (line 950) gave answer ________ to question 9. Student 7 (line 970) gave answer ________ to question 1.

— — — — — — — — — —

4; 3

43. Complete the following table showing the number of students giving each answer (1, 2, 3, or 4) to questions 1, 2, and 3.

	Answer 1	Answer 2	Answer 3	Answer 4
Question 1	0	5	2	0
Question 2	1	1	______	______
Question 3	______	______	______	______

— — — — — — — — — —

		4	1
2	3	0	2

44. In frame 43, with your help, we have shown how the 7 students answered the first 3 questions. The totals look like a 3 by 4 array. If we had continued for all 10 questions the totals would have looked like a __________ by 4 array.

— — — — — — — — — —

10

45. Let's define an array T with 10 rows and 4 columns to hold the totals. Complete the following DIM statement.

```
100 REM***QUIZ ANALYSIS PROGRAM
110 DIM________________
```

— — — — — — — — — —

```
110 DIM T(10,4)
```

46. For each student there are 10 answers. Let's define a *list* of answers A(1) through A(10). Complete the following DIM statement.

```
120 DIM________________
```

— — — — — — — — — —

```
120 DIM A(10)
```

47. We can save space by *combining* the two DIM statements into one DIM statement.

```
110 DIM T(10,4),A(10)
```

The above DIM statement defines a ______________________ called T with at most 10 rows and 4 columns, and a ______________________ called A with at most 10 members.

— — — — — — — — — —

two-dimensional array, matrix or table
one-dimensional array, list, or vector

Note that a comma is used to separate T(10,4) and A(10).

48. Here is the beginning of a program to read the students' answers and compute the totals array.

```
100 REM***QUIZ ANALYSIS PROGRAM
110 DIM T(10,4),A(10)
```

Next, we want to initialize the totals array. That is, we want it to be a *zero* array. You do it.

```
120 REM ** INITIALIZE
130 ______________________
140 ______________________
150 ______________________
```

— — — — — — — — — —

```
120 REM ** INITIALIZE
130 FOR X=1 TO 10:FOR Y=1 TO 4
140 T(X,Y)=0
150 NEXT Y:NEXT X
```

49. Write a statement to read the *list* A of answers for one student.

```
200 REM ** READ ONE SET OF ANSWERS
210 ______________________
220 ______________________
230 ______________________
```

— — — — — — — — — —

```
200 REM ** READ ONE SET OF ANSWERS
210 FOR X=1 TO 10
220 READ A:A(X)=A
230 NEXT X
```

50. Now, is this a real student or a fictitious student? Recall that a fictitious student signals the end of data. If this is the case we want to print the answers, beginning with line 510. Complete the IF-THEN statement.

```
140 REM***CHECK FOR END OF DATA

250 IF________________THEN 510
```

— — — — — — — — — — —

A(1)= -1

51. If the data are for a real student, we want to update the running tally in the T array. We did it this way.

```
300 REM ** UPDATE THE TOTALS ARRAY
310 FOR Q=1 TO 10
320 T(Q,A(Q))=T(Q,A(Q))+1
330 NEXT Q
```

Here are the answers for one student. These are the values of A(1) through A(10).

2,3,1,1,1,2,4,3,4,1

Suppose Q=1. Then A(Q)=________ and T(Q,A(Q)) is T(________,________).

— — — — — — — — — — —

2; T(1,2) (since Q=1 and A(Q)=2)

52. In the above case (frame 51), what happens when the computer obeys line 320?____

— — — — — — — — — — —

The total in T(1,2) is increased by one. (It's just like counting votes!)

53. Since line 320 is in a FOR-NEXT loop, it will be done for each value of Q specified by the FOR statement. That is, it will be done for Q=1, 2, 3, 4, 5, 6, 7, 8, 9, and 10. When Q=10, which element of the T matrix is increased by one? T(________,________).

— — — — — — — — — — —

T(10,A(10)) or T(10,1) for the data in frame 51.

54. Let's move on. After tallying the answers for one student, we want the computer to return to line 210 and read another set of answers. (See frame 49.)

```
400 REM**ANOTHER SET OF ANSWERS
410 GOTO 210
```

Then the IF-THEN statement (frame 50) is encountered again. The IF-THEN statement causes the computer to go to line 510 if a fictitious student has been read. In that case, we want to print the headings and results, then stop.

Here is what the RUN should look like:

```
RUN
      A#1     A#2        A#3          A#4
S#3    0       5          2            0

S#2    1       1          4            1

S#3    2       3          0            2

S#4    4       0          1            2

S#5    7       0          0            0

S#6    0       5          1            1

S#7    0       0          2            5

S#8    1       2          4            0

S#9    2       0          0            5

S#10    5       2          0            0
```

Complete this section of the program.

```
500 REM ** PRINT THE TOTALS ARRAY
501 REM ** A#=ANSWER NUMBER
502 REM ** S#=STUDENT NUMBER
510 PRINT "    A#1","    A#2","    A#3",
"    A#4"
520 FOR X=1 TO 10:PRINT "S#";X;" ";

530 ____________________________________________

540 ____________________________________________
```

— — — — — — — — — — —

```
530 FOR Y=1 TO 4:PRINT T(X,Y),
540 NEXT Y:PRINT :NEXT X
```

Here is a complete listing of the program.

```
100 REM ** QUIZ ANALYSIS PROGRAM
110 DIM T(10,4),A(10)
120 REM ** INITIALIZE
130 FOR X=1 TO 10:FOR Y=1 TO 4
140 T(X,Y)=0
150 NEXT Y:NEXT X
200 REM ** READ ONE SET OF ANSWERS
210 FOR X=1 TO 10
220 READ A:A(X)=A
230 NEXT X
240 REM ** CHECK FOR END OF DATA
250 IF A(1)=-1 THEN 510
300 REM ** UPDATE THE TOTALS ARRAY
310 FOR Q=1 TO 10
320 T(Q,A(Q))=T(Q.A(Q))+1
330 NEXT Q
400 REM ** ANOTHER SET OF ANSWERS
410 GOTO 210
500 REM ** PRINT THE TOTALS ARRAY
501 REM ** A#=ANSWER NUMBER
502 REM ** S#=STUDENT NUMBER
510 PRINT "    A#1","    A#2","    A#3",
"    A#4"
520 FOR X=1 TO 10:PRINT "S#";X;" ";
530 FOR Y=1 TO 4:PRINT T(X,Y),
540 NEXT Y:PRINT :NEXT X
900 REM ** STUDENT ANSWERS TO QUIZ
910 DATA 2,3,1,1,1,2,4,3,4,1
920 DATA 2,3,2,4,1,2,4,2,1,1
930 DATA 2,3,2,4,1,2,4,2,1,1
940 DATA 3,2,4,1,1,2,3,3,4,1
950 DATA 2,3,4,1,1,3,4,3,4,1
960 DATA 2,1,2,3,1,2,4,3,4,2
970 DATA 3,4,1,1,1,4,3,1,4,2
980 DATA -1,0,0,0,0,0,0,0,0,0,
```

SELF-TEST

Good for you! You have reached the Chapter 8 Self-Test. These problems will help you review the BASIC instructions you have learned for dealing with arrays of numbers, using variables with double subscripts.

1. Indicate which of the following are legal BASIC doubly-subscripted variables.

   _____ (a) X(2+2) _____ (b) X(5,5)

   _____ (c) X1(100,100) _____ (d) X(A+B,C)

   _____ (e) X(X(1,2),X(2,1)) _____ (f) X(A,A)

Questions 2 through 7 refer to the following array A.

	Column 1	Column 2
Row 1	1	2
Row 2	3	4
Row 3	5	6

2. What are the dimensions of A? _______,_______

3. Write a DIMension statement for A, using line number 100.

   100 ____________________

4. What variable locates the "box" in row 3, column 2 of A? __________

5. What is the value of the following?

   (a) A(1,1) _________ (b) A(3,1) _________

6. Let X = 2, Y = 3. What is the value of:

   (a) A(X,X) _________ (b) A(X + 1,Y–1) _________

7. What is the value of A(A(1,2),A(2,1)–1)? _______________

8. Write a program which uses two FOR-NEXT loops to fill a 10 by 10 array (M) with zeros.

9. Your city officials seek to conduct a census of the citizenry. Among other things, they want to analyze the age and sex breakdown of the community. They ask you to program your home computer to take data from the form below and prepare a report like the RUN shown.

CITY CENSUS REPORT
DATA FORM
(check one box for each question)

Question one — Age Group	Question two — Sex
☐ 1. less than 10	☐ 1. male
☐ 2. 10-15	☐ 2. female
☐ 3. 16-21	
☐ 4. 22-30	
☐ 5. 31-40	
☐ 6. 41-50	
☐ 7. 51-65	
☐ 8. over 65	

Use the following DATA statements in your program.

```
900 REM ** DATA: BY AGE GROUP, SEX
910 DATA 1,2,2,1,3,2,4,1,5,2,6,2,7,2
920 DATA 8,1,1,2,1,1,2,1,2,2,3,1,3,1
930 DATA 3,2,3,1,3,2,4,1,4,2,5,1,5,1
940 DATA 5,2,5,2,6,1,6,2,7,1,7,2,7,2
950 DATA 7,2,8,1,8,1,8,2,8,2,3,1,4,2
960 DATA 5,2,6,1,6,1,7,1,8,2,-1,-1
969 REM ** TABLE HEADINGS
970 DATA <10,10-15,16-21,22-30,31-40,41-
50,51-65,>65
```

```
RUN
AGE         TOTAL       MALE        FEMALE
<1Ø         3           1           2

1Ø-15       3           2           1

16-21       7           4           3

22-3Ø       4           2           2

31-4Ø       6           2           4

41-5Ø       5           3           2

51-65       6           2           4

>65         6           3           3


TOTALS      4Ø          19          21
```

10. Your brother-in-law owns the local "jeans" store. He carries a large inventory with tremendous variety but now finds he must cut back. The question is *which* items to cut back. He asks you to use your computer to analyze his sales and help him make the "which-item" decisions. He wants to analyze sales of children's pants first. He carries 9 styles in children's pants, each style with 3 colors. For your program, you should number the styles 1 through 9 and the colors 1 through 3, so that each piece of data will look like that below.

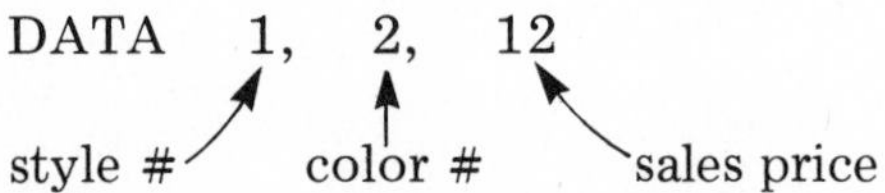

Write a program to analyze the sales and prepare a report like the one below. Use the following DATA statements in your program.

```
9ØØ REM ** STYLE,COLOR,DOLLAR SALES
91Ø DATA 1,1,12, 1,2,13, 1,3,14
911 DATA 2,1,22, 2,2,1Ø, 2,3,12
912 DATA 3,1,45, 3,2,14, 3,3,32
913 DATA 4,1,13, 4,2,1Ø, 4,3,15
914 DATA 5,1,12, 5,2,13, 5,3,12
915 DATA 6,1,12, 6,2,12, 6,3,12
916 DATA 7,1,13, 7,2,13, 7,3,13
917 DATA 8,1,14, 8,2,14, 8,3,14
918 DATA 9,1,15, 9,2,15, 9,3,15
919 DATA 3,2,35, 5,1,5Ø, 6,1,36
92Ø DATA 9,3,12, 2,3,4Ø, 5,1,24
921 DATA 3,3,14, 4,1,48, 1,1,12
922 DATA 2,1,12, 3,1,13, -1,-1,-1
```

Here is the REPORT segment of our solution—you do the rest!

```
3ØØ REM ** PRINT REPORT
31Ø PRINT "S# TOT$","COLOR 1","COLOR 2"
 "COLOR 3"
32Ø FOR S=1 TO 9
33Ø PRINT S;" ";T(S,Ø),
34Ø FOR C=1 TO 3
35Ø PRINT T(S,C),
36Ø NEXT C;PRINT
37Ø NEXT S
38Ø FOR X=Ø TO 3
39Ø PRINT "T=";T(Ø,X),
4ØØ NEXT X
```

```
RUN
S#    TOT$   COLOR 1    COLOR 2    COLOR 3
1     51     24         13         14

2     96     34         1Ø         52

3     153    58         49         46

4     66     61         1Ø         15

5     111    86         13         12

6     72     48         12         12

7     39     13         13         13

8     42     14         14         14

9     57     12         15         27

T=7Ø7        T=353      T=149      T=2Ø5
```

Answers to Self-Test

The frame numbers in parentheses refer to the frames in the chapter where the topic is discussed. You may wish to refer back to these for quick review.

1. (b), (d), (e), and (f) are legal (Longer variable names such as item (c) may be legal on *your* computer. Check the reference manual for your computer.) (frames 5–7)

2. 3,2 meaning 3 rows, 2 columns (frames 2–4)

3. 100 DIM A(3,2) (frame 12)

4. A(3,2) (frames 9–11)

5. (a) 1; (b) 5 (frame 11)

6. (a) 4; (b) 6 (frame 11)

7. 4 (frame 11)

8.
```
1Ø DIM M(1Ø,1Ø)
2Ø FOR R=1 TO 1Ø
3Ø FOR C=1 TO 1Ø
4Ø M(R,C)=Ø
5Ø NEXT C
6Ø NEXT R
```
(frame 12)

9.
```
1ØØ REM ** POPULATION AGE/SEX ANALYSIS1Ø
Ø REM ** POPULATION ANALYSIS
11Ø REM ** INITIALIZE
12Ø DIM V(8,2),A$(6)
13Ø FOR A=Ø TO 8:FOR S=Ø TO 2
14Ø V(A,S)=Ø
15Ø NEXT S:NEXT A
2ØØ REM ** READ DATA,TEST,ACCUMULATE
21Ø READ A,S:IF A=-1 THEN 31Ø
22Ø V(A,S)=V(A,S)+1:V(Ø,Ø)=V(Ø,Ø)+1
23Ø V(Ø,S)=V(Ø,S)+1:V(A,Ø)=V(A,Ø)+1
24Ø GOTO 21Ø
3ØØ REM ** PRINT REPORT
31Ø PRINT "AGE","TOTAL","MALE","FEMALE"
32Ø FOR A=1 TO 8
33Ø READ A$:PRINT A$,V(A,Ø),
34Ø FOR S=1 TO 2
35Ø PRINT V(A,S),
36Ø NEXT S:PRINT :NEXT A:PRINT
37Ø PRINT "TOTALS",V(Ø,Ø),V(Ø,1),V(Ø,2)
9ØØ REM ** DATA: BY AGE GROUP,SEX
91Ø DATA 1,2,2,1,3,2,4,1,5,2,6,2,7,2
92Ø DATA 8,1,1,2,1,1,2,1,2,2,3,1,3,1
93Ø DATA 3,2,3,1,3,2,4,1,4,2,5,1,5,1
94Ø DATA 5,2,5,2,6,1,6,2,7,1,7,2,7,2
95Ø DATA 7,2,8,1,8,1,8,2,8,2,3,1,4,2
96Ø DATA 5,2,6,1,6,1,7,1,8,2,-1,-1
969 REM ** TABLE HEADINGS
97Ø DATA <1Ø,1Ø-15,16-21,22-3Ø,31-4Ø,41-
5Ø,51-65,>65
```
(frame 19)

10.
```
100 REM ** SALES ANALYSIS
110 REM ** INITIALIZE
120 DIM T(9,3)
130 FOR S=0 TO 9:FOR C=0 TO 3
140 T(S,C)=0
150 NEXT C:NEXT S
200 REM ** READ,TEST,ACCUMULATE
210 READ S,C,D:IF S=-1 THEN 310
220 T(S,C)=T(S,C)+D
230 T(0,0)=T(0,0)+D
240 T(0,C)=T(0,C)+D
250 T(S,0)=T(S,0)+D
260 GOTO 210
300 REM ** PRINT REPORT
310 PRINT "S#",TOT$","COLOR 1","COLOR 2"
,"COLOR 3"
320 FOR S=1 TO 9
330 PRINT S;" ";T(S,0),
340 FOR C=1 TO 3
350 PRINT T(S,C),
360 NEXT C:PRINT
370 NEXT S
380 FOR X=0 TO 3
390 PRINT "T=";T(0,X),
400 NEXT X
900 REM ** STYLE,COLOR,DOLLAR SALES
910 DATA 1,1,12, 1,2,13, 1,3,14
911 DATA 2,1,22, 2,2,10, 2,3,12
912 DATA 3,1,45, 3,2,14, 3,3,32
913 DATA 4,1,13, 4,2,10, 4,3,15
914 DATA 5,1,12, 5,2,13, 5,3,12
915 DATA 6,1,12, 6,2,12, 6,3,12
916 DATA 7,1,13, 7,2,13, 7,3,13
917 DATA 8,1,14, 8,2,14, 8,3,14
918 DATA 9,1,15, 9,2,15, 9,3,15
919 DATA 3,2,35, 5,1,50, 6,1,36
920 DATA 9,3,12, 2,3,40, 5,1,24
921 DATA 3,3,14, 4,1,48, 1,1,12
922 DATA 2,1,12, 3,1,13, -1,-1,-1
```

(frame 32)

CHAPTER NINE

String Variables and String Functions

In Chapter 3, we showed you a few ways to use alphanumeric string variables. We also used string variables in the chapters that followed as we introduced new programming concepts. In this chapter we will review what you already know about string variables and introduce you to some new goodies, as well. Generally you will find that there is as wide a range of manipulation for string variables as for a numeric variable.

When you have completed this chapter you will be able to use the RESTORE statement with READ and DATA statements. You will also be able to use the following string functions with the string variables you will learn about in this chapter.

VAL
STR$
CHR$
ASC
LEN

1. So far, our use of alphanumeric (mixed alphabetic and numeric) phrases has mostly been limited to the use of strings in PRINT statements such as the following.

```
10 PRINT "THIS IS A STRING"
```

Now we can add a new feature to BASIC, the string variable.

```
5 DIM T$(50)
10 LET T$="STRING FOR THE STRING VARIABLE T$"
```

This is a string variable.

You identify a string variable by using any legal variable name followed by a dollar sign ($). String variables permit you to manipulate alphanumeric data with greater ease. String variable instructions include LET, PRINT, INPUT, READ, DATA, and IF-THEN, plus special string functions.

As we noted in earlier chapters, you must use a DIM statement at the beginning of the program that is executed *only once,* to tell the computer how much memory space to save for the string variables used in the program. A string assigned to a string variable using a LET assignment statement is limited to about 99 characters. This is due to the limitations on statement line length, including the "wrap around" to the next lines on the display. How many characters in the string variable T$ above? ______________ (Did you count blank spaces?)

— — — — — — — — — — —

33 characters

2. As you know, you can assign values to a string variable using an INPUT statement that asks for one or more string variables to be entered by the user.

Example 1

```
5 DIM N$(3Ø)
1Ø PRINT "WHAT IS YOUR NAME"; <———— One string input
2Ø INPUT N$
```

Example 2

```
5 DIM N$(3Ø),S$(3Ø)
1Ø PRINT "YOUR NAME AND SUN SIGN"; <———— Two string inputs
2Ø INPUT N$,S$
```

Example 3

```
5 DIM N$(3Ø),C$(3Ø),S$(3Ø)
1Ø PRINT "YOUR NAME, CITY, AND STATE YOU <—— Three string inputs
LIVE IN";
2Ø INPUT N$,C$,S$
```

You may also assign numeric and string variables in the same INPUT statement as shown here.

Example 4

```
5 DIM N$(3Ø)
1Ø PRINT "WHAT IS YOUR NAME AND AGE";      ┌— Mixed inputs, one string
2Ø INPUT N$,A <————————————————————————————┘   and one numeric.
```

When an input statement with more than one variable, string or numeric, is encountered by the computer while executing a program, it types a question mark and waits for the user to enter the input string or value from the keyboard.

Let's say we have entered Example 2 above into the computer. We type RUN and hit the **RETURN** key. The display shows:

```
RUN
YOUR NAME AND SUN SIGN?
```

I respond by typing my name and press **RETURN**.

```
RUN
YOUR NAME AND SUN SIGN? JERALD R. BROWN
```

Now I type my sign, which is assigned to the second input variable.

```
RUN
YOUR NAME AND SUN SIGN? JERALD R. BROWN
? SCORPIO
```

If I had typed both of the things asked for after the first question mark, they would have both been assigned to N$. If I had just pressed **RETURN** without entering anything after a question mark, a "null string" (a string with no characters) would have been assigned to the string variable.

```
5 DIM N$(30)
10 PRINT "WHAT IS YOUR NAME AND AGE";
20 INPUT N$,A
30 PRINT "NAME: ";N$
40 PRINT "AGE: ";A
```

Show what the computer will print and how you should enter the information requested if the above program is RUN.

```
RUN
```

```
RUN
WHAT IS YOUR NAME AND AGE? PAUL ARMITIGE
?33
NAME: PAUL ARMITIGE
AGE: 33
```

3.
```
10 DIM N$(15)
20 PRINT "YOUR NAME";
30 INPUT N$
40 PRINT "YOUR NAME IS ";N$
```

Suppose I RUN this program.

```
RUN
YOUR NAME? JERALD RICHARD BROWN
YOUR NAME IS JERALD RICHARD
```

What happened? Did the computer forget my last name? Take a look at the DIM statement. Since string variable N$ was only dimensioned to accept 15 characters, it assigned the first 15 characters I entered (in response to the question) to the string variable N$, and just "ignored" anything beyond that.

Suppose the program is RUN again.

```
RUN
YOUR NAME? JOHN JACOB JINGLEHIEMER SCMIDT
```

Now what will the computer say? ____

____

— — — — — — — — — —

```
YOUR NAME IS JOHN JACOB JING
```

Moral: Dimension the string variables adequately.

4. Write a program to enter and print an auto license plate that has a 3-letter alphabetic string and a 3-digit number (such as SAM 123). Enter the letters as a string variable and the number as a numeric variable. Show what the RUN should look like.

— — — — — — — — — —

```
10 DIM A$(3)
20 INPUT A$,B
30 PRINT A$;B
RUN
?SAM
?123
SAM123
```

5. You can also enter string variables by using READ and DATA statements.

```
1 REM ** STRING READ/DATA COURSE LIST
5 DIM A$(18),C$(1)
10 PRINT "COURSE    ","HOURS","GRADE"
20 READ A$,B,C$
30 PRINT A$,B,C$
40 GOTO 20
50 DATA ENGLISH 1A,3,B,SOC 130   ,3,A
60 DATA BUS ADM 1A,4,B,STAT 10   ,3,A
70 DATA HUMANITIES,3,A,HISTORY 17A,3,B
80 DATA CALCULUS 3A,4,C


RUN
COURSE                     HOURS       GRADE
ENGLISH 1A                 3           B
SOC 130                    3           A
BUS ADM 1A                 4           B
STAT 10                    3           C
HUMANITIES                 3           A
HISTORY 17A                3           B
CALCULUS 3A                4           C
```

Look at line 10 of the preceding program. Notice the trailing spaces included in the string "COURSE." Since we have reserved two columns of standard print positions for course names, the extra spaces cause "HOURS" to be printed at the third print position, and "GRADE" at the last print position column. Another way we could have used would be to include an empty or "null string" for printing nothing at the second print position!

```
10 PRINT "COURSE", "" , "HOURS","GRADE"
```

Since any string of 8 characters or less will occupy one print position column, we also included trailing spaces in the DATA statements (see lines 50 and 60) where the course name was eight or less characters in length. This forces the course names to use two print position columns. The following rules pertain to strings as DATA statement items.

(1) The first string item in a DATA statement can have no leading spaces, but will include trailing spaces up to the comma that separates the first string from the second item.

```
910 DATA HOW, NOW, BROWN, COW
```

Spaces before NOW, BROWN, and COW will be included.

(2) The last string item in a DATA statement can have leading spaces between the comma that precedes it and the first displayed character of the string, but no trailing spaces can be included.

```
910 DATA HOW , NOW , BROWN , COW
```

These spaces included in the string assignment, but no trailing space.

(3) The other items in a DATA statement will include any leading or trailing spaces as part of the string assignment.

```
91Ø DATA   HOW   ,   NOW   ,   BROWN   ,   COW
```

The two spaces before and two spaces after the word NOW will be included in the string assignment.

6. In the program in frame 5, how long is the string for the fourth data item in line 50? ____________

— — — — — — — — — — —

9 characters including two trailing spaces (SOC 130).

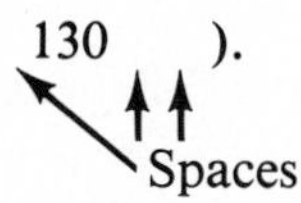

7. How many print position columns will be occupied by the string SOC 130 when it is read from the DATA statement and printed by line 30? ____________

— — — — — — — — — — —

two, because strings of 9 characters or more controlled by commas in PRINT statement will cause the computer to skip the next usual print position. This is done automatically to keep the display from one column from running into the next displayed column. In summary, if the string variable size is greater than 9 characters, the print column sequence will *not* be followed, but will skip to the next available print position.

8. The string LET assigns a particular string to a string variable. Note that you must enclose the string in quotes as in these two examples.

```
1Ø DIM A$(3),B$(2),C$(3)
2Ø LET A$="YES"
3Ø LET B$="NO"
4Ø LET C$=A$ ←——— C$ now contains "YES"
```

Show what will be printed by this program when it is RUN.

```
1Ø DIM A$(2Ø),B$(2Ø)
2Ø LET A$=" A GOOD EXAMPLE"
3Ø LET B$="THIS IS"
4Ø PRINT B$;A$

RUN
```

— — — — — — — — — — —

```
RUN
THIS IS A GOOD EXAMPLE
```

9. Next we want you to write a program similar to the one in frame 5. Instead of courses and grades, the data should be books in your office or home library. Your DATA should include author, title, and number of pages. Our data looks like this:

```
900 REM ** ORDER OF DATA:
901 REM ** AUTHOR, TITLE, PAGES
910 DATA BROWN,INSTANT BASIC,178
920 DATA WHITE,YOUR HOME COMPUTER,225
930 DATA KEMENY,BASIC PROGRAMMING,150
940 DATA OSBORNE,INTRO TO MICROCOMPUTERS
,384
950 DATA NELSON,COMPUTER LIB/DREAM MACHI
NES,186
960 DATA THIAGI,GAMES FOR THE POCKET CAL
CULATOR,54
```

Our RUN looks like the following.

```
RUN
TITLE                AUTHOR     PAGES
INSTANT BASIC        BROWN      178
YOUR HOME COMPUTER   WHITE      225
BASIC PROGRAMMING    KEMENY     150
INTRO TO MICROCOMP   OSBORNE    384
COMPUTER LIB/DREAM   NELSON     186
GAMES FOR THE POCK   THIAGI     54
```

Before you write your program, look at line 940 above, and the corresponding line in the RUN. Review frame 3. Note that we have controlled the display of long titles, in this case, by limiting the string length assigned to variables by proper dimensioning of string variables. If a title is short, i.e., less than 9 characters, include trailing spaces so that it will occupy two columns. Limit the length of authors' names in the same manner. Go to it!

— — — — — — — — — — —

```
1 REM ** STRING/DATA HOME LIBRARY
5 DIM A$(8),T$(18)
10 PRINT "TITLE","","AUTHOR","PAGES"
20 READ A$,T$,P:IF A$="END" THEN END
30 PRINT T$,A$,P:GOTO 20
900 REM ** ORDER OF DATA:
901 REM ** AUTHOR, TITLE, PAGES
910 DATA BROWN,INSTANT BASIC,178
920 DATA WHITE,YOUR HOME COMPUTER,225
930 DATA KEMENY,BASIC PROGRAMMING,150
940 DATA OSBORNE,INTRO TO MICROCOMPUTERS
,384
950 DATA NELSON,COMPUTER LIB/DREAM MACHI
NES,186
960 DATA THIAGI,GAMES FOR THE POCKET CAL
CULATOR,54
970 DATA END,0,0
```

10. Modify the program you just wrote for frame 9 so that it will only print those books with fewer than 200 pages.

— — — — — — — — — — —

```
25 IF P >= 2ØØ THEN 2Ø
```

11. The string IF-THEN allows you to compare the contents of two string variables.

```
1Ø DIM A$(3),B$(2)
2Ø B$="NO"
3Ø PRINT "DO YOU WANT INSTRUCTIONS";
4Ø INPUT A$
5Ø IF A$=B$ THEN 14Ø
6Ø PRINT "THIS SIMULATION PERMITS YOU TO
 REGULATE..."
14Ø PRINT "THE SIMULATION BEGINS..."
```

Line 50 compares the contents of the string variable A$ (YES) to the contents of string variable B$ (NO). If you responded YES to the INPUT statement, A$ and B$ are not equal (they do not have the same contents), the computer will execute the next statement, line 60, which in this case will print the instructions. If you respond NO to line 40 above, the program will branch to line 140 and continue execution there.

The comparison in line 50 is between ______________________.

— — — — — — — — — — —

the contents of two string variables, A$ and B$

12. You can compare the contents of a string variable to a string enclosed in quotes.

```
1Ø DIM A$(3)
2Ø PRINT "DO YOU WANT INSTRUCIONS? YES
OR NO";
3Ø INPUT A$
4Ø IF A$="NO" THEN 14Ø
5Ø PRINT "THIS SIMULATION PERMITS YOU TO
 REGULATE..."
14Ø PRINT "THE SIMULATION BEGINS..."
```

The comparison in line 40 above is between a______________________

and a ______________________.

— — — — — — — — — — —

string assigned to a string variable (the contents of a string variable) and a string enclosed in quotes

13. You *cannot* compare a numeric variable to a string variable.

```
11Ø IF A$ = B THEN 14Ø
```

This is not permitted. You will get an error message after you type it in.

But you *can* change a string variable into its numeric equivalent using the VAL($) function. In the above example, if A$ contained a number (entered as a string variable) you could compare it with numeric variable B by changing line 110 to read as follows.

```
110 IF VAL(A$) = B THEN 140
```

Here is another demonstration program. Circle the correct RUN for the program.

```
5 DIM A$(10),B$(10),C$(10)
10 A$="32":B$="1.115":C$="-10"
30 PRINT A$:PRINT VAL(A$)
40 PRINT B$:PRINT VAL(B$)
50 PRINT C$:PRINT VAL(C$)
```

```
RUN         RUN         RUN
32          32          32
32           32          32
1.115       1.115       1.115
1.115        1.115       1.115
-10         -10         -10
-10         -10          -10
```

First RUN is correct.

14. What will this program print when it is RUN?

```
5 DIM A$(10),B$(10),C$(10)
10 A$="32":B$="1.115":C$="-10"
30 PRINT VAL(A$)+VAL(B$)+VAL(C$)

RUN
```

```
RUN
23.115
```

15. Using the STR$ function, you can convert a numeric variable to a string or place a numeric variable into a string variable.

```
10 PRINT STR$(X) ◄———— Will print the string equivalent of the numeric content of variable X.
20 LET A$ = STR$(X)◄——— Will place into string variable A$ the numeric content of variable X.
```

What will this program print?

```
10 V = 112 : PRINT V : PRINT STR$(V)
RUN
```

```
RUN
112
112
```

16. In a string IF-THEN, the comparison is made one character at a time. For example, if a space is introduced in the wrong place, it may cause a comparison other than what you expect.

```
5 DIM A$(20)
10 INPUT A$
20 IF A$="MCGEE" THEN 140
```

If the user enters MC GEE in response to the computer's prompt during the RUN, the comparison will not be equal. Why will this comparison not be equal?

____

____

— — — — — — — — — — —

The space between C and G is a character which is not present in "MCGEE."

17. You can compare strings using the same symbols you used earlier: <>, <, >, <=, >=, and =. It's a little tricky so you should use caution with these comparisons. The comparison is still made one character at a time from left to right. The *first* difference found determines the relationship. The relationship is based on position in the alphabet; C is "less than" S; T is "greater than" M.

```
5 DIM A$(5),B$(5)
10 A$="SMITH"
20 B$="SMYTH"
30 IF A$<B$ THEN 100
```

In line 30 above, will the program branch to line 100 or continue to the next statement in sequence? _______________

— — — — — — — — — — —

Jump to line 100. The first difference is the third character and since I is "less than" Y, the IF-THEN condition is TRUE.

18. Here is another example.

```
100 DIM D$(20),E$(20)
120 D$="COMPUTE"
130 E$="COMPUTER"
140 IF D$<E$ THEN 180
150 PRINT D$
160 END
180 PRINT E$
```

Which statement will be executed after the comparison in line 140? __________

— — — — — — — — — — —

Line 180. D$ is "less than" E$. It is smaller in size, therefore "less than" E$.

19. Change line 140 in frame 18 to read as follows.

```
140 IF D$ = E$ THEN 180
```

Now which statement will be executed after the comparison of line 140?

____

— — — — — — — — — — —

Line 150. D$ is not equal to E$.

20. In frame 18 change line 140 to read as follows.

```
140 IF E$ > D$ THEN 180
```

Which statement will be executed after the comparison? _______________

— — — — — — — — — — —

Line 180. E$ is "greater than" D$.

21. To expand your understanding of string comparisons, we would like to introduce you to the ASCII (pronounced ASKEE) code. Who's ASCII, you ask? ASCII stands for the American Standard Code for Information Interchange. For each character you type on the keyboard, an ASCII code number for that character is sent to the computer. The computer sends back an ASCII code number for each character that appears on your printer or screen. That's the "information interchange" referred to by ASCII.

ATARI BASIC allows us to enter ASCII code numbers instead of keyboard characters with the use of the CHR$ function and allows us to convert a character into its ASCII code number using the ASC function.

CHR$(X) — The ASCII number to be converted is placed in X before you use this function. Or you can place the number directly into the parentheses instead of X, as in CHR$(65).

ASC(X$) — The string character to be converted to ASCII code is placed in X$ before execution.

For example, the uppercase letters we use in BASIC correspond to ASCII code numbers 65 to 90 inclusive: A = 65, B = 66, C = 67, . . . X = 88, Y = 89, Z = 90. A complete table of ASCII code numbers and the characters they represent can be found in the Appendix.

The little program below prints a quotation from John Wayne that is found in the DATA statement in ASCII code numbers.

```
10 READ X : IF X = -1 THEN END
20 PRINT CHR$(X); : GOTO 10
30 DATA 89,85,80,-1

RUN
YUP
```

Referring to that table of ASCII code numbers, tell what the following program will print when RUN.

```
10 READ A : IF A = -1 THEN END
20 PRINT CHR$(A); : GOTO 10
30 DATA 72,65,80,80,89,32,67,79,77,80,85,84,73,78,71,-1
```

```
RUN
HAPPY COMPUTING
```

22. Using the ASC function you can find out the ASCII code number for a string character. Here's a demonstration.

```
5 DIM X$(1),Y$(1),Z$(1)
10 X$="A":Y$="B":Z$="C"
20 PRINT "A = ";ASC(X$),"B = ";ASC(Y$),"
C = ";ASC(Z$)

RUN
A = 65     B = 66     C = 67
```

Write a program using the ASC function to provide you with the ASCII code for the following characters, so that the RUN looks like this.

```
RUN
CHAR          ASCII CODE

$              36
=              61
?              63
```

Here are two possible solutions.

```
5 DIM A$(1),B$(1),C$(1)
10 A$="$":B$="=":C$="?"
20 PRINT "CHAR.","ASCII CODE"
30 PRINT
40 PRINT A$,ASC(A$)
50 PRINT B$,ASC(B$)
60 PRINT C$,ASC(C$)
```

```
10 PRINT "CHAR.","ASCII CODE"
20 PRINT
30 PRINT "$",ASC("$")
40 PRINT "=",ASC("=")
50 PRINT "?",ASC("?")
```

23. Now, let's return to string comparisons using the IF-THEN statement. Strings are compared using a character by character process and the computer uses ASCII code numbers to do the comparing. For example, in frame 12, we saw this program segment.

```
5 DIM A$(10)
10 INPUT A$
20 IF A$ = "MCGEE" THEN 140
```

When the program is RUN and the user enters MC GEE, the computer compares ASCII code numbers as follows.

"MCGEE"		A$ (user-entered)
M = 77	———	M = 77
C = 67	———	C = 67
G = 71	———	space = 32
E = 69	———	G = 71
E = 69	———	E = 69
		E = 69

The computer finds the two strings equal for the first two characters, but the third character comparison is unequal (71 *vs.* 32).

Show how the computer, using ASCII codes, will compare the strings in the following segment, just as we did above.

```
5 DIM A$(3)
10 INPUT "DO YOU WANT INSTRUCTIONS? YES OR NO"; A$
20 IF A$ = "NO" THEN 140

RUN
DO YOU WANT INSTRUCTIONS? YES OR NO? YES.
```

A$ "NO"

Is the comparison true or false? __________

— — — — — — — — — — — —

A$	"NO"
Y = 89	N = 78
E = 69	O = 79
S = 83	

The comparison is false.

24. Before you proceed, we need to introduce the RESTORE statement and its use in connection with READ and DATA statements. A READ statement causes the next item(s) of data to be read from the DATA statements. You may find that you want the program to read through the data from the beginning again.

To do so, use a RESTORE statement, which causes the next DATA item to be READ to be the first piece of data in the *first* DATA statement. In other words, with the next READ statement that the computer comes to, it starts at the beginning of the DATA. See Line 30 below.

Now that you have seen how to use string variable comparisons, you can understand this simple information retrieval program that permits retrieving information from DATA statements.

The program in frame 5 prints courses, hours, and grades. The program below permits the operator to enter the course: the computer will then print the course, hour, and grade.

```
1 REM ** COURSE INFO RETRIEVAL
5 DIM A$(18),D$(18),C$(1)
1Ø PRINT "ENTER COURSE NAME";
2Ø INPUT D$
3Ø RESTORE
4Ø READ A$,B,C$: IF A$=D$ THEN 6Ø
5Ø GOTO 4Ø
6Ø PRINT A$,B,C$:PRINT :GOTO 1Ø
9ØØ REM ** COURSE,UNITS,GRADE
91Ø DATA ENGLISH 1A,3,B,SOC 13Ø,3,A
92Ø DATA BUS ADM 1A,4,B,STAT 1Ø,3,C
93Ø DATA HUMANITIES,3,A,HISTORY 17B,3,B

RUN
ENTER COURSE NAME? HUMANITIES
HUMANITIES     3              A

ENTER COURSE NAME? STAT 1Ø
STAT 1Ø        3              C

ENTER COURSE NAME? ECON 1A ←
ERROR-    6 AT LINE 4Ø
```

← Whoops, no such course. The computer read through all the data and found no such course; therefore, it printed this error message.

Let's look at another RUN of the program.

```
RUN
ENTER COURSE NAME? SOC13Ø
ERROR-    6 AT LINE 4Ø
```

Why did we get an error message this time? ______________________________

____

— — — — — — — — — —

The course name is stored SOC 130, but the user typed SOC130 without a space between SOC and 130.

Note also that you *cannot* leave leading and trailing spaces when you INPUT from the keyboard, so do not leave leading or trailing spaces in DATA statement string items that are to be compared to INPUT items, or the comparisons will not work as expected.

25. Refer back to the program in frame 24.

(a) What is the purpose of this part of line 40?

```
...IF A$=D$ THEN 6Ø
```

(b) Under what conditions will line 50 be executed? 50 GOTO 40

____

— — — — — — — — — —

(a) to test whether or not the course read from the DATA statement is the course requested in the INPUT statement
(b) when the course read by line 40 is not the course requested in the INPUT statement

26. Modify the program in frame 24 so it will print the message "NO SUCH COURSE" instead of the data error message, indicating that the course entered by the user does not exist in the computer's information system. You should put a flag at the end of the regular data.

— — — — — — — — — —

Add these statements (or ones similar to them).

```
45 IF A$ = "END" THEN PRINT "NO SUCH COURSE" : GOTO 1Ø
94Ø DATA END,Ø,Ø
```

Remember, the end-of-data signal must contain a string, followed by a numeric value, followed by a string, because the READ statement calls for three variables at once.

27. It's your turn. Write a program that contains the names and phone numbers of your friends and business associates that you would like to "retrieve" using your computer. When you type in a name, the computer should respond with the correct phone number, as shown below.

```
NAME? ADAM OZ

ADAM OZ        415-555-2222

NAME? JUDY WIL

JUDY WIL       112-555-ØØ75

NAME? JERRY
ERROR-   6 AT LINE 4Ø
```

— — — — — — — — — — —

```
1 REM ** TELEPHONE NUMBER RETRIEVAL
10 DIM N$(8),D$(8),T$(12)
20 PRINT "NAME";:INPUT N$
30 RESTORE
40 READ D$,T$
50 IF N$=D$ THEN PRINT :PRINT D$,T$:PRIN
T :GOTO 20
60 GOTO 40
900 REM ** DATA:NAME,PHONE NUMBER
910 DATA TONY BOD,415-555-8117
920 DATA MARY JAY,213-555-0144
930 DATA MARY MMM,213-555-1212
940 DATA JUDY WIL,112-555-0075
950 DATA ADAM OZ,415-555-2222
960 DATA BOBBY ALL,312-555-1667
970 DATA END,END
```

28. Next, we will show you another function that allows you to manipulate and examine parts of strings, called *substrings.* A substring is a part of a string and is defined by using subscripts after the string variable, A$(10) or A$(1,5).

```
5 DIM A$(30)
10 LET A$="MY HUMAN UNDERSTANDS ME"
20 PRINT A$(10)  <———— The substring begins at the 10th
                       character and includes all the characters
RUN                    that follow

UNDERSTANDS ME
```

Replace Line 20 with PRINT A$(15). What will be printed when the new Line 20 is RUN? ______________________

— — — — — — — — — — —

```
STANDS ME
```

29. Now look at these examples. To isolate one character you need to use the value twice indicating the first and the last character of the substring.

```
5 DIM A$(30)
10 LET A$="MY HUMAN UNDERSTANDS ME"
20 PRINT A$(4,4)  <———— Will print H, the 4th character in the
                        string. (A space counts as one character)
RUN

H
```

Here we have a substring that starts at character 1 and includes all of the characters through and including the 9th character.

```
5 DIM A$(30)
10 LET A$="MY HUMAN UNDERSTANDS ME"
20 PRINT A$(1,9)

RUN
MY HUMAN
```

In the program directly above, change Line 20 to read PRINT A$(4,8). What will be printed when the new Line 20 is executed? ______________________

— — — — — — — — — — —

```
HUMAN
```

30. What will be printed by the following program?

```
10 DIM A$(20)
20 LET A$="GAMES COMPUTERS PLAY"
30 PRINT A$(7,15),A$(17),A$(1,5)
```

— — — — — — — — — — —

```
RUN
COMPUTERS           PLAY      GAMES
```

31. Here are parts of a program to print the string variable A$ backwards, one character at a time. Fill in the blanks and show the RUN.

```
5 DIM A$(__)

10 LET A$="ABCDEFGHIJKLMNOPQRSTUVWXYZ"

20 FOR X=__TO__STEP -1

30 PRINT A$(X,____);

40 ________________________
```

— — — — — — — — — — —

```
5 DIM A$(26)
10 LET A$="ABCDEFGHIJKLMNOPQRSTUVWXYZ"
20 FOR X=26 TO 1 STEP -1
30 PRINT A$(X,X);
40 NEXT X

RUN

ZYXWVUTSRQPONMLKJIHGFEDCBA
```

32. Let's go all the way back to frame 9 of Chapter 1 and change our number guessing game to a *letter* guessing game. Here's the old program. All its logic should still apply.

```
100 REMARK***THIS IS A SIMPLE COMPUTER GAME
110 LET X = INT(100*RND(1))+1
120 PRINT
130 PRINT "I'M THINKING OF A NUMBER FROM 1 TO 100."
140 PRINT "GUESS MY NUMBER!!!"
150 PRINT : INPUT "YOUR GUESS"; G
160 IF G<X THEN PRINT "TRY A BIGGER NUMBER" : GOTO 150
170 IF G>X THEN PRINT "TRY A SMALLER NUMBER" : GOTO 150
180 IF G=X THEN PRINT "THAT'S IT!!! YOU GUESSED MY NUMBER." : GOTO 110
```

We should first add line 101 to DIM A$ and INPUT variable G$; also X$ to store the computer's letter to be guessed. Line 105, a LET statement with all the letters of the alphabet assigned to A$.

101 ____________________

105 ____

— — — — — — — — — — —

```
101 DIM A$(26),G$(1),X$(1)
105 LET A$ = "ABCDEFGHIJKLMNOPQRSTUVWXYZ"
```

33. Now change line 110 to randomly select a number between 1 and 26.

110 ____

— — — — — — — — — — —

```
110 LET X = INT(26*RND(1))+1
```

34. Let's place our selected choice into X$.

115 LET X$=____

— — — — — — — — — — —

```
115 LET X$ = A$(X,X)
```

35. You complete lines 140 and 150.

```
130 PRINT "I'M THINKING OF A LETTER FORM A TO Z"
```

140 ____

150 ____

— — — — — — — — — — —

```
140 PRINT "GUESS MY LETTER!!!" :PRINT
150 PRINT "YOUR GUESS": INPUT G$
```

36. Change lines 160, 170, and 180 as necessary. RUN your new game.

160 ______________________________

170 ______________________________

180 ______________________________

— — — — — — — — — — — —

Here's the entire LIST and a RUN.

```
100 REMARK***A SIMPLE COMPUTER GAME
101 DIM A$(26),G$(1),X$(1)
105 LET A$ = "ABCDEFGHIJKLMNOPQRSTUVWXYZ"
110 LET X = INT(26*RND(1))+1
115 LET X$ = A$(X,X)
120 PRINT
130 PRINT "I'M THINKING OF A LETTER FROM A TO Z"
140 PRINT "GUESS MY LETTER!!!";PRINT
150 PRINT "YOUR GUESS";INPUT G$
160 IF G$<X$ THEN PRINT "TRY A BIGGER LETTER." : GOTO 150
170 IF G$>X$ THEN PRINT "TRY A SMALLER LETTER." : GOTO 150
180 IF G$=X$ THEN PRINT "THAT'S IT!!! YOU GUESSED MY LETTER." : GOTO 110
```

```
RUN
I'M THINKING OF A LETTER FROM A TO Z
GUESS MY LETTER!!!


YOUR GUESS? L
TRY A SMALLER LETTER.

YOUR GUESS? G
TRY A BIGGER LETTER.

YOUR GUESS? H
TRY A BIGGER LETTER.

YOUR GUESS? K
TRY A SMALLER LETTER.

YOUR GUESS? I
TRY A BIGGER LETTER.

YOUR GUESS? J
THAT'S IT!!! YOU GUESSED MY LETTER.
```

37. Using the data from the program in frame 27, write a program that will print a list of phone numbers of people whose first name begins with the letter M.

```
RUN
MARY JAY        213-555-0144
MARY MMM        213-555-1212
ERROR-    6 AT LINE 40
```

— — — — — — — — — — — —

```
1 REM ** TELEPHONE DIRECTORY
10 DIM D$(8),T$(12)
20 RESTORE
30 READ D$,T$:IF D$(1,1)="M" THEN PRINT
D$,T$
40 GOTO 30
900 REM ** DATA: NAME, PHONE #
910 DATA TONY BOD,415-555-8117
920 DATA MARY JAY,213-555-0144
930 DATA MARY MMM,213-555-1212
940 DATA JUDY WIL,112-555-0075
950 DATA ADAM OZ,415-555-1667
960 DATA BOBBY ALL,312-555-1667
970 DATA END,999
```

38. Modify your program in frame 37 so that the computer will print telephone numbers and names located in area code 415 (you are going there for a visit and want to call old friends).

```
RUN
415-555-8117       TONY BOD
415-555-2222 ADAM OZ
ERROR-    6 AT LINE 40
```

```
1 REM ** TELEPHONE DIRECTORY
10 DIM D$(8),T$(12)
20 RESTORE
30 READ D$,T$: IF T$(1,3)<>"415" THEN 30
40 PRINT T$,D$:GOTO 30
900 REM ** DATA: NAME, PHONE #
910 DATA TONY BOD,415-555-8117
920 DATA MARY JAY,213-555-0144
930 DATA MARY MMM,213-555-1212
940 DATA JUDY WIL,112-555-0075
950 DATA ADAM OZ,415-555-1667
960 DATA BOBBY ALL,312-555-1667
970 DATA END,999
```

39. Sometimes we need to know the length of the contents of a string variable (how many characters). And, of course, BASIC has a special function, LEN, to help you find the answer. LEN(A$) will tell you the number of characters including blanks in the string A$. Here are some examples.

```
10 LET A = LEN(A$)
20 PRINT LEN(C$)
30 IF LEN(A$)<>LEN(B$) . . .
```

You can use the substring specifier to check answers to questions, to "edit" responses, and a host of other things. Below is a portion of a history teaching program. The program asks a question, requests a user response, and then checks the answer and makes an appropriate remark.

```
10 DIM A$(30)
20 PRINT "WHO WAS THE FIRST PRESIDENT OF
 THE U.S.";:INPUT A$
30 FOR X=1 TO LEN(A$)-9
40 IF A$(X,9+X)="WASHINGTON" THEN PRINT
"CORRECT":END
50 NEXT X
60 PRINT "YOUR ANSWER IS WRONG"
70 GOTO 20

RUN
WHO WAS THE FIRST PRESIDENT OF THE U.S.?
```

If you answer GEORGE WASHINGTON, what will the computer respond?

— — — — — — — — — —

CORRECT. To see how the computer checks through your response, add this line and RUN the program with the same input response.

```
39 PRINT A$(X,X+9)
```

40. Using the program in frame 39, if the user answered WASHINGTON IRVING to the question, what will the computer print? ____________________

— — — — — — — — — —

CORRECT (We only tested for WASHINGTON. Think of what might happen if we only tested for WASH—even WASHING MACHINE would qualify for a correct answer!)

41. The LEN function can be used to "edit" data entered by users that might have to be a certain size, and no bigger because of forms you use or because of the size of your computer memory. Examine the example below and answer the questions which follow.

```
10 DIM A$(30),N$(30)
20 PRINT "YOUR NAME";:INPUT N$
30 IF LEN(N$)>20 THEN PRINT "LIMIT YOUR
NAME TO 20 CHARACTERS PLEASE":GOTO 20
40 PRINT "YOUR ADDRESS";:INPUT A$
50 IF LEN(A$)>15 THEN PRINT "PLEASE ABBR
EVIATE YOUR ADDRESS":GOTO 30
```

How many characters are allowed for name? ________ For address? ________

— — — — — — — — — —

20; 15

SELF-TEST

Try this Self-Test, so you can evaluate how much you have learned so far.

1. Write a program to permit INPUT of a 5-letter word and then print the word backwards.

2. Write a program to read a series of 4-letter words from DATA statements and print only those words that begin with the letter A.

3. Modify the program in question 2 to print only words that begin with A and end with S.

4. Some years ago, the auto industry was hard-pressed to come up with names for new cars. They used a computer to generate a series of 5-letter words. Write a program to generate 100 5-letter words with randomly selected consonants in the first and third and fifth places and randomly selected vowels in the second and fourth places.

Answers to Self-Test

1.
```
10 REM ** STRING SELF-TEST 9-1
20 DIM A$(5)
30 INPUT A$
40 FOR X=5 TO 1 STEP -1
50 PRINT A$(X,X);
60 NEXT X
70 PRINT :GOTO 30
```

2.
```
10 REM ** STRING SELF-TEST 9-2
20 DIM A$(4)
30 READ A$:IF A$(1,1)<>"A" THEN 30
40 PRINT A$:GOTO 30
50 DATA ANTS,GNAT,LOVE,BALD,APES
60 DATA BAKE,MIKE,KARL,BARD,ALAS
```

3.
```
10 REM ** STRING SELF-TEST 9-3
20 DIM A$(4)
30 READ A$:IF A$(1,1)<>"A" THEN 30
35 IF A$(4,4)<>"S" THEN 30
40 PRINT A$:GOTO 30
50 DATA ANTS,GNAT,LOVE,BALD,APES
60 DATA BAKE,MIKE,KARL,BARD,ALAS
```

4.
```
10 REM ** STRING SELF-TEST 9-4
20 DIM A$(5),B$(21)
30 A$="AEIOU"
40 B$="BCDFGHJKLMNPQRSTVWXYZ"
50 FOR X=1 TO 20
60 FOR Z=1 TO 2
70 B=INT(21*RND(1))+1
80 PRINT B$(B,B);
90 A=INT(5*RND(1))+1
100 PRINT A$(A,A);
110 NEXT Z
120 B=INT(21*RND(1))+1
130 PRINT B$(B,B)
140 NEXT X
```

CHAPTER TEN

Color Graphics and Sound

In this chapter we introduce one of the most exciting capabilities of the ATARI computer. You will learn to control the color of the objects that appear on the video screen and also the color of the background on which the objects appear. In addition, you will learn to "paint" pictures which you have designed yourself. Several new graphic and color statements and commands will aid these enhancements to the output of your programs. When finished with this chapter, you will be able to:

- change the background color of the video screen to any one of 16 colors;
- draw designs on the video screen using any one of 16 colors;
- print text along with your pictures in a special text 'window';
- change the color of the text window to any one of 16 colors;
- change the number of plotting positions so that pictures can be drawn in more detail.

There are 256 colors available because of the luminosity (intensity) param.

1. You can draw lines on the screen by selecting a *screen mode* that allows graphics to be mixed with text in several different ways. This is done by giving the GRAPHICS command (which may be abbreviated GR.). Eight different modes are provided. They are selected by a number 0–7. For example:

```
10 GR. 3
```

would select a 40 column by 20 row graphics grid with provision for 4 lines of text.

(a) What command provides for drawing graphics? ____________

(b) What is it's abbreviation? ________

(c) How many different screen modes are there? ________

— — — — — — — — — — —

(a) GRAPHICS
(b) GR. (Yes, the period is necessary!)
(c) eight (0 through 7)

2. Type in the following and examine the video screen.

```
GRAPHICS 3
```

(a) Did the top part of the screen change color?

____

(b) What color is the bottom portion of the screen?

____

— — — — — — — — — — —

(a) yes, it blanked the top portion—no color now.
(b) light blue (this may vary with different TV sets)

3. In graphics mode 3, the top portion of the screen provides for a 40 × 20 grid for plotting points. The smaller portion at the bottom is provided for printing text material. Four lines of text can be used.

(a) Where do you plot points on the screen in graphics mode 3?

____

(b) In what area may text be printed?

____

— — — — — — — — — — —

(a) in the top area of the screen
(b) in the bottom area

4. You have been using graphics mode zero (GRAPHICS 0) throughout the book so far. When your ATARI is turned on, the screen mode is automatically set to GRAPHICS 0. When answering the following question, remember that mode 3 (GRAPHICS 3 or GR. 3) allows for 4 lines of text below the graph area. Enter and run the following program. When you have finished, type : GRAPHICS 0 and press the **RETURN** key. This returns you to the text mode.

```
10 GRAPHICS 3
20 PRINT "LINE 1"
30 PRINT "LINE 2"
40 PRINT "LINE 3"
50 PRINT "LINE 4";
60 GOTO 60
```

(Note: don't forget the semicolon)

What can you read at the bottom of the screen?

____

____

____

____

— — — — — — — — — —

```
LINE 1
LINE 2
LINE 3
LINE 4█
```

5. Here is a table of the graphic screen modes 3 through 7.

MODE NO.	NUMBER OF COLUMNS	GRAPHIC POSITIONS ROWS	TEXT WINDOW
3	39	20	4 lines
4,5	79	40	4 lines
6,7	158	80	4 lines

Which graphic mode(s) provide(s) the largest number of graphic positions?

____

— — — — — — — — — —

6 and 7 (158×80 positions)

6. Change line 10 in the program given in frame 4 to

```
10 GRAPHICS 4
```

If you run this revised program, will there be more room for text?

____

— — — — — — — — — —

No, there are still only 4 lines of text space.

7. When we are using graphics, we use the PLOT statement to tell the computer what point we want plotted. Both the column and the row desired must be given in the PLOT statement. The screen positions are numbered from the upper-left corner of the screen starting with the number zero (0). Thus, the position 2,5 would be the third position to the right (0,1,2) and the sixth position down (0,1,2,3,4,5). Suppose we execute the statement:

```
30 PLOT 2,5
```

Here is a sketch of the point plotted.

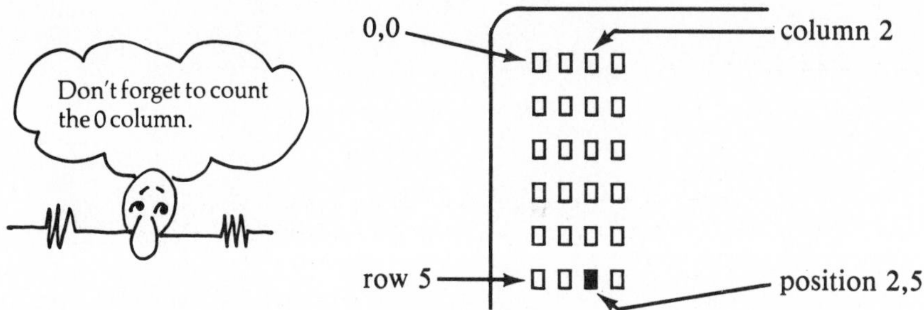

What does the PLOT statement tell the computer to do?

____

— — — — — — — — — — —

It tells the computer to plot a point at a stated position (column, row).

8. Examine this program

```
10 GR.3
20 PLOT 2,5
30 PRINT "THIS IS PLOT POSITION 2,5"
```

What does each line in the program tell the computer to do?

(a) Line 10 sets ______________________

(b) Line 20 tells where ______________________

(c) Line 30 ______________________

— — — — — — — — — — —

(a) Line 10 sets the graphic mode for a 39 × 20 grid.
(b) Line 20 tells where to plot the point.
(c) Line 30 tells what message to print in the text window.

9. To see the point, we "turn on" the color in the first color register with the statement:

```
15 COLOR 1
```

Insert this line into the program of frame 8 and run the program.

(a) Did you see the point? ___________

(b) If line 20 is changed to PLOT 10,5, would the point plotted be to the right or would it be below our original point? ___________________

— — — — — — — — — —

(a) yes, the point 2,5 is plotted in orange.
(b) to the right.

10. To return from GR.3 to the text mode: Type GR.0, then write a program to plot the four points shown below. Use GRAPHICS 3 and COLOR 1.

```
(1) 5,5
(2) 15,5
(3) 5,15
(4) 15,15
```

— — — — — — — — — —

Our program:

```
10 GR. 3
20 COLOR 1
30 PLOT 5,5: PLOT 15,5
40 PLOT 5,15: PLOT 15,15
```

We are using multiple statements per line.

11. When your program is run, which plotted point (1,2,3 or 4) is:

(a) at the upper left? ___________

(b) at the lower right? ___________

(c) at the upper right? ___________

(d) at the lower left? ___________

— — — — — — — — — —

(a) 1 (5,5) (b) 4 (15,15) (c) 2 (15,5) (d) 3 (5,15)

12. Complete the program below to put a point in each corner of the graphics area, using graphics mode 3. Remember, rows and columns start numbering with zero (0). Consult the table in frame 5. Type GR.0 to return to fullscreen text. Enter and try your completed program.

```
1Ø GR. 3
2Ø COLOR 1

3Ø PLOT Ø,Ø: PLOT ________

4Ø PLOT Ø,19: PLOT ________
```

— — — — — — — — — —

```
3Ø PLOT Ø,Ø: PLOT 38,19
4Ø PLOT Ø,19: PLOT 38,Ø
```

13. According to the table in frame 5, graphics modes 4 and 5 provide 79×40 points. This gives us 79 columns (0 through 78) and 40 rows (0 through 39).

Since the columns and rows are numbered from zero, the upper right hand corner of the screen would be plotted by the statements:

```
1Ø GR. 4
2Ø COLOR 1

3Ø PLOT ______,______
```

— — — — — — — — — —

```
3Ø PLOT 78,Ø
```

14. Write a program, using graphics mode 6, that will place a point in each corner of the graphic area for this mode. Refer to frame 12 to see how it was done for mode 3.

— — — — — — — — — —

Our sample program:

```
1Ø GR. 6
2Ø COLOR 1
3Ø PLOT Ø,Ø: PLOT 157,79
4Ø PLOT Ø,79: PLOT 157,Ø
```

15. Type GRAPHICS 0 to return to the text mode. Type NEW, enter and run the program below. Then draw a sketch of the result. Type GRAPHICS 0 when your sketch is finished to return to the text mode.

```
10 GRAPHICS 3
20 COLOR 1
30 PLOT 0,0: PLOT 1,1: PLOT 2,2
40 PLOT 3,3: PLOT 4,4: PLOT 5,5
50 PLOT 6,6: PLOT 7,7: PLOT 8,8
60 PLOT 9,9: PLOT 10,10: PLOT 11,11
70 PLOT 12,12: PLOT 13,13: PLOT 14,14
80 PLOT 15,15: PLOT 16,16: PLOT 17,17
90 PLOT 18,18: PLOT 19,19
```

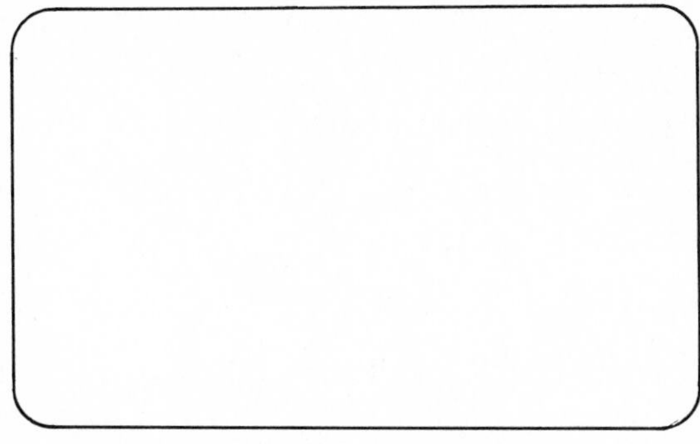

— — — — — — — — — — — —

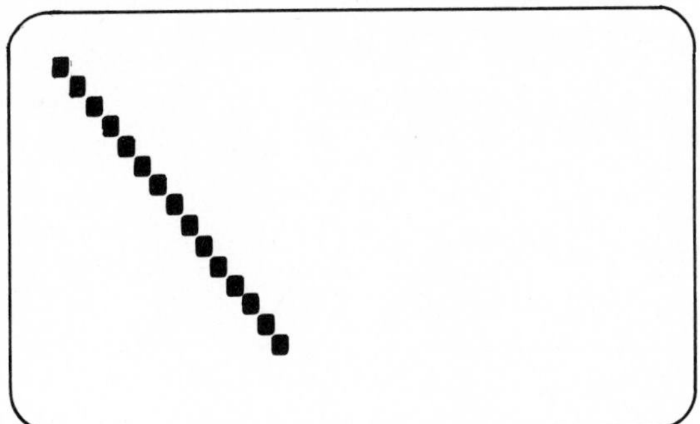

16. You can also use a FOR-NEXT loop to plot points. Type NEW, enter and run the following:

```
10 GRAPHICS 3
20 COLOR 1
30 FOR I=0 TO 19 STEP 2
40 PLOT I,I
50 NEXT I
```

How do the results of this run compare with that of frame 14?

— — — — — — — — — — — —

The results are the same.

---

17. A third way to plot a straight line is to use the DRAWTO statement along with the PLOT statement. The PLOT statement tells the computer where to start the line, and the DRAWTO statement gives the position where the line will end. The line is drawn from the PLOT position to the DRAWTO position.

Enter and run this program.

```
10 GR. 3
20 COLOR 1
30 PLOT 0,0
40 DRAWTO 19,19
```

Complete these statements.

(a) The PLOT statement tells the computer to

______________________________.

(b) The DRAWTO statement tells the computer to

______________________________.

(c) Compare the results of this program with those in frames 15 and 16.

____

____

— — — — — — — — — —

(a) start the line at the position given.
(b) end the line at the position given.
(c) the same

18. Complete this program which will draw a line from the top left to the lower right of the graphics area. Use graphics mode 4.

```
10 GR. 4
20 COLOR 1
30 PLOT 0,0

40 __________
```

— — — — — — — — — —

```
40 DRAWTO 78,39
```

19. After running the program in frame 18, the screen should look similar to this sketch.

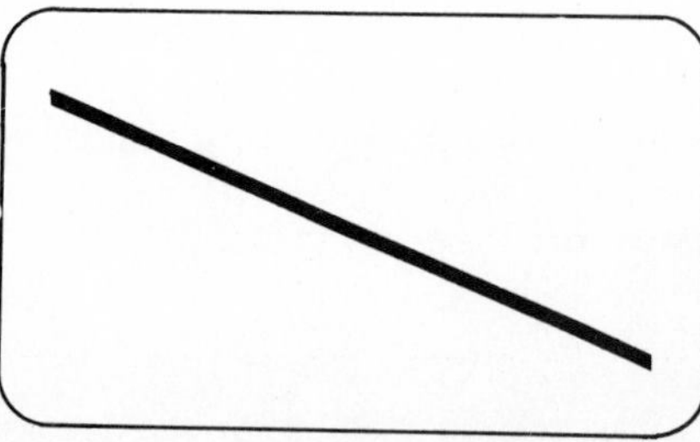

Now, add two lines to the program of frame 18 so that a second line will be drawn from the upper right corner to the lower left corner. A very large X should now be displayed as in this sketch.

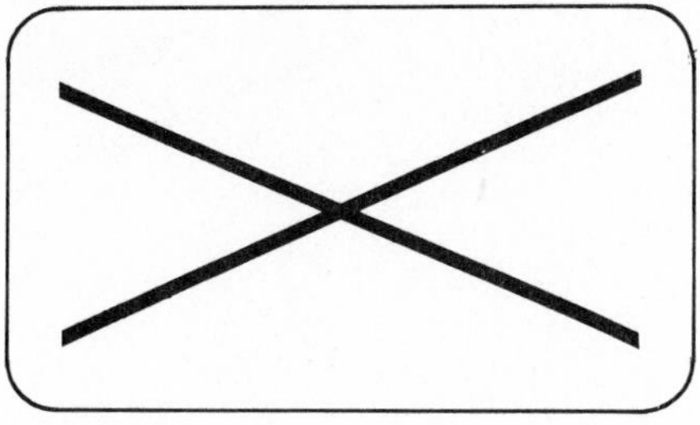

Complete these lines and add them to the program of frame 18.

```
5Ø PLOT ____________

6Ø DRAWTO ____________
```

— — — — — — — — — — —

```
5Ø PLOT 78,Ø
6Ø DRAWTO Ø,39
```

20. Add another line to the same program so that the text window will say : X MARKS THE PLOT.

```
7Ø ______________
```

— — — — — — — — — — —

```
7Ø PRINT "X MARKS THE PLOT"
```

21. Given the following program, draw a sketch of the results which will appear on the screen.

```
1Ø GRAPHICS 4
2Ø COLOR 1
3Ø FOR N= 39 TO Ø STEP -13
4Ø PLOT Ø,Ø
5Ø DRAWTO 78,N
6Ø NEXT N
```

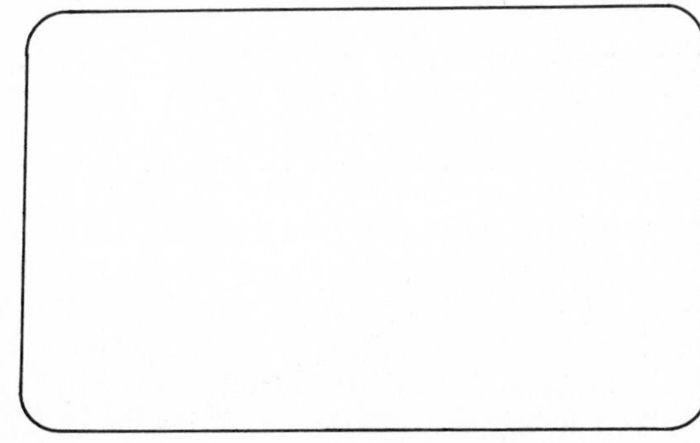

— — — — — — — — — — —

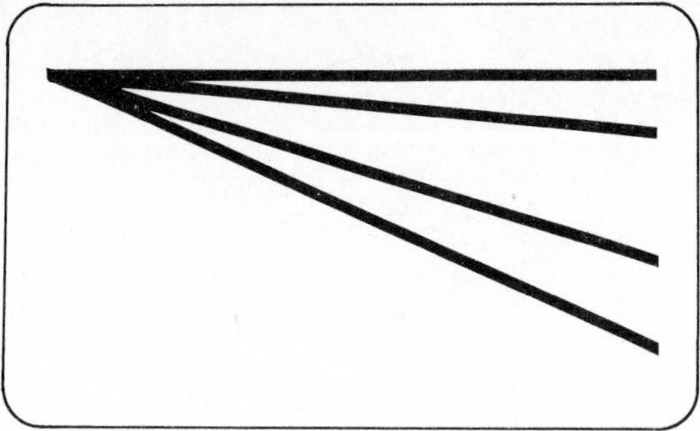

22. Add or change these lines to the program of frame 21. After running the program, press the BREAK key to stop. Then type 'GRAPHICS 0' to return to the text mode as before.

Add	`15 FOR M = Ø TO 1`
Change	`2Ø COLOR M`
Add	`7Ø NEXT M`
Add	`8Ø GOTO 15`

How do these changes effect the result? ______________________________

____

— — — — — — — — — — —

You can see each line being drawn and 'erased' repeatedly.

23. Now that you can use graphics with color, let's see how we can change the colors. We select a color with the statement:

```
SETCOLOR Ø,C,2
```

The variable C, can be any integer from 0 through 15. Each value for C will give us a different color for the plotted points.

The statement used to change color points on the screen is

______________________.

— — — — — — — — — — —

```
SETCOLOR Ø,C,2
```

24. A complete color graphics program must have the three statements: GRAPHICS, COLOR, and SETCOLOR. The GRAPHICS statement lets you pick the screen mode you want, the COLOR statement lets you get the color from the color register to the screen, and the SETCOLOR lets you change colors in the color registers. Of course, we must also plot some points.

```
10 GR. 3
20 COLOR 1
30 SETCOLOR 0,0,2
40 PLOT 0,3
50 DRAWTO 38,3
60 PRINT "WHAT COLOR DO YOU SEE?"
```

Examine the program before you run it. What do you think will appear on the screen

(a) in the graphics area? ______________________________

____

(b) in the text area? ______________________________

____

(c) Run the program to confirm your answers to (a) and (b).

— — — — — — — — — —

(a) a long grey color bar (color may vary for your TV).

(b) The words: WHAT COLOR DO YOU SEE?

(c) We trust your answers were correct. If not, you have learned something new.

25. A few changes and additions will convert the program of frame 24 to show each of the 16 colors available. The colors are changed by the values of the variable in the SETCOLOR statement in line 30.

(a) Complete the program

```
          10 GR. 3
          20 COLOR 1
Add       25 FOR N = 0 TO 15
Change    30 SETCOLOR 0,_____ _____
          40 PLOT 0,3
          50 DRAWTO 38,3
Change    60 FOR W = 1 TO 500: NEXT _______
Add       70 PRINT: PRINT: PRINT: PRINT N
Add       80 NEXT _________
```

(b) Describe what happens when you run the program.

____

____

— — — — — — — — — —

(a)
```
30 SETCOLOR 0,N,2
60 FOR W = 1 TO 500: NEXT W
80 NEXT N
```

(b) The color bar varies from grey through green with several shades of the same color.

26. You have just observed the 16 colors available on your ATARI. They were demonstrated by changing the color of the bar in the graphics area. We will now try a variation. You decide what happens on the screen.

Change line 30 in the program of frame 25 to:

```
30 SETCOLOR 2,N,2
```

Run this revised program and describe what happens.

____

____

— — — — — — — — — — —

The color bar is gold throughout the run, but the color of the text window goes through the 16 colors.

27. One more variation can be observed by changing line 30 once more.

Change line 30 to:

```
30 SETCOLOR 4,N,2
```

Run the program again with this change. Describe the new results.

____

____

— — — — — — — — — — —

This time, the background of the graphics area changes. The bar remains gold, and the text window turns dark and remains dark.

28. In frames 25, 26, and 27, we varied the values for the variables A and N in the statement: SETCOLOR A,N,2.

(a) When A was set to 0 where, on the screen, were the colors varied?

____

(b) When A was set to 2, where were the colors varied?

____

(c) When A was set to 4, where were the colors varied?

____

— — — — — — — — — — —

(a) The plotted bar
(b) The text window
(c) The background of the graphics area

29. The effects shown in frames 25, 26, and 27 can all be shown in one program.

(a) Fill in the missing blanks in lines 60, 80, 90 and 100.

```
1Ø GR. 3
2Ø COLOR 1
3Ø PRINT "WATCH MY COLORS CHANGE!!!"
4Ø FOR M = Ø TO 4 STEP 2
5Ø FOR N = Ø TO 15

6Ø SETCOLOR ___,___,___
7Ø PLOT 5,5: DRAWTO 3Ø,5

8Ø FOR W = 1 TO 2ØØ: NEXT ____

9Ø NEXT ___

1ØØ NEXT ___
```

(b) Briefly describe the results. ______________________________

____

____

— — — — — — — — — —

(a)

```
6Ø SETCOLOR M,N,2
8Ø FOR W = 1 TO 2ØØ: NEXT W
9Ø NEXT N
1ØØ NEXT M
```

(b) First the color bar varies through 16 colors, then the text window varies through 16 colors, and finally the background of the graphics area varies through 16 colors.

30. You can now plot points and create many colors on the video screen. Here is a program that combines both. Before you run the program, see if you can show where the points will be plotted. Shade the points in on the grid which is provided beside the program.

Plot the points that you think will be colored on this grid.

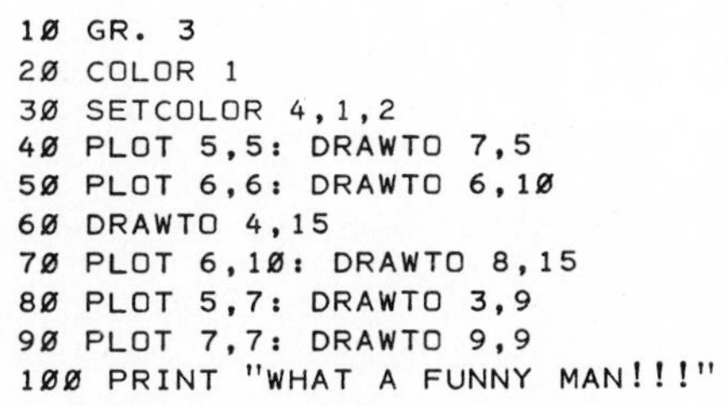

```
1Ø GR. 3
2Ø COLOR 1
3Ø SETCOLOR 4,1,2
4Ø PLOT 5,5: DRAWTO 7,5
5Ø PLOT 6,6: DRAWTO 6,1Ø
6Ø DRAWTO 4,15
7Ø PLOT 6,1Ø: DRAWTO 8,15
8Ø PLOT 5,7: DRAWTO 3,9
9Ø PLOT 7,7: DRAWTO 9,9
1ØØ PRINT "WHAT A FUNNY MAN!!!"
```

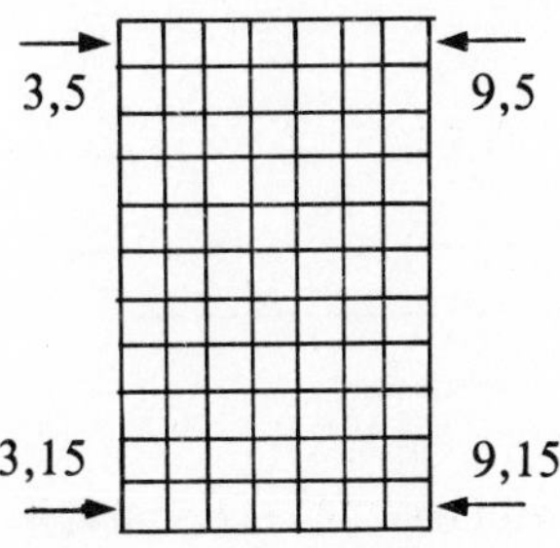

— — — — — — — — — — —

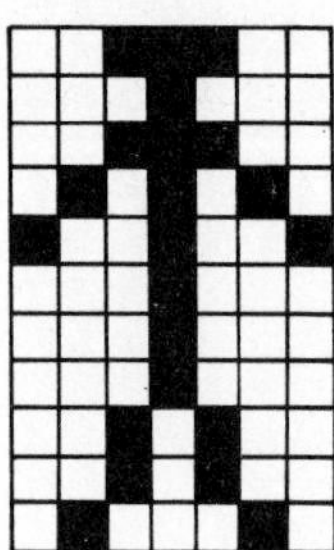

31. By changing the screen modes, we can change the size of the figure "drawn" in frame 30. Make these changes and additions to the program of frame 30.

Add	`5 FOR A = 7 TO 3 STEP-2`
Change	`10 GRAPHICS A`
Add	`93 FOR W = 1 TO 200: NEXT W`
Add	`95 NEXT A`

(a) Run the revised program and describe the results.

____

____

(b) How many screen modes were used? ______________

— — — — — — — — — — —

(a) The man appears to move from the upper left corner, and his size increases.
(b) 3

32. The program of frame 31 changed the graphics mode from many small divisions, to fewer very large divisions. Pictures can be drawn in more detail when many smaller points are used rather than larger points. In the program of frame 31,

(a) Which statement caused the change in graphics mode? __________

(b) The first value used for the variable A in the FOR-NEXT loop was __________, the second value was __________, and the third value was __________.

— — — — — — — — — — —

(a) Line `10 GRAPHICS A`

(b) first value = 7, second value = 5, third value = 3

33. The table in frame 5 shows the number of graphics positions for the screen modes. Modes 6 and 7 have 158×80, or 12,640 individual points. Modes 4 and 5 have 79×40, or 3,160 points. Mode 3 has 39×20, or 780 points. This program will allow you to examine some rectangles in the three sizes.

```
10 GRAPHICS 7
20 COLOR 1
30 SETCOLOR 0,15,2
35 X = 80:Y = 48
40 PLOT X,Y
50 PLOT X-2,Y-2: DRAWTO X+2,Y-2
60 DRAWTO X+2,Y+2: DRAWTO X-2,Y+2
70 DRAWTO X-2,Y-2
80 PLOT X-4,Y-4: DRAWTO X+4,Y-4
90 DRAWTO X+4,Y+4: DRAWTO X-4,Y+4
100 DRAWTO X-4,Y-4
```

First run the program and notice the width of the lines that were drawn and the size of the rectangle.

Second, change line 10 to: `10 GRAPHICS 5`
and line 35 to: `35 X=40: Y=24.`

Run the program again and compare the line width and rectangle size to your first run.

Third, change line 10 to: `10 GRAPHICS 3`
and line 35 to: `35 X=20: Y=12.`

Run the program again.

(a) How did the line width change for runs 1, 2, and 3?

____

(b) How did the rectangle size change?

____

— — — — — — — — — —

(a) It got wider each time.
(b) It got larger each time.

34. You can create an interesting visual effect by combining the three graphics modes in one program. Our revised program looks like this.

```
10 M = 1
20 FOR N = 7 TO 3 STEP-2
30 GRAPHICS N
40 COLOR 1
50 SETCOLOR 0,1,2
60 X = 80/M: Y = 48/M
70 PLOT X,Y
80 PLOT X-2,Y-2: DRAWTO X+2,Y-2
90 DRAWTO X+2,Y+2: DRAWTO X-2,Y+2
100 DRAWTO X-2,Y-2
110 PLOT X-4,Y-4: DRAWTO X+4,Y-4
120 DRAWTO X+4,Y+4: DRAWTO X-4,Y+4
130 DRAWTO X-4,Y-4
140 FOR W = 1 TO 200: NEXT W
150 M = 2*M
160 NEXT N
170 GOTO 10
```

Before you run the program:

(a) Which line would allow you to change the rectangle's color? ___________

(b) What key would you press to stop the program? ___________

(c) Which line would let you vary the time that each graphics mode stays on the screen? ___________

— — — — — — — — — — —

(a) line 50
(b) BREAK
(c) line 140

35. You now have color graphics under control, so we'll move on to the discovery of sound. Four variables are used with the SOUND statement. We'll call them V (for Voice), N (for Note), T (for Tone), and L (for Loudness).

```
20 SOUND V,N,T,L
```

In the line (20) above, tell what each variable represents.

(a) V = ___________

(b) N = ___________

(c) T = ___________

(d) L = ___________

— — — — — — — — — — —

(a) V = voice
(b) N = note
(c) T = tone
(d) L = loudness

36. Enter and use this two-line program to adjust the volume of your TV set to a reasonable level. Line 20 will cause the sound to continue. Press the **BREAK** key when you have the volume adjusted satisfactorily. Then type END and press the RETURN key to stop the sound.

```
10 SOUND 0,115,10,8
20 GOTO 20
```

Tell what each value used with the SOUND statement represents.

(a) 8 ____________________

(b) 115 ____________________

(c) 0 ____________________

(d) 10 ____________________

— — — — — — — — — — — —

(a) 8 = loudness
(b) 115 = note
(c) 0 = voice
(d) 10 = tone

37. We'll experiment with loudness first. Values for the variable L may be any integer from 0 through 15. Using 0 for voice, 115 for note, and 10 for tone, write a program to generate all 16 sound levels. Use an INPUT statement for L. Insert a statement: IF L = -5 THEN ________ to shut the sound off when finished.

— — — — — — — — — — — —

Our program:*

```
10 INPUT L
20 IF L = -5 THEN 50
30 SOUND 0,115,10,L
40 GOTO 10
50 END
```

* note: it may be done in other ways.

38. In the program of frame 37, each sound level will keep playing until a new input is received. Write a new program that uses a time delay to keep the note playing for a reasonable length of time. Use a FOR-NEXT loop to change the level of loudness.

— — — — — — — — — —

Our program:

```
10 FOR L = 0 TO 15
20 SOUND 0,115,10,L
30 FOR W = 1 TO 200: NEXT W
40 NEXT L
```

39. For normal use, the loudness level can be left at 8. Let's try the tone variable next. We have used a value of 10 so far. The variable N may range from 0 through 15. Write a revision of our program of frame 38 so that T (tone) will be varied. Set the loudness level at 8.

— — — — — — — — — —

Our revised program:

```
10 FOR T = 0 TO 15
20 SOUND 0,115,T,8
30 FOR W = 1 TO 200: NEXT W
40 NEXT T
```

40. Would you care to describe the sounds produced by the last program?

____

____

— — — — — — — — — —

I heard a couple of nice sounding tones, some funny noises, and some nice quiet.

41. Now let's put the tone back to 10, leave the loudness at 8, and stay with voice 0. This time we'll vary the note. The values used may range from 0 through 255. Shorten the time delay of the program of frame 39 to 50 and re-write the program to vary the notes.

— — — — — — — — — —

Our program:

```
10 FOR N = 0 TO 255
20 SOUND 0,N,10,8
30 FOR W = 1 TO 50: NEXT W
40 NEXT N
```

42. If you were writing a song, you probably wouldn't need all those 256 notes. Here is a table of values we will use that covers two and one-half octaves (when tone is set to 10).

N	Note
26	D#
27	D
29	C#
31	C
32	B
34	A#
36	A
38	G#
41	G
43	F#
46	F
48	E
51	D#
54	D
58	C#

N	Note
61	C
65	B
69	A#
73	A
77	G#
82	G
86	F#
92	F
97	E
103	D#
109	D
115	C#
122	C
129	B
137	A#
145	A

(a) From the results of the program in frame 41, which value of the note table gives the highest note? ______________

(b) Which gives the lowest? ______________

— — — — — — — — — —

(a) 26
(b) 145

43. To play a musical scale, we can store notes in a table and read them in when we need them.

Fill in the data values in this program. Do NOT use sharps (#). Start with the lowest note shown in the table in frame 42.

```
10 FOR A = 1 TO 16
20 READ N
30 SOUND 0,N,10,8
40 FOR W = 1 TO 200: NEXT W
50 SOUND 0,0,10,8
60 FOR W = 1 TO 10: NEXT W
70 NEXT A

80 DATA ____,____,____,____,____,____

90 DATA ____,____,____,____,____,____

100 DATA ____,____,____,____
```

— — — — — — — — — — — —

```
80 DATA 145,129,122,109,97,92
90 DATA 82,73,65,61,54,48
100 DATA 46,41,36,32
```

44. To make color and sound work together, add these lines to the program of frame 43.

```
5 GR. 5
15 COLOR 1
34 SETCOLOR 0,A-1,2
35 PLOT 5,11: DRAWTO 15,11
```

(a) When you run this program, how many notes will be played? ________

(b) How many colors will be displayed? ________________

— — — — — — — — — — — —

(a) 16
(b) 16

45. Blue is cold, and red is warm. Complete this program to play 8 notes. Display warm colors with high notes and cold colors with low notes. Use these colors:

dark purple	yellow-green
blue	yellow
blue-green	orange
green	red

Put both NOTE and COLOR in the data statements.

```
10 GR. 3
20 FOR A = 1 TO 8
30 COLOR 1
40 READ N,C

50 SETCOLOR 0,___,___
60 PLOT 10,9-A: DRAWTO 20,9-A

70 SOUND 0,___,10,8
80 FOR W = 1 TO 200: NEXT W
90 SETCOLOR 0,0,2
100 SOUND 0,0,10,8
110 FOR W = 1 TO 10: NEXT W
120 NEXT A

130 DATA ___,___,___,___

140 DATA ___,___,___,___

150 DATA ___,___,___,___

160 DATA ___,___,___,___
```

— — — — — — — — — —

Our choices, yours may vary.

```
50 SETCOLOR 0,C,2
70 SOUND 0,N,10,8
130 DATA 122,9,109,10
140 DATA 97,13,92,15
150 DATA 82,1 ,73,2
160 DATA 65,3,61,5
```

46. As your programming ability increases, the size of your programs also tend to increase. Long programs can be more easily written and understood if you break them up into functional parts. Often, you will find some of those functional parts being used at several places in your program. Rather than repeat them each time, a SUBROUTINE can be used. The GOSUB statement tells the computer to leave your main program and go to the subroutine. When the subroutine has been finished, a RETURN statement in the subroutine tells the computer to go back to the main program to the line that follows the GOSUB statement.

Here is a short program to demonstrate the use of the GOSUB and RETURN statements. Try it on your computer.

```
10 N = 122
20 GOSUB 100
30 N = 109
40 GOSUB 100
50 N = 97
60 GOSUB 100
70 END

100 SOUND 0,N,10,8
110 FOR W = 1 TO 200: NEXT W
120 SOUND 0,0,10,8
130 FOR W = 1 TO 10: NEXT W
140 RETURN
```

(a) Which lines contain the subroutine? ______________________

(b) How many times is the subroutine used? ________

(c) How many notes are played? ________

— — — — — — — — — —

(a) 100,110,120,130,140
(b) 3
(c) 3

47. Here is a program that uses "nested subroutines." At line 110 subroutine 1000 is called. At line 1020 in the first subroutine, subroutine 2000 is called. Subroutine 2000 returns from line 2010 to line 1030 of the first subroutine. Then the program goes back to the main program. The program below plays a one-octave scale and plots the notes on the video screen in color.

```
1Ø GR. 3
2Ø COLOR 1
3Ø SETCOLOR 1,1Ø,2
4Ø FOR N = 5 TO 13 STEP 2
5Ø PLOT Ø,N: DRAWTO 38,N
6Ø PLOT Ø,15: DRAWTO 35,15
7Ø PLOT 3Ø,15: DRAWTO 35,15
8Ø GOSUB 2ØØØ
9Ø SETCOLOR 4,4,2
1ØØ COLOR 2
11Ø X=3: Y=15: N=122: GOSUB 1ØØØ
12Ø X=5: Y=14: N=1Ø9: GOSUB 1ØØØ
13Ø X=7: Y=13: N=97: GOSUB 1ØØØ
14Ø X=9: Y=12: N=92: GOSUB 1ØØØ
15Ø X=11: Y=11: N=82: GOSUB 1ØØØ
16Ø X=13: Y=1Ø: N=73: GOSUB 1ØØØ
17Ø X=15: Y=9: N=65: GOSUB 1ØØØ
18Ø X=17: Y=8: N=61: GOSUB 1ØØØ
19Ø END

1ØØØ PLOT X,Y
1Ø1Ø SOUND Ø,N,1Ø,8
1Ø2Ø GOSUB 2ØØØ
1Ø3Ø RETURN

2ØØØ FOR W= 1 TO 2ØØ: NEXT W
2Ø1Ø RETURN
```

Replace line 190 and add lines which will come back down the scale in sound and plot the notes. (Our program only plays from low to high.)

— — — — — — — — — —

One way to do it:

```
19Ø X=15: Y=9: N=65: GOSUB 1ØØØ
2ØØ X=13: Y=1Ø: N=73: GOSUB 1ØØØ
21Ø X=11: Y=11: N=82: GOSUB 1ØØØ
22Ø X=9: Y=12: N=92: GOSUB 1ØØØ
23Ø X=7: Y=13: N=97: GOSUB 1ØØØ
24Ø X=5: Y=14: N=1Ø9: GOSUB 1ØØØ
25Ø X=3: Y=15: N=122: GOSUB 1ØØØ
26Ø END
```

48. Your ATARI sound system allows the use of four voices simultaneously by varying V in the sound statement:

```
SOUND V,N,T,L
```

We have only used one voice so far, but that is going to change now.

```
1Ø LØ = 8: L1 = Ø
2Ø NØ = 41: N1 = 129
3Ø GOSUB 1ØØØ
4Ø L1 = 8: GOSUB 1ØØØ
5Ø LØ = Ø: GOSUB 1ØØØ
6Ø L1 = Ø: GOSUB 1ØØØ
7Ø STOP

1ØØØ SOUND Ø,NØ,1Ø,LØ
1Ø1Ø SOUND 1,N1,1Ø,L1
1Ø2Ø FOR W = 1 TO 1ØØ: NEXT W
1Ø3Ø RETURN
```

(a) How many notes will you hear when line 30 is executed? ______________

(b) How many notes can be heard when line 40 is executed? ______________

(c) How many notes can be heard when line 60 is executed? ______________

(d) Which voice does line 50 turn off? ______________

— — — — — — — — — — —

(a) 1 since the loudness of voice 1 is set to zero.
(b) 2
(c) none
(d) voice 0

49. The following program demonstrates a simple tune with two voices. Three subroutines are used to play the notes for the proper length of time. Each line of the main program "calls" a subroutine to play a pair of notes.

```
1Ø NØ = 41: N1 = 129: GOSUB 2ØØØ
2Ø NØ = 32: N1 = 1Ø9: GOSUB 1ØØØ
3Ø NØ = 27: N1 = 92: GOSUB 3ØØØ
4Ø NØ = 31: N1 = 97: GOSUB 2ØØØ
5Ø NØ = 32: N1 = 1Ø9: GOSUB 1ØØØ
6Ø NØ = 36: N1 = 122: GOSUB 3ØØØ
7Ø NØ = 41: N1 = 129: GOSUB 1ØØØ
8Ø NØ = 36: N1 = 122: GOSUB 1ØØØ
9Ø NØ = 32: N1 = 1Ø9: GOSUB 1ØØØ
1ØØ NØ = 36: N1 = 122: GOSUB 3ØØØ
11Ø NØ = 27: N1 = 92: GOSUB 2ØØØ
12Ø NØ = Ø: N1 = Ø: GOSUB 1ØØØ
13Ø NØ = 41: N1 = 129: GOSUB 2ØØØ
14Ø NØ = 32: N1 = 1Ø9: GOSUB 1ØØØ
15Ø NØ = 25: N1 = 92: GOSUB 3ØØØ
16Ø NØ = 36: N1 = 122: GOSUB 2ØØØ
17Ø NØ = 32: N1 = 1Ø9: GOSUB 1ØØØ
18Ø NØ = 31: N1 = 97: GOSUB 1ØØØ
19Ø NØ = 32: N1 = 1Ø9: GOSUB 1ØØØ
2ØØ NØ = 36: N1 = 122: GOSUB 1ØØØ
21Ø NØ = 27: N1 = 92: GOSUB 2ØØØ
22Ø NØ = 41: N1 = 129: GOSUB 1ØØØ
23Ø NØ = 32: N1 = 1Ø9: GOSUB 2ØØØ
24Ø NØ = 36: N1 = 122: GOSUB 1ØØØ
25Ø NØ = 41: N1 = 129: GOSUB 3ØØØ
26Ø GOSUB 1ØØØ
27Ø GR. Ø
28Ø END
```

Fill in the missing blanks in the subroutines.

```
1000 SOUND 0,____,____,____

1010 SOUND 1,____,____,____

1020 FOR W = 1 TO 50: NEXT W

1030 ______________________________

2000 SOUND 0,____,____,____

2010 SOUND 1,____,____,____

2020 FOR W = 1 TO 100: NEXT W

2030 ________________

3000 SOUND 0,____,____,____

3010 SOUND 1,____,____,____

3020 FOR W = 1 TO 150: NEXT W

3030 __________________
```

— — — — — — — — — —

```
1000 SOUND 0,N0,10,8
1010 SOUND 1,N1,10,8
1030 RETURN

2000 SOUND 0,N0,10,8
2010 SOUND 1,N1,10,8
2030 RETURN

3000 SOUND 0,N0,10,8
3010 SOUND 1,N1,10,8
3030 RETURN
```

50. Change the subroutines in the last program so that graphics mode 3 is used. In subroutine 1000 plot a blue bar near the middle of the screen. For subroutine 2000 make the bar gold, and for subroutine 3000 make the bar red.

1Ø11 ______________________________

1Ø12 ______________________________

1Ø13 ______________________________

1Ø14 ______________________________

2Ø11 ______________________________

2Ø12 ______________________________

2Ø13 ______________________________

3Ø11 ______________________________

3Ø12 ______________________________

3Ø13 ______________________________

3Ø14 ______________________________

— — — — — — — — — —

```
1Ø11 GR. 3
1Ø12 COLOR 1
1Ø13 SETCOLOR Ø,8,2
1Ø14 PLOT Ø,12: DRAWTO 5,12

2Ø11 GR. 3
2Ø12 COLOR 1
2Ø13 SETCOLOR Ø,1,2
2Ø14 PLOT Ø,12: DRAWTO 1Ø,12

3Ø11 GR. 3
3Ø12 COLOR 1
3Ø13 SETCOLOR Ø,4,2
3Ø14 PLOT Ø,12: DRAWTO 15,12
```

51. The next program will cover frames 51 to 55. We will add some two, three, and four part harmony to our sound. The program is quite long so we'll break it up into several sections.

One of the voices plays a repeating background series of three notes. Therefore, we have used three subroutines for the sound statements with each subroutine containing one of these background notes. In addition, the subroutines also contain the sound statements for two other voices. Since the subroutines are the most important part of the program, we'll look at them first.

```
1ØØØ SOUND Ø,183,1Ø,8          first background note
1Ø1Ø SOUND 1,N1,1Ø,8           voice 1,note 1,tone,loudness
1Ø2Ø SOUND 2,N2,1Ø,8           voice 2,note 2,tone,loudness
1Ø3Ø FOR W=1 TO 25: NEXT W     time delay to hold notes on
1Ø4Ø RETURN
2ØØØ SOUND Ø,137,1Ø,8          second background note
2Ø1Ø SOUND 1,N1,1Ø,8           voice 1 again
2Ø2Ø SOUND 2,N2,1Ø,8           voice 2 again
2Ø3Ø FOR W=1 TO 25: NEXT W     hold the notes on again
2Ø4Ø RETURN
3ØØØ SOUND Ø,145,1Ø,8          third background note
3Ø1Ø SOUND 1,N1,1Ø,8           voice 1
3Ø2Ø SOUND 2,N2,1Ø,8           voice 2
3Ø3Ø FOR W=1 TO 25: NEXT W     hold the notes again
3Ø4Ø RETURN
```

Each of these subroutines provides for playing a certain number of notes simultaneously for a given period of time.

(a) How many notes at one time? ___________

(b) Which statements determine the time the note is played?

____

— — — — — — — — — —

(a) 3
(b) the FOR-NEXT loops at lines 1030, 2030, and 3030.

52. Now let's look at the main beginning of the program, which sets up the notes to be played.

```
1Ø N1=Ø: N2=Ø: GOSUB 1ØØØ      N1 and N2 set for quiet
2Ø GOSUB 2ØØØ                  N1,N2 left quiet
3Ø GOSUB 3ØØØ                  Nothing happening yet except
4Ø GOSUB 1ØØØ                    for action in the subroutines.
5Ø GOSUB 2ØØØ
6Ø N2=61:GOSUB 3ØØØ            Now turn on voice 2 with note 2
7Ø N2=46:GOSUB 1ØØØ            Change note 2
8Ø GOSUB 2ØØØ                  Leave the same except background
9Ø GOSUB 3ØØØ
1ØØ END
```

Enter this much of the program along with the subroutines and run it.

(a) How many notes heard at line 10? ___________

(b) Does line 20 change the sound? ___________________________

(c) Which line causes a second note to be heard? _______________

— — — — — — — — — —

(a) Only one, the background note (183).
(b) The background note changes to 137.
(c) Line 60 (also 2 notes at 70,80,90).

53. Replace line 100 and continue as below.

```
1ØØ N1=48:N2=41: GOSUB 1ØØØ      Voice 1 and 2 on
11Ø N1=46:N2=36: GOSUB 2ØØØ      Change notes
12Ø N1=41:N2=34: GOSUB 3ØØØ      Change again
13Ø N1=36:N2=31: GOSUB 1ØØØ        and again
14Ø GOSUB 2ØØØ                   Change only background
15Ø GOSUB 3ØØØ                   Change background again
16Ø N1=48:N2=41: GOSUB 1ØØØ      Change all three notes
17Ø GOSUB 2ØØØ                   Change only background
18Ø GOSUB 3ØØØ                   Change background again
19Ø END
```

Now run the program again.

(a) How many notes caused by line 100? ______________

(b) Do all the lines 100–180 play three notes? _______

— — — — — — — — — —

(a) 3
(b) yes

54. The next section continues in the same manner except for the last three lines.280–320.

```
19Ø N1=46:N2=36:GOSUB 1ØØØ
2ØØ GOSUB 2ØØØ
21Ø N1=48: GOSUB 3ØØØ
22Ø N1=54:N2=34: GOSUB 1ØØØ
23Ø N1=61:N2=36: GOSUB 2ØØØ
24Ø N1=69:N2=41:GOSUB 3ØØØ
25Ø N1=73:N2=46: GOSUB 1ØØØ
26Ø GOSUB 2ØØØ
27Ø N1=69:N2=54: GOSUB 3ØØØ
28Ø SOUND Ø,183,1Ø,8:
29Ø SOUND 1,82,1Ø,8
3ØØ SOUND 2,69,1Ø,8
31Ø SOUND 3,61,1Ø,8
32Ø FOR W=1 TO 5Ø:NEXT W
33Ø END
```

This time we can't use any of our three subroutines, so we do it in the main program.

(a) How many voices are heard during the execution of line 320? __________

(b) How does the time delay compare with that of the three subroutines?

____

— — — — — — — — — —

(a) 4
(b) twice as long (FOR W = 1 TO 50)

55. Here is the final portion of the program.

```
330 N1=61:N2=0:N3-0:GOSUB 3000        turn off voices 2 and 3
340 N1=73:N2=46:GOSUB 1000
350 GOSUB 2000
360 N1=46:N2=0:GOSUE 3000
370 N1=61:N2=41:GOSUB 1000
380 N1=46:N2=36:GOSUB 2000
390 N1=41:N2=34:GOSUB 3000
400 N1=36:N2=31:GOSUB 1000
410 GOSUB 2000
420 N1=46:GOSUB 3000
430 N1=48:N2=41:GOSUB 1000
440 GOSUB 2000
450 N1=0:N2=36:GOSUB 3000
460 N1=54:N2=34:GOSUB 1000
470 GOSUB 2000
480 N1=0:GOSUB 3000
490 N1=61:N2=34:GOSUB 1000
500 N2=36:GOSUB 2000
510 N1=69:N2-41:GOSUB 3000
520 N1=73:N2=61:GOSUB 1000
530 N2=46:GOSUB 2000
540 N1=82:N2=61:GOSUB 3000
550 SOUND 0,183,10,8
560 SOUND 1,92,10,8
570 SOUND 2,46,10,8
580 FOR W=1 TO 75: NEXT W
590 END
```

(a) The last tone played contained how many notes? ___________

(b) How did the duration of the last tone compare with that of each of the subroutines? ___________

— — — — — — — — — —

(a) 3
(b) three times as long

SELF-TEST

Congratulations!!! You covered a lot of ground in Chapter Ten. We have given you some fundamentals which you can use to build your understanding of the color graphics and sound capabilities of your ATARI computer. Use this self-test to demonstrate your new knowledge.

1. There are eight screen modes provided for mixing graphics and text in your ATARI computer. They are numbered from 0—7. In previous chapters all programs were printed in a pure text mode.

   (a) What graphics statement is used to provide pure text?

   ```
   10 ______________
   ```

   (b) Give a mixed text-graphics mode with approximately 160×80 graphics positions.

   ```
   10 ______________
   ```

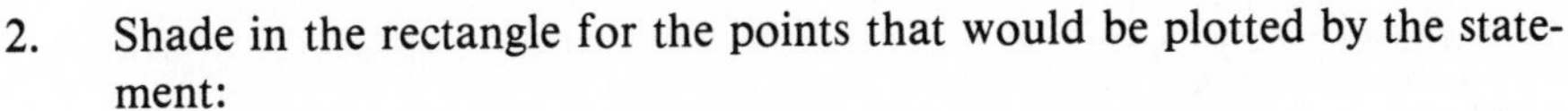

2. Shade in the rectangle for the points that would be plotted by the statement:

   ```
   20 PLOT 4,1
   ```

3. Complete this program so that it draws a vertical line from the top of the screen at the left side to the text window at the extreme right side of the screen.

   ```
   10 GRAPHICS 4
   20 COLOR 1
   30 PLOT ____________
   40 DRAWTO ____________
   ```

4. Write a program, using graphics mode 6, that will draw the largest possible rectangle in the graphics area. Also draw the diagonals of the rectangle as shown below.

5. Use the following program and your computer to answer questions 5 (a), (b), and (c).

```
10 GR. 3
20 COLOR 1
30 FOR M = 0 TO 4 STEP 2
40 FOR N = 0 TO 15
50 SETCOLOR M,N,2
60 PLOT 2,10: DRAWTO 12,10
70 FOR W = 1 TO 200: NEXT W
80 NEXT N
90 NEXT M
```

Fill in the blanks with the words BAR, TEXT WINDOW, or BACKGROUND.

(a) When the value of M is 0, what changes color? ________________

(b) When the value of M is 2, what changes color? ________________

(c) When the value of M is 4, what changes color? ________________

6. If the following program is run, describe what would happen on the video screen.

```
10 GR. 3
20 COLOR 1
30 FOR N = 0 TO 15
40 SETCOLOR 0,N+3,2
50 PLOT 2,5: DRAWTO 2,10
60 FOR W = 1 TO 200: NEXT W
70 SETCOLOR 4,N,2
80 FOR W = 1 TO 200: NEXT W
90 NEXT N
```

7. Write a program to fill the plotting area for graphics mode 3 with alternate points (that is, 0,0; 0,2; 0,4 . . . 2,0; 2,2 . . . .). Use nested FOR-NEXT loops. Choose your favorite colors.

8. Using the SOUND statement:

(a) How many different voices may be played at one time? ____________

(b) Loudness levels may be set to any integer in the range of

____________ to ____________.

(c) The note variable may range from ____________ to ____________.

9. In the following program, the SOUND statement causes a note to be played. How long will it stay on? ______________

```
10 INPUT N
20 SOUND 0,97,10,8
30 GOTO 10
```

10. Using the table in frame 42, write a program to play a one octave scale (C to C) with no sharps.

11. Given the program:

```
10 N0=36: N1=122: GOSUB 1000
20 N0=32: N1=109: GOSUB 2000
30 END
```

write the subroutines so they play the notes. Subroutine 1000 should hold the notes for a count of 50 and subroutine 2000 for a count of 100.

Answers to Self-Test

1. (a) `10 GRAPHICS 0` (frame 4)
   (b) `10 GRAPHICS 6` or `10 GRAPHICS 7` (frame 5)

2. 20 PLOT 4,1 would color the shaded rectangle in the fifth column and second row.

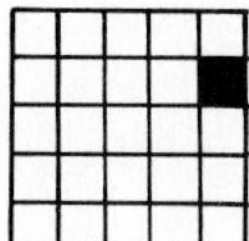

3.
```
30 PLOT 0,0
40 DRAWTO 78,39
```

4.
```
10 GRAPHICS 6
20 COLOR 1
30 SETCOLOR 0,12,2
40 PLOT 0,0
50 DRAWTO 157,0
60 DRAWTO 157,79
70 DRAWTO 0,79
80 DRAWTO 0,0
90 DRAWTO 157,79
100 PLOT 0,79
110 DRAWTO 157,0
```

(Your setcolor values may differ.)

Lines 50–110 may be different for your program. As long as your rectangle looks like the sketch, it's OK.

(frames 5,7,18,20)

5. (a) BAR (frames 23,26)
   (b) TEXT WINDOW (frames 24,26)
   (c) BACKGROUND (frames 25,26)

6. The color BAR and the BACKGROUND both change color. (frames 23–26)

7. Our program:

```
10 GRAPHICS 3
20 COLOR 1
30 SETCOLOR 0,2,2
40 FOR N = 0 TO 39 STEP 2
50 FOR M = 0 TO 19 STEP 2
60 PLOT N,M
70 NEXT M
80 NEXT N
```

(frames 5,9,23)

8. (a) 4 (frame 47)
   (b) 0 to 15 (frame 37)
   (c) 0 to 255 (frame 41)

9. Until a new note is INPUT. (frame 38)

10. Yours should be similar to this:

```
10 FOR A = 1 TO 8
20 READ N
30 SOUND 0,N,10,8
40 FOR W = 1 TO 200: NEXT W
50 NEXT A
60 DATA 122,109,97,92
70 DATA 82,73,65,61
```

lines 60 and 70 might also be:

```
60 DATA 61,54,48,46
70 DATA 41,36,32,31
```

(frame 42)

11.

```
1000 SOUND 0,N0,10,8
1010 SOUND 1,N1,10,8
1020 FOR W = 1 TO 50: NEXT W
1030 RETURN

2000 SOUND 0,N0,10,8
2010 SOUND 1,N1,10,8
2020 FOR W = 1 TO 100: NEXT W
2030 RETURN
```

Final Self-Test

Now that you're done with the book, try this final examination to test all your skills. The answers follow the test. Use separate paper for your programs and calculations.

1. STARS is a number guessing game that was first published in *People's Computer Company* newspaper. It's fun to use with players of all ages and you should find it challenging to program as well.

Here are the rules typed by the computer. You don't have to include them in your program.

> "I will think of a whole number from 1 to 100. Try to guess my number. After you guess my number, I will type one or more stars (*). The closer you are to my number, the more stars I will type. One star (*) means you are far away from my number. Seven stars (*******) means you are very, very close to my number!!"

Logic: If the guess is 64 or more away, one star; 32–63 away, two stars; 16–31 away, 3 stars; 8–15 away, 4 stars; 4–7 away, 5 stars) 2–3 away, 6 stars; 1 away, 7 stars. You will need to use the absolute value function, something new to you but easy to use.

Clues:

```
ABS(1Ø)=1Ø
ABS (-1Ø)=1Ø
IF ABS(X-Y)=1Ø THEN 1ØØ
```

```
RUN
ENTER YOUR GUESS? 10
**
ENTER YOUR GUESS? 25
***
ENTER YOUR GUESS? 50
******
ENTER YOUR GUESS? 60
****
ENTER YOUR GUESS? 45
******
ENTER YOUR GUESS? 42
*****
ENTER YOUR GUESS? 47
*******
ENTER YOUR GUESS? 48
WINNER!!!
```

2. You may have used matrix commands on some other computer. (Matrix is just another name for array.) Versions of BASIC for home computers generally do not include matrix commands. However, they are easy to simulate. Try it.

You have two 5 by 3 arrays called A and B, filled with small numbers that are read into the elements or boxes in the array from DATA statements. Write a program to add the contents of each element in array A to the corresponding element in array B, and place the results in the proper place in a third array, C.

A

7	8	9
3	4	1
6	8	2
1	4	1
8	10	2

B

3	6	8
2	4	7
1	3	1
8	4	9
6	6	6

C

10	14	17
5	8	8
7	11	3
9	8	10
14	16	8

Example: A(1,1) + B(1,1) = C(1,1)
A(1,2) + B(1,2) = C(1,2) etc.

```
RUN
A ARRAY CONTENTS

 7             8             9
 3             4             1
 6             8             2
 1             4             1
 8             1Ø            2


B ARRAY CONTENTS

 3             6             8
 2             4             7
 1             3             1
 8             4             9
 6             6             6


C ARRAY CONTENTS

 1Ø            14            17
 5             8             8
 7             11            3
 9             8             1Ø
 14            16            8
```

3. Your child plans to set up a weekend sidewalk stand selling "junk" from around the house (also known as a garage sale). Your youngster has no trouble finding merchandise and no trouble pricing it. But he or she really doesn't understand the money system and is worried about making change when people buy these "goods."

Write a program to allow the child to enter the amount of the sale and the amount of money received, and have the computer then print exactly how much and what kind of change to give back. The RUN is shown below.

```
RUN
ENTER TOTAL SALES AMOUNT? .35
ENTER AMOUNT RECEIVED? 1.ØØ
COIN CHANGE .65

1 HALF DOLLAR
 1 DIME
 1 NICKEL

ENTER TOTAL SALES AMOUNT? 3.45
ENTER AMOUNT RECEIVED? 2Ø.ØØ

BILL CHANGE IS 16
 1 $1Ø BILL
 1 $ 5 BILL
 1 $1 BILL

COIN CHANGE .55

1 HALF DOLLAR
 1 NICKEL
```

Warning: Some versions of BASIC will round off numbers in peculiar ways (deep inside the computer) because of the way the electronics perform arithmetic. So beware! 4.9999 pennies is no fair. Write your program to avoid this kind of problem by checking for integer values for change that includes pennies.

4. Write a program to perform conversions from selected U.S. standard measures to their metric equivalents and vice versa. Set up your program so that the user can select conversions as shown in the RUN below.

```
RUN
DO YOU WANT CONVERSIONS FOR
(1) METRIC TO U.S. STANDARD MEASURES
(2) U.S. STANDARD MEASURES TO METRIC
TYPE 1 OR 2? 1
WANT LIST OF CONVERSIONS (Y OR N)? Y
SELECT CONVERSION FROM THIS LIST:
(1) CENTIMETERS TO INCHES
(2) METERS TO FEET
(3) KILOMETERS TO MILES
(4) KILOGRAMS TO POUNDS
(5) GRAMS TO OUNCES
(6) LITERS TO QUARTS
(7) DEGREES CELSIUS TO DEGREES FAHRENHEIT
ENTER NUMBER OF CONVERSION DESIRED? 5

HOW MANY GRAMS? 1Ø
 1Ø GRAMS = .35 OUNCES

DO YOU WANT CONVERSIONS FOR
(1) METRIC TO U.S. STANDARD MEASURES
(2) U.S. STANDARD MEASURES TO METRIC
TYPE 1 OR 2? 2
WANT LIST OF CONVERSIONS (Y OR N)? Y
SELECT CONVERSION FROM THIS LIST:
(1) INCHES TO CENTIMETERS
(2) FEET TO METERS
(3) MILES TO KILOMETERS
(4) POUNDS TO KILOGRAMS
(5) OUNCES TO GRAMS
(6) QUARTS TO LITERS
(7) DEGREES FAHRENHEIT TO DEGREES CELSIUS
ENTER NUMBER OF CONVERSION DESIRED? 3

HOW MANY MILES? 2
 2 MILES = 3.218 KILOMETERS

DO YOU WANT CONVERSIONS FOR
(1) METRIC TO U.S. STANDARD MEASURES
(2) U.S. STANDARD MEASURES TO METRIC
TYPE 1 OR 2? 1
DO YOU WANT THE LIST OF CONVERSIONS (Y OR N)? N
ENTER NUMBER OF CONVERSION DESIRED? 1

HOW MANY CENTIMETERS? 5Ø
 5Ø CENTIMETERS = 19.5 INCHES

DO YOU WANT CONVERSIONS FOR
```

← Since the list was printed above, no need to repeat it again.

And so on.

We suggest the following manner of organizing the program, making extensive use of subroutines. The main program is shown at the top; here the user selects which type of conversion is to be made. The program then branches to subroutines which list the specific conversions. From these subroutines, the program GOSUBs again, to one of fourteen sub-subroutines (seven for each "direction" of conversion).

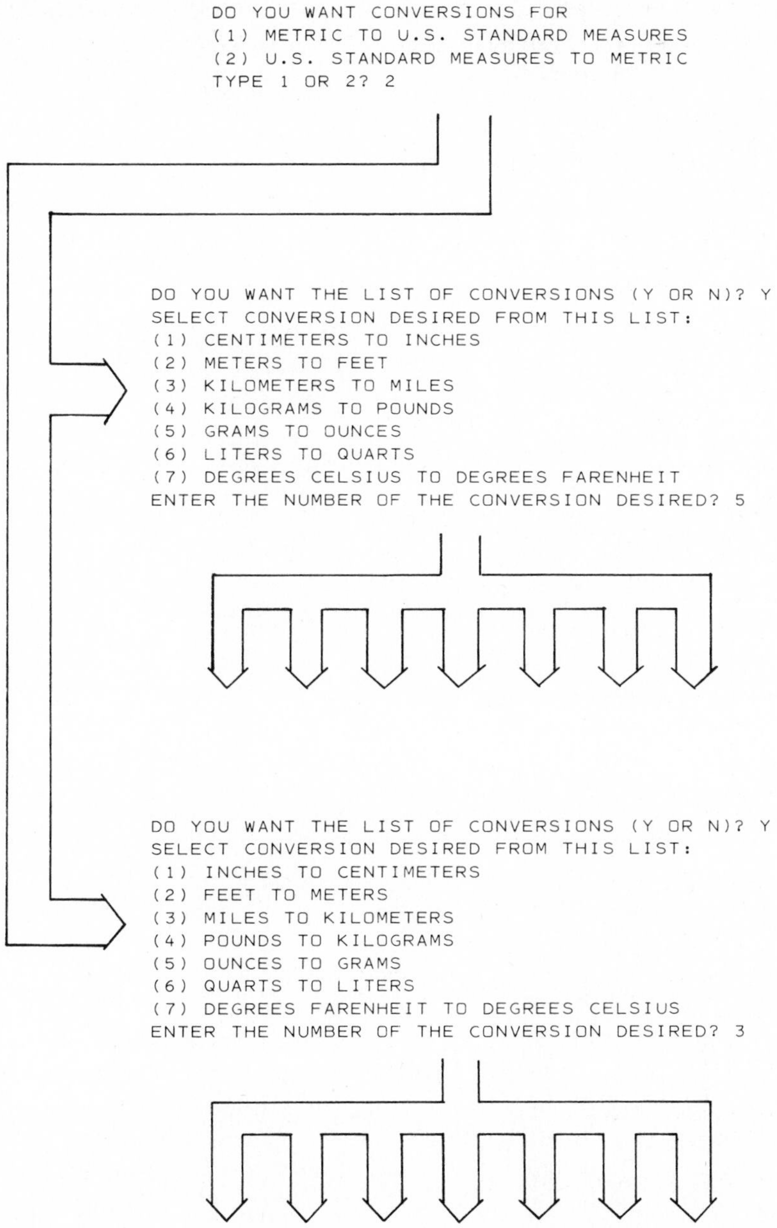

```
DO YOU WANT CONVERSIONS FOR
(1) METRIC TO U.S. STANDARD MEASURES
(2) U.S. STANDARD MEASURES TO METRIC
TYPE 1 OR 2? 2
```

```
DO YOU WANT THE LIST OF CONVERSIONS (Y OR N)? Y
SELECT CONVERSION DESIRED FROM THIS LIST:
(1) CENTIMETERS TO INCHES
(2) METERS TO FEET
(3) KILOMETERS TO MILES
(4) KILOGRAMS TO POUNDS
(5) GRAMS TO OUNCES
(6) LITERS TO QUARTS
(7) DEGREES CELSIUS TO DEGREES FARENHEIT
ENTER THE NUMBER OF THE CONVERSION DESIRED? 5
```

```
DO YOU WANT THE LIST OF CONVERSIONS (Y OR N)? Y
SELECT CONVERSION DESIRED FROM THIS LIST:
(1) INCHES TO CENTIMETERS
(2) FEET TO METERS
(3) MILES TO KILOMETERS
(4) POUNDS TO KILOGRAMS
(5) OUNCES TO GRAMS
(6) QUARTS TO LITERS
(7) DEGREES FARENHEIT TO DEGREES CELSIUS
ENTER THE NUMBER OF THE CONVERSION DESIRED? 3
```

From any one of these subroutines, return to the subroutine that sent it, and from there, return immediately to the main program to start over again.

Here are the conversion values to include in the program.

Metric to U.S. Standard	*U.S. Standard to Metric*
1 centimeter = .39 inches	1 inch = 2.54 cm
1 meter = 3.28 feet	1 ft. = .3048 meters
1 kilometer = .62 miles	1 mile = 1.609 kilometers
1 kilogram = 2.2 pounds	1 pound = .45 kilograms
1 gram = .035 ounces	1 quart = .946 liters
1 liter = 1.0567 quarts	F° = 9/5C° + 32
C° = 5/9(F°–32)	

Answers to Final Self-Test

1.

```
10 REMARK***STARS GAME
20 LET N=INT(100*RND(1))+1
30 PRINT "ENTER YOUR GUESS";:INPUT G
35 IF G=N THEN PRINT "WINNER!!!" : GOTO 20
40 LET D=ABS(G-N)
50 IF D>=64 THEN 170
60 IF D>=32 THEN 160
70 IF D>=16 THEN 150
80 IF D>=8 THEN 140
90 IF D>=4 THAN 130
100 IF D>=2 THAN 120
110 PRINT "*";
120 PRINT "*";
130 PRINT "*";
140 PRINT "*";
150 PRINT "*";
160 PRINT "*";
170 PRINT "*" : GOTO 30
```

2.

```
10 REMARK***SIMULATION OF MATRIX ADDITION
14 REMARK INITIALIZE
20 DIM A(5,3), B(5,3), C(5,3)
25 REM LOAD A AND B ARRAY FROM DATA STATEMENTS.
26 REM PRINT ARRAYS
27 PRINT "A ARRAY CONTENTS": PRINT
30 FOR X=1 TO 5
35 FOR Y=1 TO 3
40 READ X,Y: PRINT A(X,Y),
45 NEXT Y
50 PRINT
55 NEXT X : PRINT : PRINT
57 PRINT "B ARRAY CONTENTS" : PRINT
60 FOR X=1 TO 5
65 FOR Y=1 TO 3
70 READ X,Y : PRINT B(X,Y),
75 NEXT Y
80 PRINT
85 NEXT X : PRINT : PRINT
90 REM ADD A + B INTO C
95 FOR X=1 TO 5
100 FOR Y=1 TO 3
105 LET C(X,Y)=A(X,Y)+B(X,Y) : PRINT C(X,Y),
110 NEXT Y
115 PRINT
120 NEXT X
130 REM DATA FOR A ARRAY
135 DATA 7,8,9,3,4,1,6,8,2,1,4,1,8,-10,2
140 REM DATA FOR B ARRAY
145 DATA 3,5,8,2,4,7,1,3,1,8,4,9,6,6,6
```

3.

```
10 REMARK***COIN CHANGER
20 PRINT "ENTER TOTAL SALES AMOUNT";:INPUT T
30 PRINT "ENTER AMOUNT RECEIVED";:INPUT M
40 IF M<T THEN PRINT "NOT ENOUGH MONEY RECEIVED":GOTO 20
50 IF M=T THEN PRINT "EXACT CHANGE, NO CHANGE REQUIRED":PRINT:GOTO 20
60 LET C=M-T:IF C<1.00 THEN 150
65 PRINT
70 LET B=C-(C-INT(C)):PRINT "BILL CHANGE IS "; B
75 LET C=C-B
80 LET B1=INT(B/20):IF B1=0 THEN 100
85 PRINT B1; " $20 BILL"
90 LET B=B-(B1*20)
100 LET B2=INT(B/10):IF B2=0 THEN 120
105 PRINT B2; " $10 BILL"
110 LET B=B-(B2*10)
120 LET B3=INT(B/5):IF B3=0 THEN 140
125 PRINT B3; " $ 5 BILL"
130 LET B=B-(B3*5)
140 IF B<1 THEN 150
145 PRINT B; " $1 BILL":PRINT
150 LET C=INT((C+.005)*100)
152 LET C=INT(C)
155 PRINT "COIN CHANGE "; C/100:PRINT
160 IF C<50 THEN 180
170 PRINT "1 HALF DOLLAR":LET C=C-50
180 IF C<25 THEN 200
190 PRINT "1 QUARTER":LET C=C-25
200 LET C=INT(C/10):IF D=0 THEN 220
210 PRINT D; " DIME":LET C=C-(D*10)
220 LET N=INT(C/5):IF N=0 THEN 240
230 PRINT N; " NICKEL":LET C=C-(N*5)
240 IF C<1 THEN PRINT:GOTO 20
250 PRINT INT(C); " PENNY":PRINT:GOTO 20
```

4.
```
100 REM***SELECTED MEASUREMENT CONVERSIONS
110 PRINT "DO YOU WANT CONVERSIONS FOR"
120 PRINT "(1) METRIC TO U.S. STANDARD MEASURES"
130 PRINT "(2) U.S. STANDARD MEASURES TO METRIC"
140 PRINT "TYPE 1 OR 2"; : INPUT N
150 ON N GOSUB 1000,1100
160 GOTO 110

1000 REM***USER SELECTS DESIRED METRIC TO U.S. CONVERSION
1010 PRINT "WANT LIST OF CONVERSIONS (Y OR N)"; : INPUT A$
1020 IF A$="N" THEN 1040
1030 PRINT "SELECT CONVERSION FROM THIS LIST:"
1031 PRINT "(1) CENTIMETERS TO INCHES"
1032 PRINT "(2) METERS TO FEET"
1033 PRINT "(3) KILOMETERS TO MILES"
1034 PRINT "(4) KILOGRAMS TO POUNDS"
1035 PRINT "(5) GRAMS TO OUNCES"
1036 PRINT "(6) LITERS TO QUARTS"
1037 PRINT "(7) DEGREES CELSIUS TO DEGREES FAHRENHEIT"
1040 PRINT "ENTER NUMBER OF CONVERSION DESIRED"; : INPUT M
1050 ON M GOSUB 2100,2200,2300,2400,2500,2600,2700
1060 RETURN

1100 REM***USER SELECTS DESIRED U.S. TO METRIC CONVERSION
1110 PRINT "WANT LIST OF CONVERSIONS (Y OR N)"; : INPUT A$
1120 IF A$="N" THEN 1140
1130 PRINT "SELECT CONVERSION FROM THIS LIST:"
1131 PRINT "(1) INCHES TO CENTIMETERS"
1132 PRINT "(2) FEET TO METERS"
1133 PRINT "(3) MILES TO KILOMETERS"
1134 PRINT "(4) POUNDS TO KILOGRAMS"
1135 PRINT "(5) OUNCES TO GRAMS"
1136 PRINT "(6) QUARTS TO LITERS"
1137 PRINT "(7) DEGREES FAHRENHEIT TO DEGREES CELSIUS"
1140 PRINT "ENTER NUMBER OF CONVERSION DESIRED"; : INPUT S
1150 ON S GOSUB 3100,3200,3300,3400,3500,3600,3700
1160 RETURN

2100 REM***CM TO INCHES
2110 PRINT "HOW MANY CENTIMETERS"; : INPUT C
2120 PRINT C; "CENTIMETERS ="; C*.39; "INCHES"
2130 PRINT : RETURN

2200 REM***METERS TO FEET
2210 PRINT "HOW MANY METERS"; : INPUT M
2220 PRINT M; "METERS ="; M*3.28; "FEET"
2230 PRINT : RETURN

2300 REM***KM TO MILES
2310 PRINT "HOW MANY KILOMETERS"; : INPUT K
2320 PRINT K; "KILOMETERS ="; K*.62; "MILES"
2330 PRINT : RETURN

2400 REM***KG TO POUNDS
2410 PRINT "HOW MANY KILOGRAMS"; : INPUT K
2420 PRINT K; "KILOGRAMS ="; K*2.2;"POUNDS"
2430 PRINT : RETURN

2500 REM***GRAMS TO OUNCES
2510 PRINT "HOW MANY GRAMS"; : INPUT G
2520 PRINT G; "GRAMS ="; G*.035; "OUNCES"
2530 PRINT : RETURN
```

continued on the next page

```
2600 REM***LITERS TO QUARTS
2610 PRINT "HOW MANY LITERS"; : INPUT L
2620 PRINT L; "LITERS ="; L*1.0567; "QUARTS"
2630 PRINT : RETURN

2700 REM***DEGREES C TO DEGREES F
2710 PRINT "HOW MANY DEGREES CELSIUS"; : INPUT D
2720 PRINT D; "DEGREES CELSIUS ="; 9*D/5+32; "DEGREES FAHRENHEIT"
2730 PRINT : RETURN

3100 REM***INCHES TO CM
3110 PRINT "HOW MANY INCHES"; : INPUT I
3120 PRINT I; "INCHES ="; I*2.54; "CENTIMETERS"
3130 PRINT : RETURN

3200 REM***FEET TO METERS
3210 PRINT "HOW MANY FEET"; : INPUT F
3220 PRINT F; "FEET ="; F*.3048; "METERS"
3230 PRINT : RETURN

3300 REM***MILES TO KM
3310 PRINT "HOW MANY MILES"; : INPUT M
3320 PRINT M; "MILES ="; M*1.609; "KILOMETERS"
3330 PRINT : RETURN

3400 REM***POUNDS TO KG
3410 PRINT "HOW MANY POUNDS"; : INPUT P
3420 PRINT P; "POUNDS ="; P*.45; "KILOGRAMS"
3430 PRINT : RETURN

3500 REM***OUNCES TO GRAMS
3510 PRINT "HOW MANY OUNCES"; : INPUT O
3520 PRINT O; "OUNCES ="; O*28.35; "GRAMS"
3530 PRINT : RETURN

3600 REM***QUARTS TO LITERS
3610 PRINT "HOW MANY QUARTS"; : INPUT Q
3620 PRINT Q; "QUARTS ="; Q*.946; "LITERS"
3630 PRINT : RETURN

3700 REM***DEGREES F TO DEGREES C
3710 PRINT "HOW MANY DEGREES FAHRENHEIT"; : INPUT D
3720 PRINT D; "DEGREES FAHRENHEIT ="; 5/9*(D-32); "DEGREES CELSIUS"
3730 PRINT : RETURN
```

Appendixes

BASIC FUNCTIONS

This Appendix describes some of the more common and useful functions included in most versions of BASIC used on personal computers. It is by no means an exhaustive list, and the functions may perform differently on the computer you use. Check the reference manual for your computer system for the complete list of functions available in your version of BASIC.

Arithmetic Functions

(In the following, "exp" stands for any BASIC expression, variable, or number.)

ABS(exp): Gives the absolute value of the expresion, i.e., ABS(A)=A if A>=0, ABS(A)=-A if A<0.
Example: IF ABS(X-G)>=64 THEN PRINT "*"

EXP(exp): Computes the exponential function, base e, where e=2.71828. . . . Usually there is an upper limit on the value of the variable. In BASIC, the value in the parentheses must be less than 87.3365.
Examples: B=EXP(X)
Y=C*EXP(-A*T)

FRE(0): Used to determine how much space is left in the computer's memory that is not being used by BASIC or the program stored in memory. Enter it in a print statement, with zero in the parentheses, and the number of unused bytes is given.
Example: PRINT FRE(0)
See also FRE(string variable) under String Functions.

INT(exp): Computes the greatest integer less than or equal to exp. Notice that INT(3.14) = 3, but INT(-3.14) = -4. You may wish to check the reference manual for your version of BASIC for the similar function FIX.

LOG(exp): Gives the natural logarithm, base e, of exp.
Example: D = LOG(1 + X↑2)

RND(parameter): Generates a random number between 0 and 1 with control by the parameter value. For example, in BASIC, any positive value in the parentheses gives a new random number each time. A zero in the parentheses gives the same random number as was last generated by a RND function. Each different negative number (including fractions) gives a different random number, but the same random number is always given for the same negative value in the parentheses. The RND function may not work as described above for other versions of BASIC, so check your reference manual for details.

SGN(exp): Gives a 1 if the expression evaluates to a positive value (>0); gives a 0 if the expression evaluates to zero (=0); gives a -1 if the expression evaluates to a negative value (<0).
Example: ON SGN(X) + 2 GOTO 100, 200, 300
If X is negative, the above statement will branch to line 100; If X = 0, it will branch to line 200; if X is positive, it will branch to line 300.

SQR(exp): Gives the positive square root of exp. Expression in parentheses must be zero or a positive value (no negative values).

Trigonometric Functions

SIN(exp), COS(exp), TAN(exp), ATN(exp): The SIN, COS, and TAN functions give the sine, cosine, or tangent of exp, where exp is assumed to be given in radians. ATN computes the principal value of the arctangent, in radians. The value of ATN(exp) will be in the range: $-\pi/2 < ATN(exp) < \pi/2$.

String Functions

ASC(string): Gives the ASCII code numeric value for the first character in a string.
Example: PRINT ASC(B$)

CHR$(exp): Converts a number to the corresponding ASCII character.
Example: The ASCII code number 7 rings the bell on a teletypewriter or causes a beep on many CRT's. To ring the bell, use CHR$(7) in a PRINT statement, like this: PRINT CHR$(7)

FRE(string variable: Gives the number of free (unused) bytes in the memory's reserved string space. See also FRE function under Arithmetic Functions.

LEN(string): Gives the number of characters included in the string; spaces are always counted as characters.
Examples: FOR K-1 TO LEN(X$)

STR$(exp): Converts a numeric expression to a string. The minus sign in a negative value is included in the string, and the leading space for the assumed "+" in a positive value is included in the string.
Example: B$=STR$(X*Y)

VAL(string): Converts a string representation of a number to a numeric value. String must be numeric character.
Example: X$="33.3"
X=VAL(X$)

ASCII CHARACTER CODES

Decimal	Character	Decimal	Character	Decimal	Character
000	NUL	043	+	086	V
001	SO11	044	‘	087	W
002	STX	045	–	088	X
003	ETX	046	.	089	Y
004	EOT	047	/	090	Z
005	ENQ	048	0	091	[
006	ACK	049	1	092	\
007	BEL	050	2	093	]
008	BS	051	3	094	↑
009	HT	052	4	095	←
010	LF	053	5	096	`
011	VT	054	6	097	a
012	FF	055	7	098	b
013	CR	056	8	099	c
014	SO	057	9	100	d
015	SI	058	:	101	e
016	DLE	059	;	102	f
017	DC1	060	<	103	g
018	DC2	061	=	104	h
019	DC3	062	>	105	i
020	DC4	063	?	106	j
021	NAK	064	@	107	k
022	SYN	065	A	108	l
023	ETB	066	B	109	m
024	CAN	067	C	110	n
025	EM	068	D	111	o
026	SUB	069	E	112	p
027	ESCAPE	070	F	113	q
028	FS	071	G	114	r
029	GS	072	H	115	s
030	RS	073	I	116	t
031	US	074	J	117	u
032	SPACE	075	K	118	v
033	!	076	L	119	w
034	“	077	M	120	x
035	#	078	N	121	y
036	$	079	O	122	z
037	%	080	P	123	{
038	&	081	Q	124	|
039	’	082	R	125	}
040	(	083	S	126	~
041	)	084	T	127	DEL
042	*	085	U		

LF = Line Feed FF = Form Feed CR = Carriage Return DEL = Delete

ERROR MESSAGES

Errors will cause a message of the form:

"ERROR xx at LINE nnnn."

The error number ("xx" above) may be in the range 1 to 199.

ERRNUM 1 ; POWER NOT ON

ERRNUM 2 ; MEMORY FULL

ERRNUM 3 ; VALUE ERROR

ERRNUM 4 ; VARIABLE TABLE FULL (TOO MANY VARIABLES)

ERRNUM 5 ; STRING LENGTH ERROR

ERRNUM 6 ; READ OUT OF DATA

ERRNUM 7 ; VALUE NOT + INTEGER

ERRNUM 8 ; INPUT STMT ERROR

ERRNUM 9 ; ARRAY/STRING DIM ERROR

ERRNUM 10 ; ARG STACK OVERFLOW

ERRNUM 11 ; FLOATING POINT OVERFLOW

ERRNUM 12 ; LINE NOT FOUND (GOSUB/GOTO)

ERRNUM 13 ; NO MATCHING FOR

ERRNUM 14 ; LINE TOO LONG

ERRNUM 15 ; GOSUB/FOR LINE DELETED

ERRNUM 16 ; BAD RETURNS

ERRNUM 17 ; EXECUTION OF GARBAGE

ERRNUM 18 ; STRING DOES NOT START WITH VALID NUMBER

ERRNUM 19 ; LOAD PGM TOO BIG

ERRNUM 20 ; DEVICE NUMBER GRATER THAN 7

ERRNUM 21 ; NOT A LOAD FILE

Index

NOTES